Law, Crime and Law Enforcement

New York

Law, Crime and Law Enforcement

Conundrums of Paternalism in International Criminal Justice
Farhad Malekian
2024. ISBN: 979-8-89113-284-9 (Hardcover)
2024. ISBN: 979-8-89113-743-1 (eBook)

Concreting Righteousness in International Criminal Justice
Farhad Malekian
2024. ISBN: 979-8-89113-297-9 (Hardcover)
2024. ISBN: 979-8-89113-677-9 (eBook)

International Criminal Vacations: Tears of Justice
Farhad Malekian
2024. ISBN: 979-8-89113-282-5 (Hardcover)
2024. ISBN: 979-8-89113-670-0 (eBook)

Exploitation of Christian Islamic International Criminal Justice
Farhad Malekian
2024. ISBN: 979-8-89113-285-6 (Hardcover)
2024. ISBN: 979-8-89113-668-7 (eBook)

Tour de force of Moral Virtue in International Criminal Justice
Farhad Malekian
2023. ISBN: 979-8-88697-368-6 (Hardcover)
2023. ISBN: 979-8-88697-567-3 (eBook)

More information about this series can be found at
https://novapublishers.com/writer/farhad-malekian/

Michael K. Reyes
Editor

Understanding the Fentanyl Crisis

snova
New York

NOTICE TO THE READER

Library of Congress Cataloging-in-Publication Data

ISBN: 979-8-89113-830-8 (Hardcover)
ISBN: 979-8-89113-869-8 (eBook)

Published by Nova Science Publishers, Inc. † New York

Contents

Preface

Fentanyl and other synthetic opioids have devastated communities all over the United States, fueling the worst drug crisis in American history. Over 150 people die every day from overdoses related to synthetic opioids like fentanyl. America's drug crisis is so severe compared to other countries because of its position in drug supply chains. Mexican cartels import synthetic chemicals from China and make synthetic drugs like fentanyl at very low cost, which are then smuggled through the southern border. Every day, transnational criminal organizations use America's complex highway systems to smuggle illicit drugs, such as deadly fentanyl, into our country. These criminal organizations pose an enormous threat to the United States, as they undermine public safety and flood the streets with drugs.

Chapter 1

The Fentanyl Crisis in America: Inaction Is No Longer an Option*

Committee on the Judiciary and Subcommittee on Crime and Federal Government Surveillance

House of Representatives Subcommittee on Crime
and Federal Government
Surveillance
Committee on the Judiciary

Washington, DC

The Subcommittee met, pursuant to notice, at 9 a.m., in Room 2141, Rayburn House Office Building, Hon. Andy Biggs [Chair of the Subcommittee] presiding.

Members present: Representatives Biggs, Gaetz, Tiffany, Nehls, Moore, Kiley, Lee of Florida, Fry, Lee of Texas, McBath, Dean, Bush, Cohen, and Cicilline.

Mr. BIGGS. [Presiding.] The Subcommittee will come to order.

We have asked Congressman Barry Moore of Alabama to lead us in the Pledge of Allegiance.

* This is an edited, reformatted and augmented version of Hearing Before the Subcommittee on Crime and Federal Government Surveillance of the Committee on the Judiciary, U.S. House of Representatives, Serial No. 118–5, dated Wednesday, March 1, 2023.

In: Understanding the Fentanyl Crisis
Editor: Michael K. Reyes
ISBN: 979-8-89113-830-8

ALL. I pledge allegiance to the Flag of the United States of America, and to the Republic for which it stands, one Nation, under God, indivisible, with liberty and justice for all.

Mr. BIGGS. Thank you, Representative Moore.

Without objection, the Chair is authorized to declare a recess at any time.

Everyone, we welcome you to today's hearing on the fentanyl crisis in America.

I will now recognize myself for an opening statement. I thank the Members and witnesses for coming today.

As you know, this is the first hearing of this Subcommittee this Congress, and I welcome our new and returning Members.

The business before us today is this hearing which is entitled, "The Fentanyl Crisis in America: Inaction is No Longer an Option." I hope my colleagues will agree that inaction is truly no longer an option concerning this crisis.

The first wave of opioid deaths began in the late 1990's with an increase in overdose deaths involving prescription opioids. The second wave began in 2010 with a noticeable rise in overdose deaths involving heroin. The third, most recent, and deadliest wave began in 2013 with a sharp increase in overdose deaths involving synthetic opioids, particularly illicitly manufactured fentanyl, and related substances. Just two milligrams of fentanyl, the amount that fits on the tip of a pencil, is considered a potentially lethal dose.

As a Committee, we began looking at this crisis years ago. We have heard from too many parents who have tragically lost their children to this poison. Between 1999 and 2020, approximately 564,000 people died from overdoses involving an opioid prescription or illicit. In 2021, however, overdose deaths surpassed 100,000, with 67 percent of those deaths involving fentanyl. Let that sink in. It took 20 years to record a total of 564,000 opioid overdose deaths, and in just 1one year, we saw over 100,000 opioid overdose deaths.

You will hear today how communities across this country are suffering from this poison. During the last four years, while we have seen these overdose deaths rise, our colleagues across the aisle have been presented with opportunities to permanently schedule fentanyl-related substances in a bipartisan manner. Instead, they have punted the problem by temporarily scheduling fentanyl-related substances. It is long past time for Congress to perma- nently schedule fentanyl analogs and other related substances.

Unfortunately, my home State of Arizona has become the entry point for much of the illicit fentanyl entering our country. Over half of the fentanyl pills seized by the DEA last year were seized in Arizona.

Two weeks ago, law enforcement seized enough fentanyl to kill nearly 800,000 people.

If we can roll that video? [Video.]

This was seized in the Tempe suburb of the Phoenix metro area. This was found in just one pickup truck.

An individual traveling nearly 150 miles from the border was involved in a single vehicle accident, an auto accident, not a drug bust. When law enforcement arrived, they found 286 pounds, 1.3 million pills, of fentanyl.

Just this week, another 232 pounds of fentanyl worth $3 million was seized by San Diego Border Patrol from a car in San Clemente, California—75 miles from the border—most of which were pills.

I commend that these drugs were seized, but this just makes me more concerned about how many more of these hundreds-of-pounds hauls we never identify that reach their point of distribution—the point where it can enter American towns, often through the mail via sales that occur on social media.

Now, I know our Democrat friends want us to believe that farcical notion that all the fentanyl crossing our borders is coming in through our ports of entry. They have said as much in recent hearings. They want you to believe that we are doing a good job detecting and seizing it before it can enter the country and destroy and take American lives. That is simply not true.

I remind them that it is the fentanyl that is actually seized that is found at legal border-crossing points or interior checkpoints. That does not account for fentanyl that is not seized. In fact, in talking to CBP and other DEA officials, I have been told that the actual amount seized is estimated to be somewhere between 10–15 percent of the overall amount of fentanyl that is being introduced into the United States.

If we are being honest, it is the fentanyl that is not seized, obviously, that is killing and endangering our children and other mem bers of our society. To ignore the smuggling that occurs between our ports of entry is simply irresponsible and dangerous.

Just last month, Chief Patrol Agent John Modlin of the Tucson sector testified that, quote, Last year, we seized about 700 pounds of fentanyl. To give you an idea, that's enough to kill everyone in Arizona 21 times or half the population of the United States.

Fifty-two percent of that was encountered, so the majority of that was encountered in the field, predominantly being backpacked across the border.

I'm going to emphasize that: Fifty-two percent came across being backpacked across at the border. The other 48 percent was caught at the administrative check point.

Will you roll the other tape, please?

The video you are about to see takes place in Arivaca, just a few miles off Nogales, about 70 miles as the crow flies southwest of Tucson—nowhere near a port of entry, you can see. This is ranchland.

[Video.]

Those backpacks are not because they are going to go camping in the desert. They are bringing in illicit drugs.

According to CBP statistics, December was the worst month in our Nation's history for illegal migration, as measured by encounters of people, and a huge percentage of the drugs apprehended that month were between the ports of entry.

When we talk about being between the ports of entry, we refer to drugs not found at a port of entry. In fact, nearly 9,000 pounds of drugs, or 44 percent of that month's seizures, were found between the ports of entry—contrary to what you hear from our colleagues across the aisle.

Jobe Dickinson, president of the Border Security Alliance, hit the nail on the head when he said that the cartels have, quote, . . . developed a multi-pronged approach as to how to smuggle illegal drugs into this country. They don't just use one avenue, such as the ports of entry. They also use established smuggling routes and remote parts of the borders to get more drugs across.

Cartels are smart enough to avoid sending their inventory through our X-ray and drug-sniffing dogs at the border. They walk it through the gaping, unguarded holes in our border. The No. 1 sector for opioid smuggling is the Tucson sector.

Combating this poison and those who smuggle, manufacture, and sell it should be a bipartisan issue. We need to act together to stop this scourge.

I recognize in our audience today, Mr. Donald Holman. He previously testified on this topic more than three years ago. Tragically, like the Rachwals and too many parents across America, he and his family have been forever impacted by this crisis. Mr. Holman lost his son Garrett in 2017 after he took a synthetic opioid delivered through the mail. Since then, Mr. Holman has courageously been a tireless advocate to keep these dangerous drugs out of our communities.

I ask unanimous consent to enter a statement from Mr. Holman into the record, and I thank him for his presence here today.

Entered into the record.

Mr. BIGGS. At this point, I now recognize the Ranking Member, the gentlewoman from Texas, Ms. Jackson Lee, for her opening statement.

Ms. JACKSON LEE. Good morning, Mr. Chair, and good morning to my colleagues.

This is a very important moment, a very serious moment, and a moment of reasoned bipartisan to fight the scourge of fentanyl.

Let me, as I begin, take this opportunity at the outset to express my condolences, Ms. Rachwal, for the tragic loss of your son Logan. Thank you for courage of being here. It is not easy for a mother to speak of the loss of her son.

It is not the same thing, but I spent time with the mothers in Uvalde, and it is simply painful. So, your presence here today is a stark reminder, as I said as I walked into this room, that we must be determined to fight the scourge of fentanyl. We must break the cycle as well of drug addiction, and we must stop the loss of life from this deadly and terrible plague. Thank you for your presence here today.

We must also, as we go forward in this illicit fentanyl, work with our families, work with the Nation, on drug demands fueled by addiction. We must require the Federal Government to acknowledge the lessons that they have previously learned, and they must embrace and work bipartisan and include and embrace inclusive strategies that involve aggressive interdiction and community-based treatment. We should not leave families alone. They must have support.

The unprecedented COVID–19 pandemic contributed to the rise in fentanyl-related overdoses beginning in 2019, as treatment, recovery, and prevention services were interrupted and schools, jobs, and mental health support halted, especially for those suffering from substance abuse disorders.

While the previous administration was focused on China and building a wall on the southern border, fentanyl came in through the front door and exploded in this country. It is recognizable that China has a major involvement with fentanyl, communicating with Mexico. That is, of course, a response that we have to deal with as it relates to that interaction.

In 2021, fentanyl was linked to more than 1,600 fatal overdoses in Texas, with African Americans becoming the face of a second national wave of fentanyl-related overdoses. Around the country, many faces were the faces of fentanyl overdoses.

Newly released data shows a heightened rate of overdoses in our minority communities, especially among seniors, disproportionately affected by fentanyl addiction, despite an overall decline of overdose rates.

Far from the inaction, as they hearing title implies, the Biden Administration and Congress have both taken decisive steps to address the scourge of fentanyl. To disrupt the supply chain of fentanyl, Democrats passed the Fiscal Year 2023 omnibus spending package, which included $60 million to hire 125 additional CBP officers and support personnel at ports of entry and $70 million to strengthen nonintrusive inspection systems to scan vehicles.

I have just come back from the border, and talking to our very fine officers, they are working without ceasing. They are going more than the extra mile. We need to give them the resources they need to be the Superman, Batman, and Mighty Man at the border, to be able to assure that fentanyl has a stop sign before it comes into this country.

This investment in interdiction resources is critical because the fentanyl supply chain crosses an ocean and several international borders, as I have said. China, and increasingly, India, export most of the chemical precursors to Mexico that are used in the early stages of fentanyl production, where Mexican cartels produce illicit fentanyl products for smuggling to the United States.

That is why the Biden Administration is working with the Mexican government through several initiatives and redoubling diplomatic efforts to engage China to interrupt the deadly supply chain. Contrary to some expressed opinion, the Mexican cartels primarily use U.S. citizens to drive vehicles and trucks filled with hard-to-detect packages of synthesized fentanyl through lawful ports of entry, while couriers carry and send packages through the U.S. mail and private carriers. We have got to stomp that out.

There is one major danger posed by the illicit supply of fentanyl that is particularly troubling: Production of fake or counterfeit pills which have been found in every State and hold an often deadly secret. It has to be a collective effort.

Last year, DEA agents said four out of every 10 pills on Houston's streets were laced with fentanyl, leading users, including teenagers, to die without knowing what they took. That is why I intend to introduce a bill that will provide grant funding for teachers and other schools to have the necessary adverse drugs that help and other overdose reversal drugs on hand and receive training to administer them properly. My bill will also provide enhanced pen alties that do not include mandatory minimums for online sales for the manufacturers of fake pills if death or serious bodily injury occurs.

To educate the public, particularly young people and their parents, the Biden Administration launched the One Pill Can Kill public awareness campaign to raise awareness of the dangers of fake prescription pills laced with fentanyl.

Because the cartels mass produce fake pills to resemble other Schedule II prescription opioids, such as OxyContin and Percocet; depressants such as Xanax, or stimulants like Adderall. Even careful users of illegal drugs can be drawn into the web of the fentanyl trade with deadly consequences.

The hard truth is that we can only temporarily disrupt the supply of illicit fentanyl temporarily before another cartel trafficking method or analog moves in to take over the market that addiction creates. There is scientific basis to this. We are well aware of this chain of events.

We can disrupt the flow, but we must also reduce the demand. For far too long, our country has chosen the wrong approach in fighting drug abuse alone. We have left parents and families and communities alone.

Criminalizing addiction, when people need treatment, is a difficult and challenging pathway, and it impacts all our communities—young and communities of color. That is why in the last Congress we passed the Rural Opioid Abuse Prevention Act, which several Republicans who sit on this very Subcommittee voted against. That legislation provided funding to rural communities to combat the fentanyl crisis that they were facing, in addition to $104 million in grants and assistance the Biden Administration allocated to a Rural Communities Opioid Response Program. I can assure you that those rural communities welcomed this help that they had not gotten before.

It is important to stress that we must not make the same mistakes with fentanyl and the now related substances of the synthetic opioids that we have seen happen before and have not gotten the job done. We have got to get the job done. We cannot have mothers coming to tell us the story of their beloved and beautiful child.

As we learned through the crack epidemic of the 1980's, followed by amphetamine in the 1990's, and prescription drugs, and back to heroin once again, we cannot incarcerate our way out of this, out of the scourge of fentanyl and synthetic opioids.

I am concerned that banning the entire class of fentanyl-related substances without safeguards significantly may impact what we have to do in research and finding a way to stop this addiction.

I am really opposed to the expansion of mandatory minimums— penalties that prevent judges from considering the unique facts and circumstances of that addicted person who comes before them. According to the most recent statistics from the U.S. Sentencing Commission, there are already significant racial disparities in the prosecution of fentanyl trafficking cases for people of color, comprising more than 78 percent of those sentenced in 2021. The same is true for Federal convictions involving fentanyl analogs, of which 86 percent of those people were people of color. We must also be reminded that people who are young are the victims, and we must save them because they must have a future.

Of those prosecuted for fentanyl trafficking, less than five percent received a guideline increase for a leadership or supervisory role, and less than 10 percent of those prosecuted for fentanyl analog trafficking received a leadership or supervisory increase.

There is no doubt that we are currently experiencing a crisis, but it is a crisis that Congress and the Biden Administration have responded to with urgency and clear eyes. I would certainly like to emphasize that we should do so on this Committee.

Just a statistic: In the past year, CBP seized over 260,000 pounds of illicit drugs at the border, including more than 13,000 pounds of fentanyl. In December 2022, as we passed the fiscal year, as reported, we did $60 million and supported another $70 million to strengthen nonintrusive inspection systems that scan vehicles and cargo to disrupt the flow of drugs.

We are working intensely. Of course, the Customs and Border Protection data shows that, since fiscal 2020, more than 90 percent of fentanyl, heroin, and amphetamine seizures occurred at U.S. ports of entry, with almost 97 percent of all fentanyl seizures happening at ports of entry this fiscal year.

We are working to stop the death. In 2021, U.S. citizens accounted for 86.3 percent of fentanyl trafficking convictions compared to just 8.9 percent of undocumented migrants.

Let's get the facts to save lives. Therefore, let's work together.

I look forward to hearing from our witnesses today, and I hope to have an earnest discussion about solutions to reduce the supply of fentanyl and combat and prevent addiction and overdoses. We must save lives.

I yield back.

Mr. BIGGS. The gentlelady yields back.

Without objection, all other opening statements will be included in the record.

Oh, I'm sorry. I'm sorry, Mr. Chair—Mr. Ranking Member. Mr. Nadler, the former "Mr. Chair," I now recognize you for your opening statement.

Mr. NADLER. Thank you, Mr. Chair.

Mr. Chair, according to the Centers for Disease Control and Prevention, over 100,000 Americans are dying of drug overdoses each year. Most of these deaths are from fentanyl.

The seriousness of the fentanyl crisis cannot be denied. That is why Democrats have been working on solutions to address fentanyl trafficking, addiction, and overdose since it emerged as a threat to our communities.

Last Congress, under a Democratic majority, we passed multiple bills to address the opioid epidemic. We passed the Rural Opioid Abuse Prevention Act, which expanded grant eligibility to fund pilot programs in rural that focus on reducing overdose deaths.

We passed the bipartisan FENTANYL Results Act, which authorizes two State Department program that combat global drug trafficking.

As part of the Consolidated Appropriations Act, we enacted two bills that make it easier for providers to offer addiction treatments that combine medication with other services.

We passed the Infrastructure Investment and Jobs Act, which included $430 million to modernize our ports of entry and help improve CBP's ability to detect illicit drugs.

Much of these legislations were bipartisan, but the Republicans on this Subcommittee seem to have forgotten that work, and some of them actively opposed it. They titled this hearing, "The Fentanyl Crisis in America: Inaction is No Longer an Option." Republicans suggest that there has been no action to address this crisis, but they could not be more wrong.

There has been action in Congress and by the Biden Administration. Some Republicans would prefer different actions. Some Republicans want to incarcerate our way out of this problem, but we know from past experience that this simply does not work.

Drug prosecutions generally catch low-level dealers, but very rarely reach the leaders of trafficking organizations. Since cartel leaders can often recruit new dealers, more arrests and longer sentences for low-level dealers does not stop the flow of drugs into our communities.

Other Republicans say tough immigration policies and a border wall will stop fentanyl, but the facts are not on their side. While it is true that a great deal of fentanyl comes into the United States from Mexico, it is overwhelmingly U.S. citizens, not migrants, who are bringing it in.

Fentanyl is not carried across the border in the middle of the desert generally. It is driven in commercial trucks and passenger vehicles passing through legal ports of entry. That's why Democrats have supported investments in more law enforcement tools to detect illicit drugs.

The fentanyl crisis cannot be used as another justification for mass incarceration or an excuse for harsh immigration policies that do nothing to prevent addiction. While fentanyl is especially deadly, addiction and overdose are not new. We must learn from the failures of our past to treat the fentanyl crisis not as a crime problem, but as a public health problem. We must get to the root causes of addiction and substance abuse, or we will end the war on fentanyl, only to have a war on the next, even deadlier drug.

We have begun to better understand the nature of addiction, and the public health approach is beginning to take hold. We have shifted the focus from how we lock more people up to how do we save more lives. This shift has led us to get overdose prevention drugs, like naloxone or Narcan, to more first responders, to more community members. These drugs are saving hundreds of thousands of lives.

We are also making sure that those who do come into the criminal justice system because of their addiction receive appropriate treatment, whether through diversion programs that help people rejoin the community without incarceration or through treatment while incarcerated.

These programs are not just about helping individuals suffering from addiction. They improve our communities because those who receive treatment are less likely to commit crime and more likely to find employment.

Fentanyl continues to be a crisis, but it is a crisis that Members of both parties are working to address. Today, I hope we can explore more actions that we might take together to prevent addiction and get to the root causes of drug abuse. I welcome my colleagues' concern about this issue, and I hope they are sincere in their interest in joining this effort.

Thank you, Mr. Chair, and I yield back the balance of my time.

Mr. BIGGS. Thank you, Ranking Member Nadler.

Without objection all other opening statements will be included in the record.

Mr. BIGGS. We will now introduce today's witnesses.

Today, we will first hear from Dr. Tim Westlake, who is an emergency room physician, the immediate past Chair of the Wisconsin Medical Examining Board, a former member of the Wisconsin Controlled Substance Board, and former member of the Governor's Task Force on Opioid Abuse.

Thank you for being here, Dr. Westlake.

After Dr. Westlake, we will hear from Ms. Erin Rachwal, who, tragically, lost her son Logan to fentanyl poisoning on Valentine's Day 2021. Since then, she and her family have founded the Love Logan Foundation, which seeks to raise awareness and educate on drug addiction and mental health.

We appreciate you and your husband being here today. Thank you for coming.

We will, then, hear from Dr. Jeffrey Singer, who is a senior fellow at the CATO Institute, president emeritus and founder of Valley Surgical Clinics, Ltd., the largest and oldest group private surgical practice in Arizona, who has been in private practice as a general surgeon for more than 35 years.

Then, he will be followed by Mr. Derek Maltz, a former Special Agent in Charge at the DEA, the Drug Enforcement Administration. He is a national security and public safety expert who retired from the DEA after 28 years of service, including 10 years overseeing the Department of Justice Special Operations Division. He also previously served as chief of the New York Drug Enforcement Task Force.

We welcome all our witnesses here today. We thank you for appearing.

We will begin now by swearing you in; if each of you would please rise and raise your right hand.

Do each of you swear or affirm, under penalty of perjury, that the testimony you are about to give is true and correct to the best of your knowledge, information, and belief, so help you God?

The record will reflect the witnesses answered in the affirmative. Thank you. You may be seated.

Please know that your written testimony will be entered into the record in its entirety. Accordingly, we ask that you summarize your testimony in five minutes.

The microphones in front of you have a clock and a series of lights on them. When the lights turn yellow, you should begin to conclude your statement. When the light turns red, your time has expired.

If you hear me tap just a little bit, that means you are getting close, and we want to respect your statement and your time, but we do also want to make sure that we stay within that five minutes, if possible.

Our first witness will be Dr. Tim Westlake. Dr. Westlake?

Statement of Dr. Timothy Westlake

Dr. WESTLAKE. Chair Biggs, distinguished Members of the Subcommittee, thank you for inviting me to testify and for your leadership.

Let me start by clarifying what fentanyl-related substances are and why scheduling them as a class is a critical policy tool.

Fentanyl-related substances, or FRSs, are highly active opioids almost identical to fentanyl, except for a tiny difference in their chemical structure created by changing a single chemical ingredient during synthesis in Chinese labs. The result of this tweak is a new, potent opioid with the same deadly effects as fentanyl and, without FRS class scheduling, would be legal, until causing numerous deaths, raising them on the radar to be scheduled reactively by DEA.

Strong FRS scheduling penalties will not stop users from using or traffickers from trafficking. The only thing it does is stop chemical companies from legally producing them, which has, in fact, halted the very existence of new FRSs.

For me, an emergency physician, telling parents, tragically, on more than one occasion, even friends, that their child will never come home is the worst part of my job. Inspiration for FRS class scheduling reform arose out of the tragedy of my friend Lauri Badura's son Archie.

Archie was an altar server with my daughters. It started with prescription opioids, then snorting heroin, and unknowingly, fentanyl. I resuscitated Archie on his second-to-last overdose. At that time, I pulled out a body bag, laid it down next to him, and warned him that that is where he would end up if he didn't accept help. He stayed clean for six months, until illicit fentanyl ended his life. One of the last things my friend Lauri saw of her son Archie was him being zipped up into a body bag.

Motivated to act by hundreds of such deaths, FRS scheduling legislation which is proactive and not reactive, as had previously been the case, came together quickly and was enacted with a unanimous vote in the Wisconsin State Legislature in 2017. Almost immediately, DEA adopted it as national policy, but only temporarily.

Before that, scheduling new fentanyls was like a lethal game of Whac-A-Mole. We literally had to wait for people to die before action could be taken.

So, why isn't the Wisconsin law permanent Federal law yet? Some who oppose point to the recent spike in deaths from illicit fentanyl as proof that it doesn't work. In reality, this is a misunderstanding and confabulation of the facts.

FRS scheduling does not address illicit fentanyl. It was never designed to do so. Rather, it removed the incentive for legal Chinese chemical companies to create new FRSs; thus, stopping them from ever existing in the first place.

There is no quick and easy solution to the scourge of illicit fentanyl. The solution to FRSs is a simple legislative fix. At its core, it is not an extension of the war on drugs, or a law enforcement tool designed to put criminals in jail. There has been a total of eight Federal prosecutions under the language, half of whom already had known ties to drug cartels.

However, if Schedule I penalties were removed for FRS trafficking, then it would reincentivize their creation and significantly weaken the law's most powerful, proactive, and preventative effects. It truly is the ultimate form of overdose prevention and harm reduction.

To be clear, there has never been a prosecution for a non-bioactive FRS. Why is this? It's because there are no non-bioactive FRSs. All fentanyl-related substances encountered and researched to date have been found to have potent opioid activity. One of them that was recently investigated is 7,000 times more potent than morphine.

It is interesting to note that the major groups opposing scheduling are, in fact, mainly criminal justice reform and drug-legalization-based activist organizations. There is a time and a place for criminal justice reform, but FRS scheduling is neither.

Concerns raised about negative impact on research are purely theoretical and have already been addressed by discussions with stakeholders. These proposed research accommodations that have been signed off on are supported by the very agencies and organizations representing academic scientific research in the U.S., including the National Institutes of Drug Abuse, the National Institutes of Health, the Department of Health and Human Services, and the FDA. These agreed-upon accommodations would significantly loosen researchers' directions into studying all Schedule I substances, not just FRSs, and open promising areas of substance abuse research.

In conclusion, for five years now, FRS class scheduling has been Federal policy, albeit temporary. I could not be more pleased about that and the big impact my small ideas had. According to NFLIS, the National Forensic Laboratory Information System, in a matter of a few short years, the creation and distribution of new FRSs from China has ground to a halt. For comparison, in New York City alone in 2016–2017, there were 900 deaths from FRS poisons. In the devastating battle we are in against the scourge of fentanyl, the elimination of related substances that had previously escaped our scheduling and made their way to devastated communities across the Nation is surely one bright spot.

Fentanyls are so toxic and lethal that they can be classified and actually have been used as chemical weapons. The lethal dose is merely two milligrams, which is the equivalent of five grains of sand. This means that one teaspoon can kill 2,000 people. That is the amount that's in this packet of sugar. This is why our kids are dying. Imagine trying to have a lab in a basement or in a garage to mix this into 4,000 doses and have it been effective.

FRS schedule reform is only temporary until Congress takes action to make it permanent. It's imperative we work together to deploy every successful harm-reduction tool in our arsenal. I urge you to permanently close the spigot of FRSs. The fact is you can't die from ingesting something that wasn't created—

Mr. BIGGS. Dr. Westlake, thank you.

Dr. WESTLAKE. —nor can you be incarcerated for trafficking something that does not exist. That is the beauty and simplicity of FRS scheduling.

Thank you for your time, and I look forward to answering questions.

[The prepared statement of Dr. Westlake follows:]

Statement of Timothy W. Westlake, M.D., FFSMB, FACEP

FORMER WISCONSIN MEDICAL EXAMINING BOARD CHAIRMAN FORMER WISCONSIN CONTROLLED SUBSTANCES BOARD MEMBER
BEFORE THE COMMITTEE ON THE JUDICIARY SUBCOMMITTEE ON CRIME AND FEDERAL GOVERNMENT SURVEILLANCE U.S. HOUSE OF REPRESENTATIVES
THE FENTANYL CRISIS IN AMERICA: INACTION IS NO LONGER AN OPTION

March 1, 2023
Release Upon Delivery

Dear Members,

Thank you for the opportunity to testify at this hearing and contribute to the discussion on this topic.

The Issue

What Congress Can Do

As Congress grapples with how best to address opioid poisoning deaths, it should start by making permanent a proven strategy to eliminate the creation and supply of all new deadly fentanyl related substances (FRSs) by passing the SOFA Act or HALT Fentanyl Act. After FRS Class Scheduling was enacted in Wisconsin in 2017, the U.S. Drug Enforcement Administration enacted temporary FRS class scheduling federally in 2018, authorization of which has been extended multiple times since (including 6 times by the current administration, the most recent being a 2-year extension passed in the omnibus). In short, these efforts have resulted in shutting down the creation and flow and very existence of new fentanyl related substances into the U.S. It's why Congress must act to finally make permanent this temporary policy. The fact is, no one can die from ingesting something never created or be incarcerated for trafficking something that does not exist.

Background on Fentanyl Class Scheduling Legislation

By design, FRS class scheduling is preventative, not punitive. As the primary architect of current FRS class scheduling policy, my goal was to stop the creation and spread of deadly new fentanyl related substances from transnational drug trafficking organizations. It was not to incarcerate people with substance use disorder.

I am a full-time emergency physician and recent part-time medical regulator in Wisconsin. I provide medical direction for a statewide peer-to-peer recovery program that provides naloxone training and I also prescribe medication-assisted treatment when needed. I'm the immediate past Chairman of the Wisconsin Medical Examining Board and a former member of the Wisconsin Controlled Substances Board (responsible for controlled substance scheduling at the state level) and was architect of the State of Wisconsin prescription opioid reform strategy. Since 2016, I have testified four times before the US House of Representatives and Senate in hearings focused on opioid reforms.

As well, I have been on the front lines in the opioid battle for more than 30 years. One of the most heartbreaking aspects of my job is to inform parents and other family members that their loved one is never coming home due to an opioid poisoning. Inspiration for the fentanyl class scheduling reform arose out of the tragedy of my friend Lauri Badura, whose son Archie died of an overdose. Archie was an altar server with my daughters. He got hooked on prescription medicine and then snorting heroin. I was able to resuscitate Archie on his second to last overdose. On that occasion, I showed him a body bag and warned he would end up in it if he didn't accept help. He attended rehab and stayed clean for six months. Sadly, fentanyl caught up with him once more. One of the last memories my friend Lauri has of her son Archie is his lifeless body being zipped up into a body bag.

At the time I originated FRS class scheduling legislation over six years ago, doctors and other health care professionals -- in Wisconsin alone -- were battling more than nine nearly identical fentanyl variants.

While each was responsible for dozens or more poisoning deaths in our state and across the U.S., they were still considered "legal" substances, having not yet been scheduled federally by the DEA or at the state level by the Controlled Substance Board (CSB). In Wisconsin, when deaths result from new novel substances, the CSB can use its emergency scheduling authority. It was like a lethal game of "Whack a Mole". We literally had to wait for the body count to pile up before we could find and schedule new fentanyl variants individually.

I knew something had to change, thus my idea to selectively schedule likely bioactive fentanyls as a class and remove the incentive foreign transnational drug trafficking organizations and chemical/ drug manufacturers had in modifying the fentanyl molecule. Knowing these entities could simply add or delete one minor chemical group and stay ahead of U.S. scheduling, my calculus was simple: stop the drugs at their source. If we could get it done in Wisconsin, we could then scale it nationally and impact global production, with the end game of stopping it in China and elsewhere where these lethal fentanyl variants have largely been manufactured.

Working with the DEA, FRS class scheduling language was created. In part, the Stopping Overdoses of Fentanyl Analogues (SOFA) Act, or Wisconsin Act 60, which passed unanimously in the state legislature, memorialized Archie Badura. It was named after the Saving Others for Archie organization (SOFA) that his mom Lauri created after his death to help other families in crisis. State Senate Leader, now Wisconsin Congressman Scott Fitzgerald (R-WI), shepherded the bill through the state process. It was signed into law on November 9, 2017. Within its first week on the books, the DEA published its intent to use emergency scheduling powers to temporarily schedule FRSs as a class federally. This took effect February 2018. The results have been incontrovertible: the creation of new fentanyl related substances has ground to a halt internationally.

To date, DEA has found 36 new FRSs found to have caused thousands of poisoning deaths in multiple states across the country. Since 2018, 12 new fentanyl related substances were found and with significantly fewer deaths attributed; it is suspected that many of these new FRSs may have already been in development prior to the temporary scheduling. The NFLIS (National

Forensic Lab Information System) data show 7,058 encounters for FRSs in 2016-2017, and a decrease in 2018-19 to 758 encounters [a 90% decrease], and of these, the vast majority were for previously scheduled FRSs. Most importantly, the fentanyl/FRS flow from China has ground to a halt, and reports to NFLIS of overdose deaths related to new fentanyl-related substances have essentially ceased.

Table 1. Examples of recent structural modifications to fentanyl observed on the illicit market.

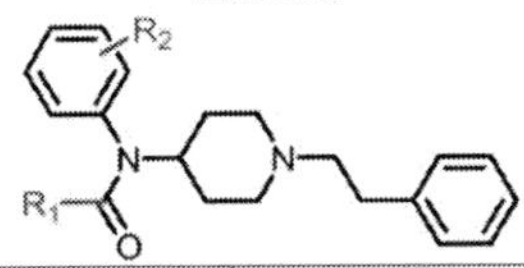

Substance	R_1	R_2
fentanyl[14]	$-CH_2CH_3$	H
acetyl fentanyl	$-CH_3$	H
butyryl fentanyl	$-CH_2CH_2CH_3$	H
furanyl fentanyl	-furan-2-yl	H
4-fluoroisobutyryl fentanyl	$-CH(CH_3)_2$	*para*-F
acryl fentanyl	$-CH{=}CH_2$	H
ortho-fluorofentanyl	$-CH_2CH_3$	*ortho*-F
tetrahydrofuranyl fentanyl	-tetrahydrofuran-2-yl	H
methoxyacetyl fentanyl	$-CH_2OCH_3$	H
cyclopropyl fentanyl	-cyclopropyl	H
valeryl fentanyl	$-CH_2CH_2CH_2CH_3$	H
isobutyryl fentanyl	$-CH(CH_3)_2$	H
para-chloroisobutyryl fentanyl	$-CH(CH_3)_2$	*para*-Cl
para-methoxybutyryl fentanyl	$-CH_2CH_2CH_3$	*para*-OCH_3
cyclopentyl fentanyl	-cyclopentyl	H
ocfentanil	$-CH_2OCH_3$	*ortho*-F
para-fluorobutyryl fentanyl	$-CH_2CH_2CH_3$	*para*-F

Concerns Raised and Considered

Increased Incarceration?

The goal of fentanyl class scheduling is singularly laser focused: to remove the incentive for the creation and therefore halt development of deadly fentanyl poisons at their origin, namely, in drug labs overseas.Those opposed to fentanyl class scheduling initially suggested there would be a large increase in societal costs due to increased incarceration of people suffering from substance use disorder, but that has not proven to be the case. According to a 2021 GAO report, in the three years since FRS class scheduling wasplaced into regulation, there have been exactly eight prosecutions in the U.S. using the temporary scheduling language and half of these defendants had known ties to transnational criminal organizations. *It is important to note that removing the schedule I penalties for FRSs would actually incentivize their creation and significantly weaken the law's most powerful proactive and preventative effects.*

Opposition also mischaracterizes FRS scheduling as a partisan matter at the federal level given the years in which the policy has taken hold. I beg to differ. I have talked with federal and state policymakers acrossthe political spectrum who care deeply about this issue and are determined to do what they can to help fix it. Plain and simple, by halting the creation and existence of new fentanyl variants, there has been significantly less availability and supply, causing a reduction in harm, overdose deaths and incarceration.

This underscores the primary strategy of overdose prevention and harm reduction. When considering societal effects, we must also consider the impact on mortality rates. In New York City alone, in 2016 and 2017, there were over 900 deaths from FRSs. Since 2018, FRS related deaths in the US have been almost nonexistent. As such, those who have opposed this policy because of concerns related to incarceration, now suggest it is unnecessary because of the low number of prosecutions. Their pivot proves the policy is working. We have already witnessed the positive societal impacts of the fentanyl class scheduling including that thousands more Americans are alive today who would otherwise not behad new fentanyl related substances been created and trafficked in the U.S. Not only are people with opioid use disorder not being incarcerated as a result of FRS scheduling, they are alive today, in part, because of this policy.

Other false claims used by opponents of FRS class scheduling include that deaths and incarcerations dueto fentanyl and FRSs have sharply increased in recent years. As mentioned previously, deaths and incarcerations from new FRSs have ground to a halt. Increases are due to illicit fentanyl which FRS scheduling is not designed to stop. Rather, it is to prevent overdoses at the hands of new FRSs by removing the incentive for their creation and distribution at foreign points of origin. *FRS class scheduling is the ultimate form of harm reduction and overdose prevention: you can't die from ingesting something never created, nor can you be incarcerated for selling something that doesn't exist.*

Effect on General Research

Concern about not wanting to impede general research was thoughtfully considered, and great care was given to ensure the language would be specific and narrowly crafted. We looked at more than structural similarity when arriving at the definition of fentanyl related substances. Structure-Activity

Relationship (SAR) considers the relationship between changes in chemical structure relative to changes in pharmacological activity; it was the basis of the definition to make sure substances meeting this definition have a high probability of retaining opioid-like pharmacological and psychoactive activity. The detailed scheduling language includes specific modifications to only those portions of the fentanyl molecule with documented high likelihood of bioactivity. The language is the equivalent of a surgical scalpel, not a hand grenade.

Concerns raised about the potential negative impact of FRS scheduling on research are purely theoretical and have already been addressed by discussions with stakeholders. These proposed research accommodations have been signed off on and are supported by the agencies and organizations representing academic scientific research in the US - including the National Institute of Drug Abuse, the National Institutes of Health, HHS and the FDA. Why would they all support FRS class scheduling if it would harm research? The agreed upon accommodations would significantly loosen research restrictions on all schedule 1 substances (not just FRSs) and open up wide areas of substance abuse research.

- Those who oppose FRS scheduling point to increased numbers of illicit fentanyl deaths as reason for why FRS scheduling is not working. Some have said that "Temporary scheduling is a failed experiment that hasn't curbed the devastation of the opioid crisis." At best, this is disingenuous and a misunderstanding of the issue. In fact, the opposite is true. FRS scheduling has accomplished the one and only thing it is designed to do: stop the creation and very existence of new FRSs and therefore shut down all new FRS related deaths.
- Tragically, poisoning deaths from illicit fentanyl have skyrocketed, but deaths from illicit fentanyl are a separate issue from FRSs and FRS scheduling, and one that could never be impacted by FRS class scheduling. Arguing that FRS class scheduling has not worked because illicit fentanyl deaths have risen is a complete confabulation and misrepresentation of the facts on the effects of FRS scheduling. The correct question should be about what has been the effect on deaths and trafficking arrests from new FRSs, which have ground to a halt, exactly as intended.
- Opponents of permanent FRS scheduling have said that "Temporary scheduling has preemptively criminalized potentially life-saving antidotes to fentanyl overdoses and impeded the medical, research

and scientific community's ability to develop solutions we need to effectively tackle this crisis", and that "One FRS has been shown to have similar properties to naloxone." But this is a misrepresentation and is based on one FRS (Mirfentanil) that was studied in the early 1990s that had antagonistic properties at low levels, but agonist effects at high levels and has never passed beyond phase 2 studies. Again, a purely theoretical argument about a theoretically negative effect on research when weighed against the actual death of thousands of Americans from FRSs when they were left to be reactively scheduled individually. The fact is, academic scientific research would actually be significantly advanced if research accommodations similar to the ONDCP proposal in the HALT Fentanyl Act were to be enacted allowing easier access to research on all controlled substances.

Others have held up that FRS scheduling would impede research into new opioid versions of fentanyl. But seriously, is anyone arguing we need a new opioid more powerful than fentanyl?

Similarly, some suggest research into new lifesaving treatments such as a FRS reversal agent or medication assisted treatment would be impeded.

- The scientific basis for this argument seems to be based on one line in testimony by Dr. Throckmorton, Deputy Director of the Center for Drug Evaluation and Research at the FDA, at a December 2021 Energy and Commerce Committee hearing, "The Overdose Crisis: Interagency Proposal to Combat Illicit Fentanyl-Related Substances": "Among the individual FRS for which pharmacological activity has been studied, FDA has identified examples of substances lacking in mu-opioid agonist activity, the presumed pharmacology that would lead to opioid-related harms."
- While it is true there is a single FRS that is a predominant kappa receptor stimulator at low levels (which are thought to have lower abuse potential and theoretically beneficial antagonistic properties) as cited by Dr. Throckmorton, however at high levels it does stimulate mu receptors which cause euphoria and the respiratory suppression that kills.
- However, when reviewing research into FRSs, every substance studied and classifiable under the FRS class scheduling language has been found to have opioid receptor bioactivity. Almost all are dozens

to hundreds and even thousands of times more potent than heroin and morphine. More complete information is forthcoming from federal chemists at DEA conducting FRS research. It is my understanding this research will show that as of August, 2022 the DEA has encountered 36 FRSs and completed preliminary pharmacological investigations on 27 of them, with additional testing ongoing. It was found that all FRSs studied to date bind and activate at least one opioid receptor with varying affinities and efficacies. In short all FRSs are bioactive.

- To date, and over the past 60 years of exhaustive structure-activity relationship studies on fentanyls, research has failed to highlight any activity leading to the development of a fentanyl based antagonist/ reversal agent or medication assisted treatment.
- In contrast, prior to FRS class scheduling, legal FRSs pouring across our borders took the lives of countless Americans.

Fentanyls fall into the 4-anilinopiperidine class (defined by the aniline ring in the 4-position of the piperidine ring). By definition, in order to structurally classify as a fentanyl related substance under the FRS language, the base chemical structure must be that with Nitrogen at the 4-position of the piperidine ring (highlighted in yellow below).

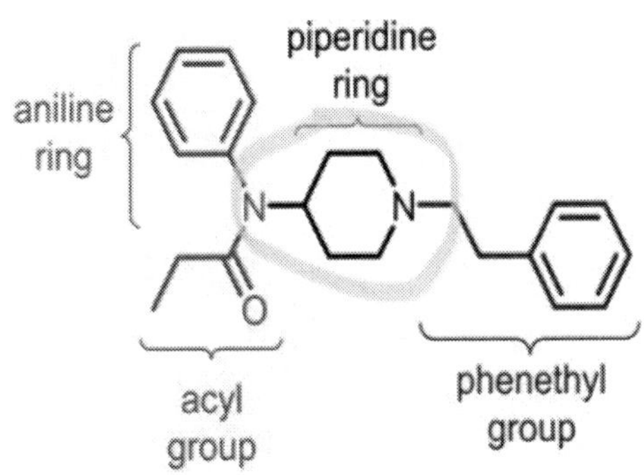

Any chemical without that exact base structure and without any of the specified modifications would not be included in the scheduling. All elements of the basic fentanyl molecular chemical scaffolding must be present. If there are any deletions from the scaffold, the chemical wouldn't be included, and if there are any substitutions not specifically included in the specific language, those chemicals would also not be included in scheduling. FRS Class Scheduling Language: must include one or more of the following-

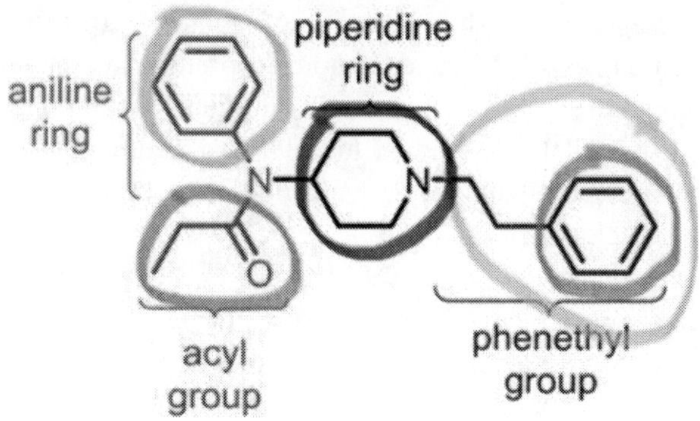

(A) By replacement of the phenyl portion of the phenethyl group by any monocycle,whether or not further substituted in or on the monocycle;
(B) By substitution in or on the phenethyl group with alkyl, alkenyl, alkoxy, hydroxy, halohaloalkyl, amino or nitro groups;
(C) By substitution in or on the piperidine ring with alkyl, alkenyl, alkoxy, ester, ether,hydroxy, halo, haloalkyl, amino or nitro groups;
(D) By replacement of the aniline ring with any aromatic monocycle whether or notfurther substituted in or on the aromatic monocycle and/or
(E) By replacement of the N-propionyl group by another acyl group.

The targeted language was intentionally designed to capture only the modifications [already well described in the scientific and medical literature] being used by transnational criminal organizations to exploit the legitimate research information on structure activity relationships. By staying one step ahead of the CSA and Analogues Act, they continued the spread of these deadly poisons in the U.S. and internationally. There is an excellent detailed discussion on the chemistry and history of fentanyl and fentanyl related substances in a statement from Michael Van Linn, PhD taken from testimony before the United States Sentencing Commission in December, 2017: https://www.ussc.gov/sites/default/files/pdf/amendment-process/public-hearings-and-meetings/20171205/Van-Linn.pdf.

Fentanyl was first created in 1960 and has been studied extensively since then. As noted in the Van Linn testimony, many of the new FRSs responsible for recent overdose deaths in the U.S. are well described in the patent and scientific literature, often accompanied by pharmacological data and detailed instructions on synthesis. Essentially, these are precise maps or recipes that guide legal -- as well as illicit – drug labs and chemical manufacturers in creating new FRSs that are almost certain to be bioactive.

The pathway to synthesize fentanyl and FRSs is relatively straight forward and well-defined, and creation of a new FRS is as simple as plugging in or removing a different chemical at one step or another in the process of synthesis. The path to create new bioactive FRSs is easy straightforward to medicinal chemists and, unfortunately, also illicit chemists.

Reversing Overdoses and Medication Assisted Treatment

Some opposition in the research community suggest FRS class controls would hamper research into possible chemicals that could be used to reverse poisonings or treat opioid use disorder. To date, in over 60 years of extensive research done on fentanyls during which exhaustive structure activity relationship studies have been conducted, registered researchers and published research have failed to highlight any activity in developing a fentanyl based antagonist/ reversal agent or medication assisted treatment.

It should also be noted that the pharmacological and poisoning effects including lethal respiratory depressant effects of fentanyl/FRSs are similar to those of other all other opioid agonists. Naloxone (Narcan) has been shown to be effective in reversing the respiratory depression that leads to death caused by opioids like heroin, as well as semisynthetic and synthetic opioids including fentanyl. In other words, Naloxone is a very effective reversal agent/ antagonist. Deaths do not occur because naloxone doesn't work or isn't strong enough. Rarely it can wear off and if it does, the solution is to give more.

Poisoning deaths occur because of the ingestion of lethal doses of highly potent and toxic opioids, and not due to lack of potency or effectiveness of naloxone in reversing opioid toxicity when given in time.

With regard to medicinal treatment of opioid use disorder (medication assisted treatment/ MAT), relapse rates have no correlation with current MAT options. Relapse or drop-out rate of patients is attributed to many factors such as cost, access to doctors/ treaters and/ or lack of behavioral treatments among other factors, and are not related to the specific opioid being abused. Nor have there been discovered or created any fentanyl/FRS based medication assisted treatments. To recap, not one reversal agent/antagonist or MAT has been found or investigated in the six decades of research done into fentanyls. All current research is focused on detection, analysis and understanding the harm of these substances. The fentanyl class is not being researched as a possible therapeutic prior or since the DEA emergency control in 2018.

Sufficient Oversight and Collaboration Across Agencies

In the normal sequence of scheduling, DEA reviews and investigates chemical compounds individually, then collaborates with HHS and the FDA in making a final decision in the scheduling process. Concerns about bypassing consultation with HHS and the FDA in this circumstance by which the DEA can schedule certain fentanyl-related substances based on the specific, limited, targeted criteria were thoughtfully considered. As a result, the language was narrowly crafted to only include likely bioactive modifications based on the already well known fentanyl structure activity relationship body of research.

Lethal Doses of Chemical Warfare Agents and Narcotics

ChemicalAgent/ Drug	Lethal Dose	Route
Botulinum Toxin	.00007mg	Inhaled/Ingested/Injected
Tetanus Toxin	.0001mg	Inhaled/Ingested/Injected
CARFENTANIL	.02mg	Inhaled/Injected
Tabun NerveAgent	1-1.5mg	Inhaled/Ingested/Percutaneous
Ricin	1.78mg; 10mg	Inhaled/Injected;Percutaneous
FENTANYL	2mg (approx. equalto 4 grains of	Inhaled/Injected
VX Nerve Agent	2.1mg; 10mg	Inhaled/Injected; Percutaneous
Strychnine	70-140mg	Ingested
HEROIN	70mg	Inhaled/Injected
Cyanide	100-200mg	Ingested
MORPHINE	200mg	Inhaled/Injected
Methamphetamin	200mg	Inhaled/Injected
Cocaine	200mg	Inhaled/Injected
MDMA (Ecstasy)	1000mg	Ingested
THC/Marijuana	4000mg (pure THC)	***Not realistically achievable in humans by all methods of marijuana consumption per the
	One teaspoon of Fentanyl is enough to kill 2,000 people	

Proactively, and also in response to research concerns raised by the Department of Health and Human Services (HHS) and other stakeholders, DEA has already addressed and significantly simplified the research requirements for FRSs including, for example, requiring a single registration for all chemicals in the fentanyl class instead of separate registrations for each individual substance like it does for all other substances. It is significant to note that the majority of research registrants for the new FRS class were for DEA subcontractor chemical analysis or submitted through the Department of Defense. Ultimately, research is driven by funding and there does not appear to be a current investment in FRS research after 6 decades of studying the class. A final point on this: nearly all development of new fentanyl-related substances has been done oversees [in China mostly] and not by American scientists and researchers.

The table on the previous page is a representation of the precise level of lethality [how much is required to kill an average human] of common narcotics and chemical weapons agents. It is almost incomprehensible how small a dose of fentanyl will kill someone: 2mg or approximately the equivalent of 4 grains of sand.

Lethality and Potency, as Deadly as Chemical Weapons

The most accurate way to view fentanyl-related substances is as weapons of mass destruction, not as recreational drugs or intoxicants like marijuana, cocaine, and even heroin. In a 2019 paper by John P. Caves, Jr., a Distinguished Research Fellow in the Center for the Study of Weapons of Mass Destruction (CSWMD) at the Institute for National Strategic Studies at the National Defense University, called "Fentanyl as a Chemical Weapon" covers the topic well. https://www.hsdl.org/?view&did=832803.

Opposition to fentanyl class scheduling has likened it to cocaine legislation in the 1980s and as an extension of the war on drugs, but this perspective fails to account for the chemical weapon-like level of lethality that exists with fentanyl and FRSs.

In September 2018, 52 members (including all 50 states) of the National Association of Attorneys General (NAAG) sent a letter urging Congress to adopt the Wisconsin law on scheduling FRSs. When Congress failed to act, in December 2019 a second unanimous letter from all 56 members of the NAAG was sent urging Congress to adopt FRS class scheduling showcasing the strong bipartisan support for this policy. https://1li23g1as25g1r8so 11ozniw-wpengine.netdna-ssl.com/wp-content/uploads/2020/10/Letter-to-Congress-SOFA-Act-8.23-1.pdf, https://1li23g1as25g1r8so11ozniw-wpengine.netdna-ssl.com/wp-content/uploads/2020/10/NAAG-Support-for-FIGHT-Act-Letter.pdf.

A signatory of both letters included HHS Secretary Xavier Becerra in his capacity as California Attorney General, who actually signed them both. This speaks to the importance of this matter as a critical national public safety measure which is completely non-partisan at it's core.

Theoretical Research Concerns

It is interesting to note that the main groups opposing FRS scheduling for reason of theoretical negative effects on research are in fact mainly criminal justice reform and drug legalization based activist organizations. These are the same organizations who initially opposed FRS scheduling due to concerns of theoretical effects of mass incarceration preferentially affecting of people of color. This did not happen. A report by the GAO in 2021 said there were eight prosecutions for drug trafficking in the U.S. in the 3 years FRS scheduling had been temporarily enacted, four of which were known cartel traffickers. As designed, *"No one can die from ingesting something never created or be incarcerated for trafficking something that does not exist."*

Targeted control of specific fentanyl-related substances as a class and not as discrete chemicals is not a minor change to the U.S. Controlled Substance Act (CSA). It has been carefully and thoughtfully crafted and wouldn't even be considered, but for its significant impact already seen in the worst drug epidemic in the modern era. Annualized deaths caused by illicit fentanyl and known analogues now surpass heroin and are responsible for the overdose/poisoning death spike and lowering of the average life expectancy for Americans for the first time since development of immunizations and antibiotics.

Analogues Act of the CSA is Not Sufficient

Some suggest the Analogues Act of the CSA is sufficient to give DEA and DOJ the power needed to act against fentanyl-related substances. That is simply not accurate. In order to use the Analogues Act, a substance must be proven substantially similar to a listed schedule I or II, and also must be proven to be intended for human consumption. This is highly problematic because those findings must be adjudicated (and re-adjudicated) in court in each and every case, even when the substance has been proven to be an analogue in a previous case. In addition, the usual threshold to trigger looking at a substance as an analogue is purely reactive when it is found to be killing people, usually many people across multiple states. It is simply not preventative or proactive in any way. If the Analogues Act was sufficient, then the thousands of Americans killed by FRS poisoning would be alive, and there would have been no need for me to come up with FRS class scheduling in the first place.

Between 2017 and 2018 in New York City alone there were over 900 deaths from FRSs. According to the 2019 Florida Medical Examiners Commission Report, deaths in the Sunshine State directly attributable to FRS overdose rose 65 percent in just one year: 965 in 2016 to 1,588 in 2017, that is over 2,500 lives lost in just 2 years from FRSs…in just one state. Untold thousands have already died due to the existence and availability of fentanyl related substances. It's why the former Governor of New York called for fentanyl class scheduling language in NY and why other states and nations including our neighbors to the north in Canada are following Wisconsin's lead. We cannot go back to the way it was before fentanyl class scheduling was put in place.

Concerns over Prosecutions for Non-Bioactive FRSs

Concerns raised about increased prosecution of people distributing non-psychoactive FRSs that would be inappropriately classified as schedule I is an extremely unlikely scenario for the following reasons:

1) First and foremost - every substance classifiable under the FRS class scheduling language (all 27 studied to date) has been found to have potent opioid bioactivity - dozens or more times more potent than morphine.
2) Simple charges of possession and lowest level dealing of FRSs are simply not aggressively prosecuted by federal prosecutors.
3) FRSs do not exist naturally. They are synthesized in illicit clandestine overseas labs by chemist suppliers to transnational criminal organizations. The process of FRS synthesis is intentional and based on researched and readily available information of the roadmaps of the Structure-Activity Relationships: it isn't grown in a backyard; there is no bathtub lab manufacturing occurring; and, there is never going to be accidental synthesis, manufacturing and distribution of a new FRS.

The low likelihood of transnational criminal organizations/drug cartels synthesizing, manufacturing, and distributing new FRSs that aren't bioactive/

psychoactive. It's simply not plausible they would decide not to test their product lest they put new FRSs in their distribution networks that were duds [non- psychoactive]. How long would they be able to sell them if they didn't have potent opioid bioactivity?

Due to the specific and targeted nature of the SOFA language based on stopping the exploitation of known fentanyl/FRS structure activity relationships, it is almost certain that a newly developed FRS covered under this fentanyl related substance class scheduling language that is then manufactured and internationally trafficked would be bioactive. If the bioactivity were similar to fentanyl, it would be at the level of chemical weapons lethality: one teaspoon deadly enough to kill 2,000 people.

Those opposed to enacting permanent fentanyl class scheduling suggest a drug trafficker could be incarcerated for distributing a FRS that was actually beneficial or an antagonist like naloxone. This is simply not the case. As previously mentioned, in the over 60 years of research done on fentanyls, not one substance with antagonistic properties has ever been researched. Of importance to note, if Congress were to enact the rapid de-scheduling pathway proposed by President Biden in his ONDCP FRS scheduling recommendations (also in the HALT Fentanyl Act), rescheduling could be done rapidly in the highly unlikely circumstance of a substance being trafficked turns out to be non-psychoactive.

Sentencing Guidelines

Under current federal guidelines, the sentence is 5 years for 10 grams of fentanyl/ FRS, and 10 years for more than 100 grams. On first glance, that may seem harsh, but it is important to remember the lethalityand consider that 10 grams of a FRS is enough to kill 5,000 people, and 100 grams of a FRS could kill 50,000. I would venture to guess that most, if not all, physicians [and Americans too for that matter] would agree: if you could have only one class of drug with associated mandatory minimums, it would be fentanyl and FRSs. *As mentioned above, it is important to note that removing the schedule I mandatory minimums for FRSs would actually incentivize their creation and significantly weaken the law's proactive and preventative effects.*

There is information being disseminated that there have been prosecutions for FRSs that are not bioactive. This is not correct. As mentioned previously, every FRS researched to date under the FRS language has been found to have opioid effect bioactivity far more potent than heroin and morphine.The most recent new FRS studied was found to be four to eight times more potent than fentanyl.

Benzyl fentanyl has often been pointed to as an example of a fentanyl analogue that was scheduled under emergency order and then unscheduled [in 1985 and 1986 respectively]. In fact, it would not havequalified under the fentanyl class scheduling language as a FRS. The benzyl fentanyl modification and similar modifications were specifically excluded from the scheduling language because of their known non-bioactivity. It is also misstated by opposition that since 2018, prosecutions of the List 1 precursor benzyl fentanyl have occurred under FRS scheduling. In fact, they have occurred under precursor controls. [This is because benzyl fentanyl can be easily modified to create fentanyl, therefore it was controlled as a List 1 precursor]. *There have been Zero prosecutions for FRSs that are not bioactive.*

In addition, on several occasions, substances that do not fall under the FRS class scheduling language have been misclassified as such by those arguing against FRS Class Scheduling: benzyl fentanyl, remifentanil, Imodium and AT202 adding to the confusion on the issue of impact on research. In fact, allare not classifiable as schedule 1 under the FRS scheduling language.

International Coordination (with China Especially)

In trade negotiations with the Chinese government, the U.S. included targeted FRS class scheduling among its priorities. As a result, China permanently enacted similar scheduling language in May 2019. The United Nations includes it in its toolkit of model opioid legislation for member nations. Several other countries [including Canada] and many American states have adopted similar scheduling language. In this case of harm reduction to benefit American citizens, even China sees the value in permanent FRS class scheduling. It is not inconceivable -- and many would say likely -- that if the U.S. doesn't permanently enact FRS class scheduling, China may not continue its prohibitions on fentanyls. The incentives for the creation and distribution of new FRSs would re-occur and that some of the thousands of chemical companies in India could/would start on the FRS creation pathway that would re-open if FRS scheduling were to sunset.

Conclusion

It is incontrovertible that temporary targeted fentanyl class control has already been an extremely effective harm reduction tool and has eliminated the incentive for traffickers to create new FRSs, closingthe FRS loophole at home and overseas and saving countless lives in the process. If Congress allows the FRS-class scheduling to expire, it's only a matter of time before other countries like China and India could restart the fentanyl-related substance creation machine and unleash the devastating consequences.

My roles as an emergency physician, parent of young adult daughters and a medical regulator, drove meto design a legislative solution to prevent the development of new FRSs by illicit overseas chemists, but at the same time not incarcerate people with substance use disorder or impede critical research. The FRSclass scheduling language that has been embraced by the Biden Administration/ONDCP and the HALT Fentanyl Act threads that needle.

I first testified on FRS scheduling at an HJC hearing 5 years ago, and my wife keeps asking me why it is necessary for me to keep coming out to Washington to get this simple legislation locked in place. I can'treally give her an answer that would make sense to most Americans. Congress has in its power the ability to permanently enact this important FRS class scheduling legislation and continue to save countless lives. There is no question, if we turn our collective backs on the progress that's been made tostem the tide of the creation of new FRSs in America, thousands more deaths will occur annually from the reemergence, existence and widespread availability of these deadly chemical agents. *Now is the time to make this crucial reform permanent and pass the SOFA Act or HALT Fentanyl Act.*

Thank you for the opportunity to contribute to the discussion and thank you for your leadership on thiscritical public health issue.

Timothy W Westlake, MD, FFSMB, FACEP
Wisconsin Medical Examining Board,
Immediate-Past Chairman
Wisconsin Controlled Substance Board, Former Member

Mr. BIGGS. Thank you. Thank you so much, Dr. Westlake. We appreciate your testimony.

Now, Ms. Rachwal, I recognize you for five minutes.

Statement of Erin Rachwal

Ms. RACHWAL. Good morning, Chair Biggs and distinguished Members of the Subcommittee.

Thank you for providing me to share our views on permanently scheduling FRSs and how it relates to our story.

My husband and I are here today because we are grieving parents walking through an unimaginable experience. We are founders of the Love, Logan Foundation and we reside in Wisconsin. I'm a mom of two beautiful boys and I'm also a licensed clinical therapist, and I've built a thriving private practice working with families and children in mental health.

Through our advocacy, we have hopes for change and actions, so that other families will not have to suffer the needless and grievous loss of child or loved one to fentanyl poisoning. We recently established this 501(3)(c) [sic] nonprofit after losing our oldest son, Logan, forever 19, to a fake pill containing fentanyl.

Logan died on Valentine's Day. We received the call that no parent ever wants to get. Logan was found dead in his dorm room at the University of Wisconsin, Milwaukee, in his freshman year. His toxicology report showed three different forms of fentanyl—three different forms. He was poisoned.

Even though my profession is so focused on helping people in various areas of mental health, I, as his mom, did not even know about fentanyl poisoning or the severity or lethality of it until his tragic death.

Unfortunately, we have met way too many parents who have lost children to this deadly poison. They were all unaware, as we also were.

Logan, he was a kind, caring, smart, and creative young man who had his whole life ahead of him. He had a great sense of humor. He loved animals and played baseball for many years.

Being a mom of two beautiful boys was the most important thing in the world to me. We raised Logan and younger brother Caden in a nurturing and loving home. We vacationed and we camped. We celebrated birthdays. We went to church. We played sports. We spent consistent time together.

I tell you these things about our family to make the point that no family is immune to this danger. This could happen to your family. Fentanyl does not discriminate. It is a poison.

Logan went to college in the fall of 2020 and he, tragically, never finished out his freshman year. His brother Caden, just 14 months younger, experiences daily battles of depression and trauma and side effects from his death. For all of us, losing Logan was like a bomb going off in the middle of our family that we had built our life around. This explosion killed our son and killed Caden's brother. The aftermath of a completely unexpected and devastating death like this is unexplainable until you actually experience it. This problem, this weapon is called fentanyl.

Through our grieving process over the past two years, we have realized the impact this crisis has had on our Nation. Today, I sit here, not only on behalf of Logan and our family, but also for every single family in this country that has suffered the loss of this tragic drug.

There is an urgent need to confront the growing threat of fentanyl from every angle in our country. According to the DEA, fentanyl is now the leading cause of death in the United States for people ages 18–45, and the kids are getting younger. These are the ages when young adults, when Logan should have been thriving and excelling, but, instead, thousands of them are dying with increasing numbers. Death leaves no opportunity to recover. These kids are not able to learn from their mistakes, as they once used to. We have connected with families all over the country through our devastation, and we have learned that coming together is a powerful way to change lives and change laws and take political action against those who are killing our children.

The temporary scheduling of FRS has shown to deter the creation of new FRSs, which is one clear way in protecting our country. Therefore, we know permanent scheduling of these substances is a solid shield we have to fight the fentanyl crisis. If you are questioning whether this bill should be passed, I'm going to ask you: How can you focus on theoretical rights of criminals over the rights of our children—children just like my son Logan?

Permanent scheduling symbolizes a proactive and bipartisan approach to this crisis. United we stand; divided we fall. "United we stand; divided we fall"—this is a phrase that has been used for hundreds of years to inspire unity and collaboration. Its once concept lies in the collectivist notion that, if individual members of a group work on their own instead of together, they are doomed to fail, and we all will be defeated.

Do you believe in any way that our country is being defeated by this poison developed in Chinese and cartel labs? I'm going to ask that question one more time. Do you believe in any way that our country is being defeated by this poison developed in Chinese and cartel labs?

Mr. BIGGS. Ms. Rachwal, if you could please—

Ms. RACHWAL. I can tell you that I believe we are, and many other—many others do as well. Wisconsin parents of Cade, forever 18; Ryan, 23; Nick; Sylvia; Katrina; Tyler, Archie, Miguel; Sam; McKenzie; Ryan.

To connect with a young adult around Logan's age, most parents simply go out to dinner, visit, call, text, Facetime, vacation, or spend a holiday. To connect with our son Logan, we have to look at a sunset, a rainbow, listen to a song, look at a picture, or wear his fingerprint around our neck. This is what fentanyl does. It changes everything—our past, present, and future.

In conclusion, our family's story, Logan's story, is just one of tens of thousands that have occurred and will keep occurring if we do not take action to slow down and, ultimately, stop the explosion of this deadly poison.

We hope by sharing our experience we can give meaning to Logan's ultimately untimely loss and honor his life and leave a significant legacy to protect other families from this devastation.

Thank you for your time and opportunity to tell our story. [The prepared statement of Ms. Rachwal follows:]

Written Statement of Erin Rachwal, MSW, LCSW

GRIEVING MOTHER OF SON, LOGAN RACHWAL, FOREVER 19
CO-FOUNDER OF LOVE, LOGAN FOUNDATION, 501c3 NON-PROFIT
BEFORE THE COMMITTEE ON THE JUDICIARY
SUBCOMMITTEE ON CRIME AND FEDERAL GOVERNMENT SURVEILLANCE
UNITED STATES HOUSE OF REPRESENTATIVES

THE FENTANYL CRISIS IN AMERICA: INACTION IS NO LONGER AN OPTION

March 1, 2023

Dear Members,

Thank you for the opportunity to testify at this hearing and share our personal story as it relates to this topic.

Why We Are Here

My name is Erin Rachwal. My husband, Rick, and I are invested in this discussion because we are grieving parents walking through an unimaginable experience. We are the founders of the Love, Logan Foundation residing in Wisconsin. I am also a Licensed Clinical Therapist and have built a thriving private practice working with families and children in mental health. We are thankful you have provided us the opportunity to share our views that strongly support permanently scheduling Fentanyl- Related-Substances, (FRS) as a class – in the hopes that other parents and siblings will not have to suffer the needless and grievous loss of a child or loved one.

We recently established our 501c3 nonprofit organization after tragically losing our 19- year-old son, Logan, to a fake pill containing fentanyl. His toxicology report showed three different forms of fentanyl in his system. Even though my profession is focused on helping people in various areas of mental health, I didn't even know much about fentanyl poisoning or the severity or lethality of it until Logan's tragic death. Unfortunately, hundreds of other parents we have personally met who have lost children to this deadly poison were as unaware as we were.

Fentanyl Doesn't Discriminate- Logan's Story

As a young boy, Logan was generally happy but did struggle with some anxiety. He found making friends extremely challenging and often felt like he was the one left out.

We had him in counseling very early on and throughout most of his life. He was always our boy who seemed to be sad, and we made countless attempts to help him. While he had his struggles, as many children do, Logan was also kind, caring, smart, and creative. He had a great sense of humor and would have done anything for anyone. He loved animals – especially his cats - and he played baseball for many years. Being a mom and having a family was the most important thing in the world to me. We raised our two boys in a nurturing and loving home. We vacationed, camped, celebrated birthdays, went to church, played sports, and spent quality time together. I tell you these things about our family and son to make the point that NO family is immune from this danger – it could happen to any family.

Logan went off to college in the fall of 2020 and tragically never finished out his freshman year. He had his whole life ahead of him. On Valentine's Day, 2021 we received the call that no parent ever wants to get. Logan was found dead in his dorm room at the University of Wisconsin – Milwaukee. The year prior (2019-2020), our relationship with Logan became very strained. Looking back, we are now able to piece together what was missing information to help us understand what was happening at that time. Logan was using pills to self-medicate for his anxiety and became irritable, dishonest, secretive, angry and extremely difficult to deal with.

There are no words to describe what it's like coping with a child who can technically make his own decisions at age 18, yet as a parent you see destruction and turmoil taking over. It is clear that at some point he was buying pills from friends and we will never really know when he may have crossed that invisible line of addiction. The availability of fake pills that are potent and driving addiction in young adults is far and wide. I remember a recent conversation with a Wisconsin DEA Agent that sat down with us and said "that ship has sailed" regarding the drug cartels and numerous analogues / forms of pills that they are making and distributing all over the United States. Cartels are driving addiction – on purpose – for their business. Logan was being used to increase sales in their business and he didn't even know it.

Once Logan's first semester of college started in fall 2020, we were working very hard repairing the relationship with him. Logan was coming home for dinners, laundry, visits, etc. Things felt better; not perfect, but much better. For the first time in a long time, I was a mom with hope. Covid prohibited a few planned visits and celebrations over the holidays that year. The day before Valentine's Day, Logan texted us both and said "Hey Mom and Dad, Happy Saturday! I just wanted to say I love you and I am at work". We both replied to him that day unbeknownst to us, that would be the last time we would ever "speak" to our 19-year-old son.

The following evening, Valentine's Day, at 8:37 pm, I received a phone call from Logan's best friend. He was frantically telling me to call the University Police Dept. I attempted to call and text Logan from my cell at 8:44 pm immediately with no answer or reply. It was at this point I knew in my gut that something was terribly wrong – I looked at my husband and said, "he's gone, I can feel it". The connection a mom has to her child is like no other. My body could actually feel his absence. We called our other son home and the three of us drove down to the university with no additional information other than a few social media posts that all seemed to point to his (possible) death. Walking into the police station in the same building Logan's dorm was is a memory I will never forget. I was physically holding my other son up so he didn't collapse on the ground. The gripping fear and pain was the most indescribable thing I have ever been through. Logan was gone. They told us he was found an hour prior, by a friend, laying in his lofted bed. It was estimated that he had been laying there for at least 12 hours.

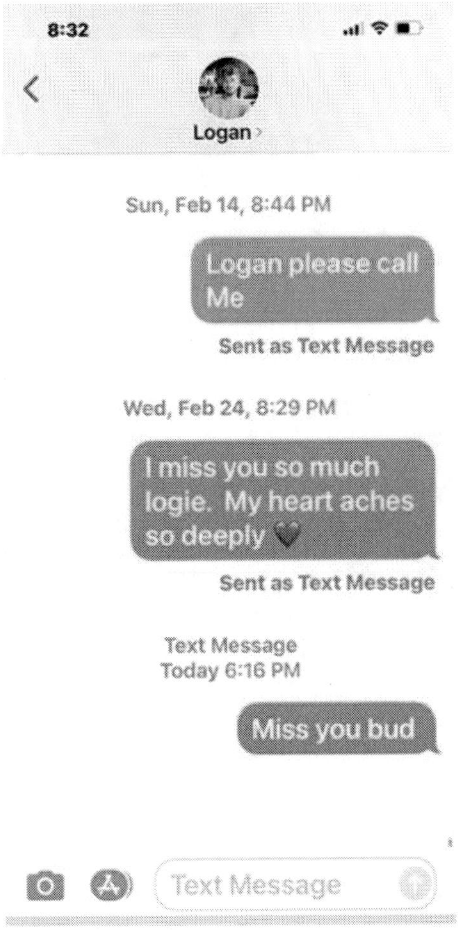

He had taken a pill while over Face Time with his girlfriend around 7:30 am earlier that morning. She told the police that within he "started snoring and fell asleep". The three of us went up to the 11th floor to his dorm room to see him that night. I can't put into words the guttural pain and emotion I felt when looking at him in his bed, his right arm half red and half blue and knowing I would NEVER see him again.

The Aftermath of an Untimely Death

As invested parents, you never expect to be burying your child. This untimely death brings up significant, life-long losses. Loss of the past, loss of the present and what would be, and loss of the future. We often wonder what Logan would have accomplished in his life. Would he have had a family? Children? Would we have beengrandparents? So many unfinished details of a life gone way too soon.

Logan leaves behind a younger brother, Caden, who now experiences daily battles of depression and side effects from seeing his family broken and forever changed. Havinglost the 4th family member is like a table leg being broken off and trying to still eat and use the table as if. Losing our child, and a brother, to this poison, was like a bomb going off in the middle of everything we had built our life around – this explosion killed our oldest son; Caden's only brother. The aftermath of a completely unexpected and devastating death like this is unexplainable until you experience it. This bomb – the weapon – FENTANYL.

Three months later, we received a phone call with the results of the toxicology reportonly to find out that Logan had *THREE different forms of fentanyl* in his system.

Logan was murdered – poisoned. He *thought* he had bought a "perc 30" and insteadreceived a fake pill, made to look real, containing fentanyl and it killed him - instantly.

Why This Is Important

Through our grieving process over the past 2 years, we have realized the impact of the loss of a child will never go away. Two weeks ago, marked two years since Logan's death. We find ourselves still in shock, still pushing through each day, breaking down unexpectedly. But this grief has given us a deeper compassion for others and especially for those suffering from losing a child to fentanyl poisoning. We are not only representing Logan's tragic death, rather every family across this nation suffering from being a victim of a horrible crime related to Fentanyl.

Our pain reminds us of the need to confront the growing threat of fentanyl from every angle in our country. According to the DEA, Fentanyl is now the leading cause of death in the U.S. for people ages 18-45. These are the ages when our young adults should be thriving and excelling, but instead, thousands of them are dying in increasing numbers. Death leaves no opportunity to recover – these kids aren't able to learn from their mistakes. Logan isn't here to learn from his mistakes because fentanyl took that opportunity away from him. We have connected with families all over the country through our devastation. Through this trauma and loss, we have learned that coming together is a powerful way to change laws and take political action against those who are killing our children.

Temporary Scheduling of FRS

The temporary scheduling of Fentanyl Related Substances (FRS) has shown to deter the creation of new FRS's which is one clear avenue protecting our country. Therefore, we know the permanent scheduling of Fentanyl Related Substances is a solid shield we have to fight the fentanyl crisis. If you are questioning whether this bill should be passed, I'd ask how can you focus on the theoretical rights of criminals over the rights of our children? Children just like my son Logan.

Permanent Scheduling of FRS

Permanent scheduling symbolizes a proactive and bi-partisan approach to this crisis. "United we Stand, divided we fall" is a phrase that has been used for hundreds of years to inspire unity and collaboration. It's core concept lies in the collectivist notion, that if individual members of a group work on their own instead of together, they are doomed to fail and will all be defeated. Do you believe in any way that our country is being defeated by this poison developed in Chinese and cartel labs?

To connect with a young adult Logan's age, most parents simply go to dinner, visit, text,call, FaceTime, vacation or spend time on Holidays together. Well, to connect with our son Logan, we have to look at a sunset, a rainbow, a picture, listen to a song, wear his sweatshirt or keep his thumbprint necklace around our neck. This is what Fentanyl does. It changes everything; our past, our present and our future. Our family's story –Logan's story - is just one of *tens of thousands* that have occurred and will keep occurring if we do not take action to slow down and ultimately stop the flood of this deadly poison. We hope by sharing our experience we can give meaning to Logan's untimely loss and – in honor of his life – leave a significant legacy to protect other families from this tragedy.

Thank you for your time and the opportunity to tell our story.

Erin Rachwal, MSW, LCSW
Logan's mom

Logan Case number 21-01270

Mr. BIGGS. Thank you, Ms. Rachwal.

Dr. Singer, you are recognized for five minutes.

Statement of Dr. Jeffrey A. Singer

Dr. SINGER. Thank you, Chair Biggs.

My deepest condolences to the Rachwals.

Members of the Committee, I've submitted written testimony which I'll summarize here.

Leaders and commentators often refer to the fentanyl overdose crisis as an epidemic or an invasion, but these are inappropriate metaphors. Fentanyl is not a viral pathogen that jumps from host to host or a hunter seeking a defenseless prey. The influx of fentanyl is a response to market demand.

More crucially, fentanyl is just the latest manifestation of what drug policy analysts call "the iron law of prohibition." The short- hand version of the law states, the harder the law enforcement, the harder the drug. Prohibition incentivizes the creation of more potent drugs that are easier to smuggle in smaller sizes and can be subdivided into more units to sell. The iron law is why cannabis THC concentration has grown over the years. It is what brought crack cocaine to the cocaine market. It is why fentanyl replaced heroin as the primary cause of overdose deaths in the United States.

Fentanyl-related overdose deaths started rising in 2012. By 2016, they eclipsed deaths from heroin and diverted prescription pain pills. By 2017, fentanyl was found in more than 50 percent of opioid-related overdose deaths, and by 2022, as we know, it was involved in roughly 90 percent.

Now, we are getting troubling reports about the veterinary tranquilizer xylazine, which users call "tranq," becoming an additive to fentanyl and other illicit narcotics. This tranquilizer greatly potentiates the opioid's effects, producing powerful highs. Adding this potentiator, again, enables illicit opioids to be smuggled in smaller sizes and be subdivided into more units.

Xylazine makes blood vessels constrict, and if it gets into the tissues surrounding blood vessels, it can cause tissue death and deadly soft tissue ulcers. Some ulcers become so severe, so severely affected, that surgeons must perform lifesaving limb amputations. What makes xylazine even more deadly is that it's not an opioid, and overdoses from it which make people stop breathing cannot be reversed with naloxone.

The iron law hasn't stopped with tranq. In 2019, health departments in Europe and the U.S. began seeing the synthetic opioid nitazene in overdose toxicology studies. Last fall, the Tennessee Department of Health reported nitazene-related overdose deaths increased fourfold between 2019 and 2021.

Ciba-Geigy developed nitazenes in the 1950's, but never brought them to market. They're estimated to be roughly 20 times more potent than fentanyl.

Fortunately, naloxone reverses nitazene overdoses, but it might require multiple doses.

Because most health departments haven't been testing for nitazenes, we're unaware if nitazenes are becoming more prevalent among black market drugs. I wouldn't be surprised if two or three years from now we're talking about the nitazene crisis instead of the fentanyl crisis.

Border closures, lockdowns, and other pandemic policies made it more challenging to transport opium to drug dealers to process into heroin. Pandemic-related supply chain problems created shortages of the commercial chemical acetic anhydride that is used to complete the process.

On the other hand, fentanyl and fentanyl analogs can be easily made in clandestine labs by modifying its fundamental ingredient, piperidine, which is in abundant supply. Because fentanyl and its analogs are entirely synthetic, drug cartels don't need to rely on growing and transporting opium.

All these factors made it an easy business decision for the drug cartels to switch out heroin for fentanyl. With pandemic policies relaxed, it still makes sense for the cartels to stick with what works. Adding fentanyl analogs to Schedule I is ill-advised. First, many fentanyl analogs are medically used to control pain and assisting anesthesia, such as sufentanil, alfentanil, and remifentanil. An outright ban on developing a category of fentanyl analogs will stifle advances in therapeutic research. Besides, placing a drug on schedule will not deter drug cartels. Heroin has been on Schedule I for more than 50 years and it's not deterred heroin trafficking. There's no evidence that placing fentanyl analogs on Schedule I drugs will work any better to reduce overdose deaths.

Threatening drug dealers with life in prison or the death penalty is also unlikely to deter the drug trade. Most drug dealers already factor in the risk of death when they get into the business and are, correctly, more afraid of getting killed by rivals than by the U.S. Department of Justice.

Prohibition makes the black market dangerous because people who buy drugs can never be sure of the drug's purity, dosage, or even if it is the drug they think they are buying. As a parent and grandparent, my heart breaks whenever I hear stories of teenagers who thought they were buying Percocet, or something like that, on the black market, and died because of an overdose because the pill contained fentanyl. Those young people were not seeking and did not know they were buying fentanyl. The black market killed those youngsters.

I urge the Subcommittee to avoid doubling down on policies that will not only fail to stem the flow of illicit fentanyl, but will fuel the development of even more deadly replacements.

Thank you very much.

[The prepared statement of Dr. Singer follows:]

Statement of Jeffrey A. Singer, MD, FACS Senior Fellow Cato Institute before the Subcommittee on Crime and Federal Government Surveillance Committee on the Judiciary United States House of Representatives

March 1, 2023

RE: "The Fentanyl Crisis in America: Inaction is No Longer an Option"

Chairman Biggs, Ranking Member Jackson Lee, and distinguished members of the subcommittee:

I want to thank the Subcommittee on Crime and Federal Government Surveillance for the opportunity to provide my thoughts on the fentanyl crisis in America.

My name is Jeffrey A. Singer. I am a Senior Fellow in Health Policy Studies at the Cato Institute. I am also a medical doctor specializing in general surgery and have been practicing that specialty in Phoenix, Arizona, for over 40 years. The Cato Institute is a 501(c)(3) non-partisan, non-profit, tax-exempt educational foundation dedicated to the principles of individual liberty, limited government, free markets, and peace. Cato scholars conduct independent research on a wide range of policy issues. To maintain its independence, the Cato Institute accepts no government funding. Cato receives approximately 80 percent of its funding through tax-deductible contributions from individuals. The remainder of its support comes from foundations, corporations, and the sale of books and other publications. The Cato Institute does not take positions on legislation.

Leaders and commentators often refer to the fentanyl overdose crisis as an "epidemic" or an "invasion." But these are inappropriate metaphors. Fentanyl is not a viral pathogen that jumps from host to host or a hunter seeking defenseless prey. The influx of fentanyl is a response to market demand.

But more crucially, fentanyl is just the latest manifestation of what drug policy analysts call "the iron law of prohibition."[1] A variant of what economists call the Alchian-Allen Effect, the shorthand version of the iron law states, "the harder the law enforcement, the harder the drug." Enforcing prohibition incentivizes those who market prohibited substances to develop more potent forms that are easier to smuggle in smaller sizes and can be subdivided into more units to sell.

During alcohol prohibition, bootleggers and dealers were not smuggling beer and wine but whiskey and other hard liquors. At football games, tailgaters drink beer and wine but smuggle flasks of hard liquor into stadiums that prohibit fans from bringing alcoholic beverages.

The iron law of prohibition is why cannabis THC concentration has grown over the years. It is what brought crack cocaine into the cocaine market. And it made fentanyl replace heroin as the primary cause of overdose deaths in the United States.

The Centers for Disease Control and Prevention began seeing fentanyl-related overdose deaths rise in 2012. By 2016 fentanyl-related deaths eclipsed deaths from heroin and diverted prescription pain pills. By 2017 fentanyl was found in more than 50 percent of opioid-related overdose deaths. By 2022 it was involved in roughly 90 percent of deaths.[2]

The iron law of prohibition cannot be repealed. Already we have been getting troubling reports of the veterinary tranquilizer xylazine—drug users call it "tranq"—becoming an additive to fentanyl and other illicit narcotics. This tranquilizer greatly potentiates opioids' effects, producing more powerful "highs." Adding this potentiator again enables illicit opioids to be smuggled in smaller sizes and subdivided into more units to sell. Xylazine causes blood vessels to constrict, and if it gets into the tissues surrounding blood vessels, it can lead to tissue necrosis and deadly soft tissue ulcers. Some users' ulcers have become so severely infected that surgeons must amputate limbs to save their lives.[3] What makes xylazine more deadly is that it is not an opioid, and overdoses from it that cause people to stop breathing cannot be reversed with naloxone.

And the iron law hasn't stopped at "tranq." In 2019, health departments in Belgium, Canada, Estonia, Germany, Latvia, Sweden, the United Kingdom,

[1] https://filtermag.org/infographic-the-iron-law-of-prohibition/.

[2] https://usafacts.org/articles/are-fentanyl-overdose-deaths-rising-in-the-us/.

[3] https://www.cato.org/blog/iron-law-prohibition-introducing-tranq.

and the United States began seeing the synthetic opioid nitazene in overdose forensic toxicology studies. Last fall, the Tennessee Department of Health reported that nitazene-related overdose deaths increased four-fold between 2019 and 2021.[4] Nitazenes were developed by Ciba-Geigy in the 1950s but never brought to market. Nitazenes are estimated to be roughly 20 times more potent than fentanyl.

Fortunately, naloxone reverses nitazene overdoses, though greater doses of naloxone are required. Because most health departments have not been testing for nitazenes, we are unaware if nitazenes are becoming more prevalent among black market drugs. Yet, I wouldn't be surprised if two or three years from now, we are talking about the "nitazene crisis" instead of the fentanyl crisis.[5]

The Covid pandemic accelerated fentanyl's prominence among black market drug users. Border closures, lockdowns, and other pandemic policies made it more challenging to transport opium and opium gum to drug dealers to be processed into heroin. Pandemic-related supply chain problems created shortages of the commercial chemical acetic anhydride—used to make cigarette filters, aspirin, and other products—which is necessary to convert the morphine in opium to diacetyl-morphine, which Bayer branded as heroin when it developed the drug in the 1890s.[6]

On the other hand, fentanyl and fentanyl analogs can be easily synthesized in clandestine labs by modifying its fundamental ingredient, piperidine. Piperidine is a chemical used to make numerous pharmaceuticals and is in abundant supply. And because fentanyl and its analogs are entirely synthetic, drug cartels don't need to rely on growing and transporting opium.

These factors, plus the tighter border controls in response to the pandemic, made it an easy business decision for the drug cartels to switch out heroin for fentanyl. With pandemic policies relaxed, it still makes sense for the cartels to stick with what works for them.

University of California, San Francisco medical school professor Daniel Ciccarone, MD told the audience at a 2019 Cato Institute harm reduction conference that most IV drug users prefer heroin to fentanyl. The fentanyl experience differs significantly from the heroin experience. In 2019, most

---

[4] https://www.cdc.gov/mmwr/volumes/71/wr/mm7137a5.htm?s_cid=mm7137a5_w.

[5] https://www.cato.org/blog/nitazene-overdose-deaths-rise-iron-law-prohibition-cannot-been-repealed.

[6] https://www.unodc.org/documents/data-and-analysis/covid/Covid-19-and-drug-supply-chain-Mai2020.pdf.

heroin users considered fentanyl an unwanted contaminant.[7] Today, however, heroin is much less available as the cartels have moved to supply fentanyl instead. Therefore, IV drug users have resigned themselves to using fentanyl, and many have come to prefer it.

Adding fentanyl analogs to the Drug Enforcement Administration's Schedule I is ill-advised. First, many fentanyl analogs are used medically to control pain and assist in anesthesia, including sufentanil, alfentanil, and remifentanil. An outright ban on developing fentanyl analogs will stifle advances in therapeutic research. Second, placing a drug on Schedule I will not deter drug cartels. Heroin has been listed on Schedule I for more than 50 years, and it has not deterred heroin trafficking or heroin use. There is no evidence that placing fentanyl analogs on Schedule I works any better.

Threatening drug dealers with life imprisonment or the death penalty is also unlikely to deter the drug trade. Most drug dealers already factor the risk of death into their decision to get into the business and, correctly, have a greater fear of being killed by rival cartels and dealers than by the United States Department of Justice.

If policymakers double down on the same prohibitionist policies they have employed for over 50 years, deaths from illicit drug overdoses will continue to rise. Doing the same thing repeatedly, with even more vigor this time, will not yield a different result.

Prohibition makes the black market dangerous because people who buy drugs on the black market can never be sure of the drug's purity, dosage, or even if it is the drug they think they are buying.

Policymakers learned how alcohol prohibition failed and came to their senses when they repealed it in 1933. Today, when I go to my legal drug dealer to purchase whiskey, it never enters my mind that it might be adulterated with fentanyl or have a greater concentration of alcohol than it says on the bottle label. That is because it is legal and regulated.

As a parent, my heart breaks whenever I hear stories of teenagers who thought they were buying a diverted prescription drug like oxycodone and then died from an overdose because the pill contained fentanyl. Those young people were not seeking and did not know they were buying fentanyl. The black market killed those youngsters.

Short of ending prohibition, federal and state lawmakers can help reduce overdose deaths by repealing drug paraphernalia laws that make it illegal to

---

[7] https://cdn.cato.org/archive-2019/cc-03-21-19-05.mp4 and also https://www.cato.org/events/harm-reduction-shifting-war-drugs-war-drug-related-deaths

distribute fentanyl test strips, which mitigate the dangers of fentanyl consumption. The Canadian company that makes fentanyl test strips has also developed strips that can test for xylazine.[8] Xylazine test strips are likely to grow in importance as "tranq" becomes more prevalent.

I urge the Subcommittee to avoid doubling down on policies that will not only fail to stem the flow of illicit fentanyl but will fuel the development of more deadly replacements.

Thank you and I look forward to answering your questions.

Mr. BIGGS. Thank you, Dr. Singer.

Now, we recognize Mr. Maltz for your five minutes.

Statement of Derek Maltz

Mr. MALTZ. Chair Biggs, Ranking Member Jackson Lee, and distinguished Members of the Committee, thank you very much for the opportunity to speak today on the fentanyl growing crisis that is killing our kids at record levels.

I'm not here representing DEA. I'm a private citizen who cares deeply about the private people in America and our national security.

The President should immediately declare a national security and public health emergency. Let's make that clear. Because we have chemical substances all over our streets. These are not overdoses. This not a red or a blue issue. It's a red, white, and blue issue. Every American should care.

As the leader of DEA's Special Operations Division for the last 10 years of my career, I had really nice optics on the growing Mexican cartels and, also, the growing role of the Chinese criminal networks that have been doing a bombing campaign on our country with synthetic drugs. They are being made in labs in China. They're also being made in labs in Mexico at record levels.

This is a game-changer for America. This is different. This is not the same opioid crisis. The Chinese criminals are providing critical money-laundering services, and they're also providing the mass amount of chemicals to make the poison. The Cartel Jalisco New Generation and the Sinaloa Cartel are the enemy of our children. In my view, fentanyl is a chemical weapon, and the narco-terrorists in Mexico are destroying our country. They need to be held

---

8 https://www.cfsre.org/nps-discovery/drug-checking/characterization-of-xylazine-test-strips-for-use-in-drug- checking.

accountable, even if it means using our U.S. military. The cartels are taking total advantage of weak security at the porous border, killing more Americans than any terrorist organization in the history of the country.

After my DEA career, I've been supporting law enforcement agencies and working closely with families like the Rachwals. We are working hard to spread awareness and save lives.

I teamed up with the Lost Voices of Fentanyl, and you'll see the collages of all the dead kids that we've made over the years—in all an effort to get awareness and save lives.

I teamed up, also, with other people in America that care about our country.

As highlighted earlier by the Chair, and also, the work done last week in Phoenix, Arizona and throughout Arizona, 4.5 million fake pills—remember what the DEA Administrator said—six out of those 10 pills have a potentially fatal dose of fentanyl. Sheila Jackson Lee, Ranking Member, the four pills, that's outdated. She updated it to six.

So, according to the DEA, this is a crisis like we've never seen. We cannot expect to end this poisoning crisis with law enforcement alone. Addicted people need help. Mental illness is on the rise, and kids are, sadly, turning to these pills for help. They're using social media platforms to get what they need. It's as simple as ordering food. The cartels have invaded our homes. They are supposed to learn from mistakes, not die from mistakes.

So, the question to everybody in America: Where the hell is the Department of Education? Where are the public service announcements? Why can't the White House team up with professional athletes and celebrities to get video reels to the kids on social media, because that's what they'll see and that's what they'll respond to? Protecting the kids must be No. 1.

There are armies of families who are dedicating every day working throughout America, spreading awareness, presenting at schools, starting nonprofits with their own money, making billboards of their deceased loved ones.

There must be a true coordinated U.S. task force using authorities and capabilities with accountability for results. You can't just give them money; you've got to ask them: Where are the results? Are the death rates going down? If not, you have to change.

The cartels in Mexico have evolved quickly from drug cartels to transnational criminals, to now terrorists like we've never seen ever. Al Quaeda, ISIS, Hezbollah, they're not killing this amount of Americans.

There's positive movement from families and State attorney generals and congressional Members to declare cartels terrorists and, also, fentanyl, a weapon of mass destruction, which I fully support. The cartels use the latest technology, weapon systems. They take total advantage of antiquated laws. They control the government of Mexico—infiltrating, intimidating, placing the highest-ranking officials on their payroll.

Look what happened last week in the Eastern District of New York. The FBI equivalent in Mexico convicted, sent to life. He's going to be sent to life—prison for life because of his role with the cartels. Sorry, ladies and gentlemen, you can no longer rely on the corrupt, soft-on-crime leaders in Mexico to save our kids.

What keeps me motivated is the courageous, selfless, inspiring families like the Rachwals, who lost loved ones, but they fight daily. Look at the amazing work of the Families Against Fentanyl. They're the ones going through the CDC data. They're the ones telling America about the rising rates of these kids dying. Isn't that the job of the U.S. Government? What am I missing?

CDC, where are the accurate and timely stats on fentanyl deaths? During COVID, we saw it every night on TV. The crisis needs an Operation Warp Speed.

Kings County, Washington, the medical examiner, 35 dead in the first 21 days. They don't have enough cooler space out there.

San Diego, 25 percent increase in fentanyl-related deaths in five years.

As the younger kids are dying, every parent is wondering: Why is there a sense of urgency from the White House? Where's the leadership on this fentanyl poisoning crisis? Why are social media companies able to get away with killing the kids on their platforms? Why is it that this continues?

Dr. Gupta—almost done—Dr. Gupta: This is the worst drug crisis in the history of the country. He said it's unacceptable to him and the President. He also said it's a direct and surging threat to national security and public health—public health.

So, I ask, if it's a new era of drug trafficking, where's the new era of aggressive action to destroy the production labs?

Thank you very much, Chair, and I apologize for going over, but it's a very important topic.

[The prepared statement of Mr. Maltz follows:]

United States House of Representatives House Committee on the Judiciary Subcommittee on Crime and Federal Government Surveillance
Hearing Titled, "The Fentanyl Crisis In America: Inaction Is No Longer an Option."

Statement Of Derek S. Maltz

March 01, 2023

Introduction

Chairman Jim Jordan, Ranking Member Jerrold Nadler, Chair Andy Biggs, Ranking Member Sheila Jackson Lee and distinguished members of the committee, I would like to thank you forthis opportunity to speak today about America's devastating and escalating fentanyl poisoningcrisis. I am grateful for the opportunity to share my experience and thoughts as America faces complex challenges with this unprecedented national security and public health disaster. I hada long rewarding 28-year career as a Special Agent in the Drug Enforcement Administration (DEA). I retired from the DEA in July 2014 but remain actively involved in the private sectorsupporting law enforcement agencies around the world as they aggressively target Transnational Criminal Organizations (TCOs). I'm also very engaged in supporting families around the country who have lost loved ones to the devastating substance fentanyl entering America at historic levels.

During the last 10 years of my career, I was the Agent in Charge of the DEA's Special Operations Division (SOD) in Northern Virginia. In that capacity, I ran the SOD operational coordination center with 30 participating agencies, to include representatives from Canada, Australia, and the United Kingdom. SOD's primary mission is to support and synchronize the investigative efforts of federal, state, local and international law enforcement agencies. Since the Mexican cartels are one of the biggest threats to the United States, SOD focused substantial resources on the Mexican cartels. SOD was instrumental in supporting the Mexican government and the U.S. agencies to capture the former leader of the Sinaloa Cartel,El Chapo Guzman, on two occasions, and coordinating the worldwide investigations against the cartel.

SOD also has a long history of coordinating the efforts of agencies around the world disrupting and dismantling major criminal networks.

Unfortunately, I watched the threat of the Mexican cartels grow over the years from drug cartels to transnational organized criminals to currently narco-terrorists. In my view they remain the greatest daily threat to the citizens of this country. They control the importation anddistribution of heroin, cocaine, methamphetamine, and now deadly fentanyl. They work closelywith Chinese Criminal Networks (CCN) and together they are destroying communities and families throughout the United States and are killing historic numbers of our future generation. Iremain committed to work with Congress, my colleagues in the government agencies and fellow citizens who have lost their loved ones to the drug crisis to help develop recommendations and solutions to build more effective approaches to eliminate the current threats. Too many Americans are dying from fentanyl poisoning and citizens all over the United States are impacted by the Mexican cartels and the CCN. It is time to work together and put politics aside. *"The current unprecedented fentanyl poisoning crisis that's killing our kids at record levels is not a Red or Blue Issue. It's a Red, White and Blue issue. We need all Americans to work together now to save lives".*

We must utilize the best and brightest patriots serving the country and combine the arsenal of capabilities and authorities to decimate the cartel's deadly production operations in Mexico. We must simultaneously dismantle their importation and distribution networks to eliminate thegrowing threat to the United States. The U.S. agencies must also work harder and smarter to shut down the flow of precursor chemicals shipped to Mexico from China, India and other countries around the globe that are used in the production of dangerous synthetic drugs. The evolving sophisticated money laundering schemes offered by the CCN to the cartels must also be shut down. Law enforcement has the important responsibility to enforce the laws of Americato keep our citizens safe and needs the full support of Congress. However, this national security threat requires a true "whole of America approach" While we must continue to treat those with mental illness and drug addiction, the Mexican cartels and the CCN must be held accountable for their devastation and damages. *They can no longer operate with impunity, and we need Congress and government leadership to step up their efforts.*

According to the recent provisional overdose data published by the Centers for Disease Control and Prevention's (CDC) National Center for Health Statistics (NCHS), it reflects approximately 106,840 predicted drug overdose deaths in the 12-month period ending September 2022. This alarming amount equates to losing almost 293 people per day (CDC, 2023).

When you look at the death statistics in San Diego, California, there was a 2375% increase in fentanyl related deaths in the 5-year period 2016-2021. (Galindo, 2022). In King County, Washington, according to the Prosecutor there were 35 fentanyl-related overdose deaths in the county in the first 21 days of the year. (Swaby, 2023). There are so many storiesaround the country that highlight the unprecedented nature of the fentanyl poisoning crisis so *please see the attached PDF document.* (Walters, 2023) (Hocker, 2023)

"The King County is experiencing a grim indicator of how bad the opioid crisis has become. Dr. Faisal Khan, director of Public Health – Seattle & King County, laid out one of the issuesstemming from rising overdose deaths during a county Board of Health meeting last week. "The Medical Examiner's office is now struggling with the issue of storing bodies because the fentanyl-related death toll continues to climb," Khan said. The examiner's office has finite space in the coolers they use, and that space is being exceeded on a regular basis. The number of overdose deaths in King County involving fentanyl have skyrocketed in the past few years." King County Public Health Director Dr. Faisal Khan also stated that many major metro areas across the country are dealing with a lack of space in morgue coolers.

According to the Families against Fentanyl who have analyzed CDC statistics and have donea tremendous job educating the public on the troubling trends involving fentanyl, they revealed the following in the recent report "The Changing Faces of Fentanyl Deaths" (The Changing Faces of Fentanyl Deaths, 2023):

- Synthetic opioid (fentanyl) poisoning was still the leading cause of death among Americans 18 to 45 in 2021.
- Synthetic opioid (fentanyl) fatalities among children are rising faster than any other age group.
- In just two years, synthetic opioid (fentanyl) deaths among children ages 1 to 4 more than tripled, and increased fourfold among infants less than one, and children ages 5 to 14.
- Since 2015, deaths among infants increased nearly 10-fold; among children ages 1 to 14 deaths increased 15-fold: an increase of more than 1400%.

These are staggering statistics, and all Americans should be alarmed and demanding accountability from the leaders.

Over the last few years while actively supporting law enforcement in the private sector, I participated in the production of documentaries, national media segments, congressional, think tank and educational sessions, and rallies with grieving families and non-profits from around America to help educate the public and bring needed awareness to the dangerous and evolving synthetic drug crisis. As a patriotic American who lost his brother Michael, fighting for America during Operation Enduring Freedom in the U.S. Air Force, I am familiar with the pain and suffering of losing a loved one. However, nothing is more difficult in life than losing a child and I remain committed to this fight.

I will continue to engage with families who lost children from these poisonous substances hitting our communities like a tsunami. It's hard to imagine the lack of engagement and action from of our national leaders in Washington especially on the education for young Americans. I have worked tirelessly with families to recruit celebrities, professional athletes, role models and social media influencers to help create a movement to get specific messages to the kids.

Sadly, these efforts to date haven't been very successful. I believe if the right celebrity pushed out short social media videos and reels, the kids would get the important messages. We must all accept that most children are not watching congressional hearings, mainstream media, cable news or listening to podcasts so it's critical to have role models step up in a big way to fill the educational void.

In addition to the troubling news on the fentanyl poisoning crisis, there are also dangerous connections between the criminal activity of the Mexican cartels and terrorist groups like Hezbollah. The cartels are also working in close partnership with CCN, operating with impunity and killing our citizens at historic levels. The threats posed by the cartels is growing rapidly as they make billions of dollars, especially benefiting from human smuggling with the porous Southern Border. The topic of narco-terrorism has been a priority of mine for many years, and the United States Government must use all tools of national power to combat and decimate these complex threats.

As the former Special Agent in Charge of SOD in Northern Virginia, the Chief of the New York Drug Enforcement Task Force in New York City and DEA Special Agent working investigations around the globe, I had the privilege of collaborating with numerous local, state, federal and international law enforcement agencies. I have witnessed the incredible results and positive impact to communities when law enforcement works together in a professional manner enforcing the controlled substances act of the United States. It's very impressive whenyou look at the seizure statistics of the Customs and Border

Protection (CBP), the DEA and law enforcement agencies around the country, but also rather alarming.

The DEA Administrator Anne Milgram last week testified at a Senate hearing and told the committee that DEA seized in 2022 over *57,000,000* fake prescription pills, over *13,000* pounds of illicit fentanyl which is equivalent to *410 million* deadly dosage units. Ms. Milgramadvised that according to the CDC, the majority of the drug poisoning deaths in the United States involve synthetic opioids, such as fentanyl. In many instances, the fentanyl is being hidden in and being mixed with other illicit drugs such as cocaine, heroin, and methamphetamine. Drug traffickers are also flooding our communities with fentanyl disguisedin the form of fake prescription pills. These fake pills are made and marketed by drug traffickers to deceive Americans into thinking that they are real, diverted prescription medications. *DEA lab testing revealed that 6 out of 10 of these fentanyl-laced fake prescription pills contain a potentially lethal dose.*

Ms. Milgram was very clear that the *Sinaloa and Jalisco Cartels pose the greatest criminal drug threat the United States has ever faced.* These ruthless, violent, criminal organizationshave associates, facilitators, and brokers in all 50 states in the United States, as well as in morethan 40 countries around the world. The DEA Administrator also provided testimony that the Sinaloa Cartel and the Jalisco Cartel and their affiliates control the vast majority of the fentanyl global supply chain, from manufacturing to distribution. The cartels are buying precursor chemicals in the People's Republic of China (PRC); transporting the precursor chemicals from the PRC to Mexico; using the precursor chemicals to mass produce fentanyl; pressing the fentanyl into fake prescription pills; and using cars, trucks, and other routes to transport the drugs from Mexico into the United States for distribution. The Administrator further indicated that drugs manufactured by the cartels often end up being marketed by dealers using social media platforms to relentlessly expand their business and deceptively sell fake prescription pills directly to young people and teenagers. Drug traffickers operate on multiple platforms simultaneously, and often drive traffic between platforms. (FULL COMMITTEE HEARING, 2023).

CBP reports the staggering seizure statistics on their website, and they reported in fiscal year2022 CBP seized *14,700* pounds of fentanyl and *175,000* pounds of methamphetamine. (US Customs and Border Protection, 2023) Although, I appreciate the incredible work and I'm totally impressed with the dedication of the men and women on the front lines, these large seizures of deadly drugs should be a "wake up call" for all Americans. It's obvious and alarming to anyone who works in drug enforcement or border security that if this is what agencies are seizing, then everyone should be concerned on how much is imported, and now onthe streets in America.

To be clear, the drug crisis can't be solved with law enforcement alone. This complex and emerging problem requires that all Americans unite. The U.S. needs more focus and resources on drug education, treatment and rehabilitation in addition to law enforcement. This is an unprecedented public health, national security and community safety matter that also has huge mental health ramifications for the addicted as well as their families. There are many great American patriots working in the medical, education, addiction, science, technology, financial,and other private sector industries that can help develop comprehensive strategies and plans to deal with this matter. *The status quo is an unacceptable option as too many lives are on the line.* There must be accountability on all resources provided to these initiatives since it'snot good enough to just provide funding. We need to see the death rates decline across the country.

Overview

Over the last 37 years, I have been honored to be an active participant as a Special Agent in theDEA and now in the private sector to work with some of the best and brightest public servants. I have been committed to DEA's mission focusing enforcement efforts on the entire criminal organization. I remain very concerned that our collective efforts have many significant challenges. The Mexican cartels are taking total advantage of our current border polices, weaknesses and vulnerabilities. I have watched the cartels evolve from drug cartels to transnational criminals to substantial narco-terrorists.

Based on the growing and devastating fentanyl poisoning disaster in the United States causedby the Mexican cartels and their partners from China, I am pleased to be here at this importantnational security and public health hearing to discuss the historic threats to the United States. The Mexican "terror" cartels are a tremendous threat to public health, safety and national security and way more aggressive action is needed. In my view based on experience, the Mexican syndicates are one of the greatest current threats to America and we need bold leadership to combat this very dangerous threat causing devastation to communities and families across the country.

Former Attorney General William Barr articulated correctly in my view during an interview onNewsmax in July 2022 when he stated, "*The United States has been relegated to working through Mexico to try to deal with the cartels, and I think that's a losing proposition. We have to be more active against the cartels. In my mind, we have to approach the cartels more like ISIS and less like the mafia." Barr compared the current policy of attempting to prosecute Mexican drug gangs and affiliated organizations as about as ridiculous as "going after ISIS in Syria on the same basis." "They are effectively terrorist organizations. They are increasingly building their connections with terrorists. Their paramilitary can take on the Mexican military, and they have so much money they can corrupt any system," the former attorney general further emphasized that with the ongoing fentanyl and migrant crisis, "the United States cannot have these cartels operating on our border, poisoning our country — over 100,000" deaths. Barr condemned the Biden administration's response to the cartels, proclaiming they "have essentially abandoned the border to them."* (Cacciatore, 2022)

America has outdated technology and laws, limited resources directed at these national securitythreats, deceptive political leadership and huge morale issues across the agencies who are responsible for keeping the country safe. There is a concerning movement involving experienced law enforcement personnel retiring rapidly. This is happening as the cartels are building up their capabilities, enhancing their weapons systems, expanding their product line and unfortunately after forming a lethal partnership with CCN. Sadly, this has resulted in increased violence and escalating deaths in the United States.

As a DEA supervisor for many years, the Agent in Charge of SOD for almost ten years and asan huge supporter of law enforcement and grieving families since retirement, I learned so much about the evolution of the opioid addiction crisis, the "bombing of America" from synthetic drugs coming from China and Mexico, the growing role of CCN in drug trafficking and money laundering and the increased threats posed to our country from the Mexican "terror" cartels.

From 2006- 2014, as reported in a comprehensive Washington Post investigative story, more than100 billion opioids were provided to Americans (Steven Rich, 2020) by the "corporate cartels" with no significant accountability despite the widespread and lasting impacts throughout the United States. Starting in the early 1990's, the Colombian cartels and then later the Mexican cartels, sold very pure white heroin all over America to maximize profits and take advantage ofthe addicted population. In my opinion, it was all about the money and greed that was driving the business opportunities. The American public didn't receive adequate education about the consequences of using and abusing these powerful and addictive opioids.

From my perspective as a new Director of SOD commencing my senior leadership assignmentin 2005, I was alarmed to hear about hundreds of deaths in the Midwest, Northeast and Mid- Atlantic regions of the United States during late 2005 and 2006 from clandestinely produced illicit fentanyl. This was a new drug trend to me as the leader of SOD. The Department of Justice, National Drug Intelligence Center, produced a valuable intelligence report at that time.It was later determined from great work by DEA in Chicago, working with their U.S. law enforcement partners along with counterparts in Mexico, that the Mexican cartels had a deadlyfentanyl laboratory in Toluca, Mexico. Thanks to the outstanding work, in May 2006 the Mexican authorities seized the lab and many lives were saved. (Fentanyl: Situation Report, 2006).

Former Drug Czar John Walters made a very astute comment about this matter when he stated,"*In effect, to be quite clear, the drug traffickers have substantially poisoned the drug supply in the United States.*" (News Drug Lab Shut Down, 2006).

In my opinion and based on the investigative developments at that time, the Mexican cartels recognized the profit potential of producing illicit fentanyl for distribution to the robust opioidaddicted market in America. Since they were greedy and ran a growing global business enterprise, they were looking to maximize profits by producing this powerful synthetic drug.

Chicago Tribune News Article Below on Huge Fentanyl Lab Seized in Toluca, Mexico in 2006

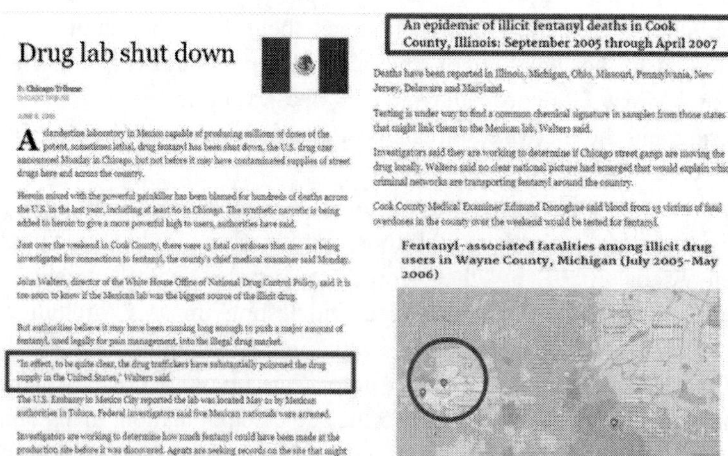

Drug lab shut down

A clandestine laboratory in Mexico capable of producing millions of doses of the potent, sometimes lethal, drug fentanyl has been shut down, the U.S. drug czar announced Monday in Chicago, but not before it may have contaminated supplies of street drugs here and across the country.

Heroin mixed with the powerful painkiller has been blamed for hundreds of deaths across the U.S. in the last year, including at least 80 in Chicago. The synthetic narcotic is being added to heroin to give a more powerful high to users, authorities have said.

Just over the weekend in Cook County, there were 13 fatal overdoses that now are being investigated for connections to fentanyl, the county's chief medical examiner said Monday.

John Walters, director of the White House Office of National Drug Control Policy, said it is too soon to know if the Mexican lab was the biggest source of the illicit drug.

But authorities believe it may have been running long enough to push a major amount of fentanyl, used legally for pain management, into the illegal drug market.

"In effect, to be quite clear, the drug traffickers have substantially poisoned the drug supply in the United States," Walters said.

The U.S. Embassy in Mexico City reported the lab was located May 21 by Mexican authorities in Toluca. Federal investigators said five Mexican nationals were arrested.

Investigators are working to determine how much fentanyl could have been made at the production site before it was discovered. Agents are seeking records on the site that might provide clues as to its production capacity and distribution channels.

An epidemic of illicit fentanyl deaths in Cook County, Illinois: September 2005 through April 2007

Deaths have been reported in Illinois, Michigan, Ohio, Missouri, Pennsylvania, New Jersey, Delaware and Maryland.

Testing is under way to find a common chemical signature in samples from those states that might link them to the Mexican lab, Walters said.

Investigators said they are working to determine if Chicago street gangs are moving the drug locally. Walters said no clear national picture had emerged that would explain which criminal networks are transporting fentanyl around the country.

Cook County Medical Examiner Edmund Donoghue said blood from 13 victims of fatal overdoses in the county over the weekend would be tested for fentanyl.

Fentanyl-associated fatalities among illicit drug users in Wayne County, Michigan (July 2005–May 2006)

Keep in mind that for more than 30 years, the Mexican cartels had a long standing partnership with Chinese chemical brokers. They benefited in a huge way as their production and distribution of methamphetamine skyrocketed throughout the years of doing business together. To illustrate the magnitude of the methamphetamine business, look at the seizure of $207 million dollars in Mexico City in 2007. This record-breaking money seizure was reported as the largest ever in the world. The subject in Mexico related to the seizure was identified as a wealthy Chinese national chemical broker who was providing precursor chemicals to the Mexican cartels as they manufactured methamphetamine in Mexico for importation into the U.S. (dea.gov, 2007)

There was another game changer for U.S. drug law enforcement commencing around 2008 and 2009 when the Chinese chemical companies started producing synthetic cannabinoids and cathinones in China. These drugs were commonly called K2, Spice and Bath Salts on the streets and were surfacing around the country. The CCN initiated a very profitable business on the internet and were selling these dangerous chemicals on websites to U.S. consumers. This trend exploded rapidly causing SOD and law enforcement partners in the Department of Homeland Security and other countries to unite and attack this developing problem. As the head of SOD, I received intelligence about the increased emergency room visits and Poison Control hotline contacts. As a result, SOD synchronized several successful enforcement operations under the names Operation Log Jam and Project Synergy to address this emerging public health threat. There were many successful law enforcement investigations around the country which exposed the global nature of this threat emanating from China that was harming and killing Americans. (Operation Log Jam Press Conference, 2012) (DEA News Huge Synthetic Drug Take Down, 2014) (Press Release Top China-Based Global Designer Drug Trafficker Arrested In U.S, 2015)

During 2012, DEA and other law enforcement agencies had investigations in America resulting in drug overdose deaths. Initially, they were reported as heroin overdoses. However, in many of these instances, specifically in the Northeast and Southeast, the medical examiner reports revealed that fentanyl was the actual cause of death. While at SOD, to address this deadly trend, we subsequently initiated a focused intelligence and enforcement program named Operation Deadly Merchant. The DEA offices in West Palm Beach (Palmer, 2019) and Gulfport Mississippi (Press Release First in the Nation Criminal Indictment of a Chinese National for Manufacturing and Distributing Fentanyl and Other Opiates, 2017) and the Immigration and Customs Enforcement in North Dakota (Chinese manufacturers indicted in deadly Fentanyl case, 2017) had very productive operations exposing the role of Chinese criminal networks and their deadly new endeavor to manufacture fentanyl analogues in Chinese labs for distribution in the United States. As the deaths started to drastically increase, DEA leadership became very concerned and briefed the former Attorney General Eric Holder in 2014 about this deadly and concerning trend emanating from China and involving Mexican and Dominican drug trafficking groups in the United States.

During the initial years of the illicit fentanyl crisis, most of the deadly substance was being shipped to the country via mail services after Chinese websites received the orders from America. The DEA produced a "Fentanyl Threat Overview" pamphlet and distributed it to federal, state and local law enforcement around the country. The law enforcement community and first responders started to become overwhelmed because of this escalating threat. CBP, DEA, ICE, FBI and foreign partners worked collaboratively to further identify the extent of the threat. There were massive amounts of these synthetic drugs being seized at the ports of entry and throughout the country.

Around 2019, officials from the United Sates Government applied significant pressure on the Chinese government regarding the fentanyl analogue exports killing Americans at alarming rates. As a result of U.S.G. engagement, on May 1, 2019, China officially controlled all forms of fentanyl as a class of drugs. This fulfilled the commitment that President Xi made during the G-20 Summit. The implementation of the new measure included investigations of known fentanyl manufacturing areas, stricter control of internet sites advertising fentanyl, stricter enforcement of shipping regulations, and the creation of special teams to investigate leads on fentanyl trafficking. The hope was that the new restrictions would severely limit fentanyl production and trafficking from China. (Fentanyl Flow to the United States, 2020). DEA further reported at that time that the Mexican organizations were producing increased quantities of fentanyl and illicit fentanyl-containing tablets, with some cartels using increasingly sophisticated clandestine laboratories and processing methods.

DEA, working in conjunction with Mexican officials, seized and dismantled numerous fentanyl pill pressing operations and fentanyl synthesis laboratories in 2018 and 2019, highlighting the role cartels started to play in supplying the US fentanyl market. Fentanyl was being smuggled across the U.S.-Mexico border. In December 2018, Mexican officials in combination with DEA authorities seized an illicit pill mill in Azcapotzalco, Mexico City. Law enforcement officials seized illicit fentanyl-laced oxycodone M-30 pills, suspected fentanyl powder, precursor chemicals and multiple other items related to the production of fentanyl-laced illicit pills. DEA reported during this critical time frame that the Sinaloa and the Cártel de Jalisco Nueva Generación (CJNG) cartels were likely the primary trafficking groups responsible for smuggling fentanyl into the United States from Mexico.

It was very apparent that the Chinese criminal networks changed their primary method of operation and turned over most of the illicit fentanyl production to the Mexican cartels. The cartels leveraged their existing relationships they had for years with the chemical brokers in China and increased their orders of critical precursor chemicals to make the fentanyl in clandestine laboratories in Mexico. The cartels dominate the country of Mexico and had the existing infrastructure to add fentanyl to their ongoing methamphetamine production operations. From their perspective this was another cost-effective way to generate massive amounts of profits.

(U) FIGURE 1. FENTANYL FLOW TO THE UNITED STATES 2019

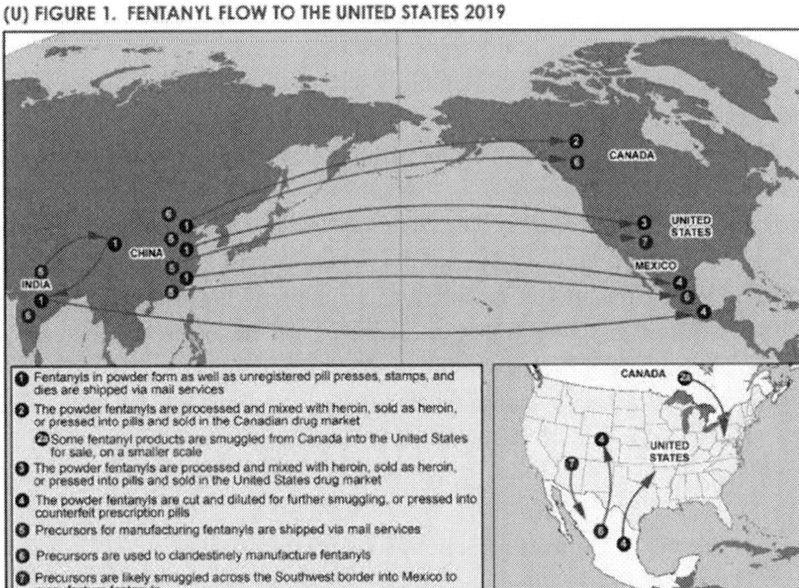

Source: DEA

Unfortunately, many Americans got addicted to the powerful pharmaceutical opioids and theMexican cartels took advantage of this greater business opportunity with a larger customer base throughout America. The cartels are now working closely with companies in China and India to acquire massive amounts of precursor chemicals to make fentanyl in large scale operations in Mexico. In a recent trip to Texas, Congressman Latta Ohio learned that it cost less than 10 cents to make a fake pill in Mexico and the pills are being distributed for $30.00 each. (Jr., 2023). Based on my discussions with DEA officials, in places like Montana on the Indian reservation, a pill is being sold for as high as $150.00. The profit potential for not only the Mexican cartels is so significant that we are also seeing pill pressing operations inside the United States. As an example, in October 2022, the York County South Carolina Sheriff's Office made a record-breaking drug bust and seized around 30 kilograms of fentanyl and 7 pill presses after a highly successful investigation into a drug trafficking organization responsible for the manufacture and trafficking of fentanyl-based pills and powder. (Snipes, 2022).

Most recently, law enforcement in Houston, Texas seized a fentanyl lab which was disguised as a car rental. Texas Department of Public Safety raided a building on Jan 30, 2023 finding pill press machines, more than 17lbs of possible fentanyl precursors from China, over 1 kilogram of suspected counterfeit Xanax pills laced with fentanyl and 0.3 lbs fentanyl-laced Oxycodone. The authorities also found cocaine, ecstasy, methamphetamine pills, a stolen vehicle, three pistols and a rifle. (Adam Shaw, 2023).

There was also a disturbing report from South Texas revealing a Nueces County traffic stop turned into the largest liquid fentanyl drug bust in U.S. history. It was reported that law enforcement located a compartment built in the gas tank of the vehicle, and inside the gas tank was a modified tank, which contained approximately 25 pounds or 3 gallons of liquid fentanyl. In my view, this is another serious trend to see the cartels importing liquid fentanyl into America. This could result in the cartels following their successful model of establishing conversion labs in the U.S. for fentanyl just like they have done successfully for years with methamphetamine. (Wes Wilson, 2022)

Chinese Money Laundering Schemes Supporting the Cartels

During the recent testimony of DEA Administrator Milgram referenced above, she explained that the Sinaloa and Jalisco Cartels utilize U.S.-based Chinese Money Laundering Organizations around the world to facilitate laundering drug proceeds. These networks use trade-based money laundering and bulk cash movement to facilitate the exchange of foreign currency. The use of Chinese networks by the cartels simplifies the money laundering process and streamlines the purchase of precursor chemicals utilized in manufacturing drugs.

Based on my discussions with law enforcement officials, the Chinese money laundering activities with the Mexican cartels started to really expand around 2015. The innovative and complex schemes established a very efficient way to move money effectively reducing the risk of losing proceeds. The wealthy Chinese businessmen benefit big time by having the ability to receive huge amounts of cash in America. This enables them to bypass the restrictions related to China's capital flight laws of transferring large sums of money held in Chinese bank accounts for use abroad. The Chinese targets in the United States, in many cases, use the cash they receive from the cartel operatives inside America to buy, real estate, land, property and make other investments.

I have received significant intelligence that the CCN's often use young Chinese nationals in America here on student visas to pick up large amounts of currency from the cartels. The cash is then turned over by the couriers throughout the country to wealthy Chinese businessmen. Subsequently, the businessmen frequently transfer the exact amount of money using their Chinese banking apps and other encrypted apps to China. In many cases they then use the traditional trade-based money laundering schemes to buy consumer goods in China and shipthem to Mexico for huge profits. This is a very effective way for the cartel leadership to get paid. In many cases, they use the funds in China to make purchases of massive quantities ofprecursor chemicals to keep the deadly cycle of production of their synthetic drugs moving quickly.

One important point to highlight knowing this growing partnership between the CCN's and the cartels, is there are numerous press reports about the very large purchases of land and real estate in the U.S. by Chinese nationals. According to the Washington Examiner release in July2022, China is the top foreign buyer of US housing at $6.1 billion last year from April 2021 toMarch 2022, which the report said was up 30% from the prior year. The article further states, "Chinese buyers flooded the American housing market with more than $6 billion last year, more than purchasers from any other foreign country and 58% of Chinese buyers made all- cash purchases."

In my view, the United States must examine this alarming national security trend of the cartels working with the CCN since there is so much cash being transferred in America from the drug business. This is even more critical when you look at the totality of the intelligence and evidence to include FBI Director Christopher Wray's statement that *"we consistently see that it's the Chinese government that poses the biggest long-term threat to our economic and national security."* (Dunleavy, July)

The Chicago Sun Times on April 30, 2021, did a comprehensive analysis, based on law enforcement sources and court files, on one of the popular and elaborate money laundering schemes used by the Mexican cartels and the CCN to move millions of drug proceeds in a very efficient manner. (Seidel, 2021). The Chinese criminals brilliantly offered these services to the cartels and undercut the other traditional money launderers by charging much less in commissions.

The latest scheme depicted below avoids a traceable paper trail and presents a huge obstacle for U.S. law enforcement infiltration. They also capitalize on the use of advanced technology to beat law enforcement who's forced to deal with antiquated laws and policies to overcome encrypted communications. The below chart was introduced in U.S. District Court and was marked as a government exhibit. The chart depicts how the cash was moved from the cartels to the Chinese money laundering organization. Based on information from law enforement, this advanced and complex scheme is extremely difficult to penetrate and provides the cartels and the Chinese criminals a huge advabntage to beat the system of Justice in America. This creative scheme also enables the cartels to produce more deadly drugs and build their business enterprise.

See the below mirror transaction scheme published in the the Chicago Sun Times article referenced above.

A great illustration of the substantial money laundering involving the Mexican cartels and their Chinese partners was documented in a New York Post article dated April 3, 2022, titled "How a crew laundered millions in cartel cash across New York City" (Feuerherd, 2022). The DEA in Atlanta, working with their law enforcement partners, were targeting a known and significant Mexican drug trafficker. During a court authorized intercept investigation, the agents established surveillance to watch a money transfer from the cartel operative. They observed the transfer of $350,000.00 in cash made to two Asian males, who were members of a large-scale money laundering network based in New York. The money was seized in August 2018 and the investigation continued. During the sentencing process in November 2021 the federal prosecutor wrote in a memo about one of the Asian targets, "By engaging in this conduct, the defendant and others played a critical role in laundering millions of dollars in drug money."

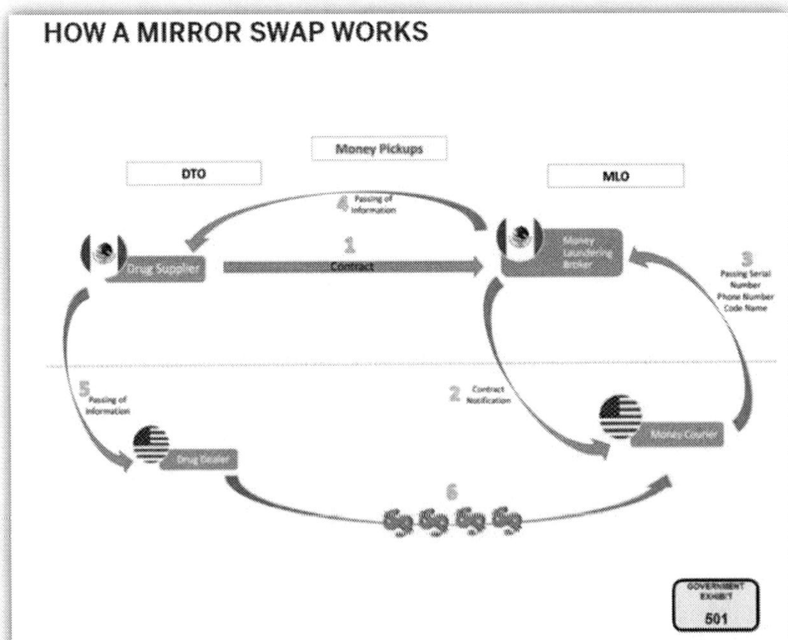

This chart, introduced in court, shows how cash from Mexican drug cartels was moved to Chinese money-laundering organizations. Xianbing Gan, a money-laundering broker in Mexico, had a bank account in China. An associate in the United States collected cash from cartel drug sales, removed an equal amount from a bank account in China and deposited it in Gan's Chinese account to get around the U.S. banking system and try to avoid detection, according to prosecutors, in what's called a mirror swap. A second swap was then done in Mexico to complete the money-laundering and try to make the illegal drug proceeds look like a legitimate business transaction. | U.S District Court trial exhibit

Narco-Terrorism and Systemic Corruption

Another disturbing aspect involving the Mexican cartels is their role as narco-terrorists and their advancement with the use of technology and weapon systems to enhance their deadly business enterprise. They are not typical crime groups as they conduct acts of terrorism not solely in furtherance of drug trafficking but for the purpose of instilling fear in the public and influencing. They are responsible for utilizing terror tactics to silence, torture and kill civilians, government officials, Catholic priests, and news reporters, who publicly speak out against the violence inflicted by the cartels. The Mexican cartels have become Mexico's insurgency's and have utilized terror tactics. They have corrupted the system and undermine the Mexican government and the rule of law. The Mexican cartels have recruited hundreds of trained law enforcement and military personnel who now carry out executions and assassinations on behalf of the cartels. The cartels routinely conduct beheadings, in which corpses and heads are hung on public display. The cartels also indiscriminately killing to scare the general population into submission and subservience.

The recent conviction of Genaro Garcia-Luna, former Director of Mexico's Public Security, in federal court in New York and the DEA arrest of Salvador Cienfuegos, former Defense Secretary of Mexico, reflects the level of corruption at the highest level of the Mexican government. (Eastern District of New York Press, 2023) (Justice News, 2020). Having the top government officials on the Mexican cartel's payroll, help the cartels operate with impunity moving tons of drugs around the world and make billions. One of the biggest obstacles for U.S. law enforcement is overcoming the presence of high-level corruption in Mexico.

In my view, the United States Government mistakenly views the Mexican cartels as only transnational crime organization, and its current strategy and policies are insufficient to end the Mexican cartels chaos and massive deaths to Americans. Look at the amounts of young Americans dying daily from their poisonous substances. The production is on the rise and the supply of these poisonous drugs are vast. The United States must accept and come to the realization that the cartels are terrorist organizations. As far as I know, there has never been a terrorist organization like Al Qaeda, Hezbollah or ISIS, that has killed this many Americans. There must be a great sense of urgency to decimate the cartels and hold them responsible for the havoc they are causing communities and families around the country. The U.S. government assessment of the cartels must be updated.

The U.S. and Mexico efforts and strategy against the Mexican cartels have been proven to be ineffective in its ability to curtail and significantly reduce the level of drug trafficking and violence inflicted by the cartels. The purpose of reclassifying Mexican drug cartels as terrorist organizations is to not only address the problem of drug trafficking, but to ultimately confront the level violence and terror carried out by the cartels. A designation would also provide the U.S. government with additional options when combating the Mexican "terror" cartels that would not be limited to the capabilities of law enforcement. Instead, it would help bridge the gap between the law enforcement, military, and intelligence community, thus providing more resources and capabilities to combat the Mexican drug cartels. The cartels utilize military grade weapons and C4 explosives and have been found to be in possession of weapons such as assault rifles, pistols, grenades, RPG rocket launchers, claymore anti-personnel mines and man portable air defense systems. The Mexican cartels have taken control of Mexico through active means of terrorism. During my recent trip to the Rio Grande Valle, Texas, I was extremely concerned to learn about the 9000 drones used by the cartels for surveillance inside America especially knowing how the cartels are now dropping C4 explosives on their adversaries in Mexico. It's a threat growing daily on our Southern border and the use of drones and explosives is a huge risk to our brave men and women of CBP who are fighting daily to keep us safe.

Some Recommendations to Address Current Crisis

(** This is certainly not a complete list)

- Immediately declare a national health and security emergency from the White House based on the historic number of deaths from fentanyl and the escalating growing lethal relationship between the Mexican "terror" cartels and the CCN.
- Declare fentanyl a weapon of mass destruction.
- Declare the Sinaloa and CJNG cartel's terrorist organizations and apply the appropriate U.S. authorities, resources and capabilities to this growing threat.
    - Work with Mexico to provide support to decimate the production labs in Mexico.
    - Hold high level security meetings with the Mexican counterparts to accurately assess their commitment to shut down the cartel's ability to kill at record levels.
    - Increase U.S. Treasury designations and sanctions to target people and businesses facilitating the deadly criminal enterprises and flooding America with poisonous drugs.
    - Develop task forces to target the supply of precursor chemicals from China and other countries to the Mexican cartels.
    - Strengthen border security with the polices that work and always place the interest of American citizens first.
        - Need additional scanning resources at border.
        - Implement border walls with appropriate technology where necessary based on Homeland Security expertise not based on political motives.

- o Develop robust strategies to attack the money laundering schemes and networks as well as seize the assets derived from criminal activity.
- o Apply pressure on Mexico for increased information sharing and bilateral investigations.
- o Increase operations to arrest and extradite the highest members of the cartels to face justice in the U.S.
  - ▪ Increase operations in Mexico to identify and destroy fentanyl and methamphetamine manufacturing labs.
  - ▪ Mandate the U.S. Department of Education to commence drug education in the schools throughout the country about the increased threats from the illicit drug supply.
- o As part of the education campaign, must develop partnerships with celebrities, role models, social media influencers and professional athletes, (NFL, MLB, NHL, NBA, WNBA, MLS, WMLS as examples) to develop videos and reels to push all over social media platforms to hit the target audience of young Americans.
  - ▪ Have the Department of Education work with the Office of National Drug Control Policy of U.S. to develop Public Service Announcements immediately and establish close partnerships with grieving families and nonprofits who are fighting daily to spread awareness and save lives.
  - ▪ Hold social media companies accountable for facilitating the movement of deadly drugs and other serious criminal activity like "sextortion" on their platforms.
  - ▪ Increase resources for mental health, treatment and rehabilitation for drug addiction and apply strict accountability for the resources. Need to articulate the results and progress.
  - ▪ Demand that the CDC provide updated and timely reporting on the synthetic drug deaths across the country.
- o Provide resources for lab analysis and medical examiners to expedite the process.
  - ▪ Set up fentanyl death task forces like Task Force 10 in San Diego to aggressively prosecute fentanyl dealers who are killing citizens.
- o Increase resources and prosecutions of synthetic drug violators.

  - Create an Operation Warp Speed for Fentanyl like we had for COVID and apply the best practices and lessons learned for the current fentanyl poisoning crisis.
  - We need a "real opioid/ Fentanyl/ task force" set up to operate with a multi-agency SOD like model using existing resources at the National Targeting Center at DOD, National Targeting Center at CBP, DOJ OCDETF Fusion Center, DEA's Special Intelligence, HIDTAs, HHS, FDA, USPS, Treasury and other key elements.
  - Must address the outdated laws and polices especially related to criminal communications.
- Work with technology companies and law enforcement to collaborate on the growing concern of encrypted communications and the impacts to national security.
- Must address the DOJ policy regarding the December 16, 2022, memorandum to all federal prosecutors on charging, pleas and sentencing on drug crimes.
  - The perception from law enforcement around America is their own DOJ is way to "soft on criminals". The dedicated law enforcement is working hard to keep citizens safe are feel strongly they are being undermined. There are huge moral issues developing.
  - Must engage with mail services companies like UPS, FEDEX, DHL and others to address the movement of deadly substances into America.
- Need updated technology at mail facilities to screen and identify contraband moving around the country.

Conclusion

Mexican cartels, Sinaloa, and CJNG, currently operate throughout the U.S. and around the globe. They are working with CCN and are flooding America with deadly synthetic drugs. They are operating with impunity and the current enforcement focus alone is not enough to stop the death and destruction. The United States must enhance the strategies to shut down the cartel's ability to operate. We must use all authorities and capabilities of not only law enforcement but the Intelligence Community, the Department of Defense and Treasury Department as one force to decimate the cartels. They are taking advantage of the porous Southern and Northern borders and overwhelming our CBP daily. The country is inundated with crime, drugs and violence fueled by the Mexican cartels. The cartels are taking advantage of the massive addiction and the demand for opioids and methamphetamines all over the United States.

During his Senate testimony on February 15, 2023, Dr. Rahul Gupta, Director, Office of National Drug Control Policy of U.S., stated the following related to the current drug situation:

- "Worst drug crisis we have ever seen."
- "Unacceptable to me"
- "Unacceptable to the President"
- "Direct threat to public health and national security"
- "New era of drug trafficking"

Based on these statements, the American public and specifically the families who have lost loved ones to poisonous fentanyl, deserve full transparency and way more action. Solving this unprecedented national security and public health crisis won't go away from just words. We need new strategies and way more action. We must recognize this is something America has never faced before and we are losing the future generation rapidly.

Terrorists will continue to tap into the incredible amounts of money generated from drug trafficking and many other criminal activities such as human trafficking, counterfeiting, weapon sales and sex trafficking so it's imperative that our hard-working law enforcement andother U.S. government personnel get the resources and support to enforce the laws and keep Americans safe.

We need the leadership of the Attorney General, the Secretary of the Department of Homeland Security, Executives from the Department of Defense and the Intelligence Community to uniteand battle these growing adversaries. We also need to work closely with our state and local counterparts who are under resourced trying to deal with this crisis on the front lines. We needto unite our agencies as the complexity of the threats continues to grow. The threats to this great country are moving at lightning speed and we need a sense of urgency at this point. It's evident that the Mexican cartels are moving extremely fast while our investigators and assets are getting "stuck in the mud" of politics, bureaucracy, and antiquated laws. *In my view, fentanyl is a chemical weapon and the narco-terrorists' Mexican cartels are destroying our country as their work closely with the CCN.*

Thanks to the relentless efforts of the Families against Fentanyl and others around the country, we now have congressional and a multi-state movement to declare fentanyl a weapon of mass destruction, and "21 states call on Biden to label Mexican drug cartels terrorist organizations." (Gans, 2023) (Paxton Signs Multistate Letter Urging Joe Biden to Declare Fentanyl a Weapon of Mass Destruction, 2022)

We need to step up the game with a sense of urgency. Law enforcement will continue to do their best in enforcing the laws, but America needs congress to further engage on these growing issues. The death rates are spiking and impacting Republicans, Democrats and Independents. We must come together and develop updated strategies to combat these threats.

Thank you for the opportunity to speak on these important topics impacting our national security and public safety.

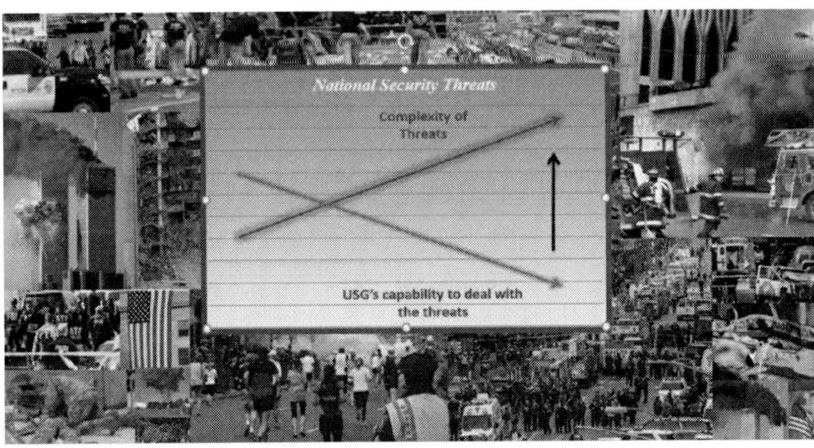

(Chart made by Derek Maltz to depict the complexity of crime in America. The gap between"good and evil" is growing rapidly resulting in a more dangerous America)

See PDF attachment which highlight some of the mass poisonings around the country since dea administrator anne milgram's announcement in april 2002 to warn america on this escalating crisis.

References

Adam Shaw, B. M. (2023, Feb 8). Texas authorities bust fentanyl lab in Houston disguised as car rental.

Retrieved from Foxnew.com: https://www.foxnews.com/politics/texas-authorities-bust-fentanyl-lab-houston-disguised-car-rental

Cacciatore, L. (2022, July 22). Bill Barr to Newsmax: US Needs to Treat Mexican Cartels 'Like ISIS'.

Retrieved from Newsmax.com: https://www.newsmax.com/newsmax-tv/newsmaxtv-billbarr-mexicancartels/2022/07/22/id/1080025/.

CDC. (2023, Feb 15). National Vital Statistics System. Retrieved from CDC.gov: https://www.cdc.gov/nchs/nvss/vsrr/drug-overdose-data.htm.

Chinese manufacturers indicted in deadly Fentanyl case. (2017, Oct 17). Retrieved from ICE.gov: https://www.ice.gov/news/releases/chinese-manufacturers-indicted-deadly-fentanyl-case.

DEA News Huge Synthetic Drug Take Down. (2014, May 07). Retrieved from DEA.gov: https://www.dea.gov/press-releases/2014/05/07/dea-news-huge-synthetic-drug-takedown.

dea.gov. (2007, March 07). Retrieved from News Release from DEA: https://www.dea.gov/sites/default/files/divisions/hq/2007/pr032007p.html.

Dunleavy, J. (July, 2022 21). China is top foreign buyer of US housing at $6.1 billion last year. Retrieved from Washingtonexaminer.com: https://www.washingtonexaminer.com/foreign-policy/news/china-top-foreign-buyer-us-housing-6-billion-2021.

Eastern District of New York Press. (2023, Feb 21). Retrieved from Justice.gov: https://www.justice.gov/usao-edny/pr/ex-mexican-secretary-public-security-genaro-garcia- luna-convicted-engaging-continuing.

Fentanyl Flow to the United States. (2020, Jan 01). Retrieved from DEA.gov: https://www.dea.gov/sites/default/files/2020-03/DEA_GOV_DIR-008-20%20 Fentanyl%20Flow%20in%20the%20United%20States_0.pdf.

Fentanyl: Situation Report. (2006, Jun 05). Retrieved from Justice.gov: https://www.justice.gov/archive/ndic/pubs11/20469/index.htm.

Feuerherd, B. (2022, April 3). Metro Exclusive How a crew laundered millions in cartel cash across New York City. Retrieved from NYPOST.com: https://nypost.com/2022/04/03/how-a-crew-laundered-millions-in-cartel-cash-across-nyc/.

FULL COMMITTEE HEARING. (2023, Feb 15). Retrieved from foreign.senate.gov: https://www.foreign.senate.gov/hearings/countering-illicit-fentanyl-trafficking.

Galindo, R. (2022, Sep 24). Imperial Beach Teen Who Died From Fentanyl Overdose Remembered by Friends and Family. Retrieved from NBCSanDiego.com: https://www.nbcsandiego.com/news/local/imperial-beach-teen-who-died-from-fentanyl- overdose-remembered-by-friends-and-family/3054903/.

Gans, J. (2023, Feb 8). 21 states call on Biden to label Mexican drug cartels terrorist organizations.

Retrieved from TheHill.com: https://thehill.com/homenews/state-watch/3849600-21-states-call-on-biden-to-label-mexican-drug-cartels-terrorist-organizations/

Hocker, C. (2023, Jan 24). LOCAL NEWS Fatal overdoses, staffing contributing to morgue capacity issues. Retrieved from KING5.com: https://www.king5.com/article/news/local/fatal-overdoses-staffing-morgue-capacity-issues/281-d31b1957-2707-4ba1-825a-22a98b772728.

Jr., T. H. (2023, Feb 23). Rep. Latta: U.S. must empower prosecutors, tighten border security to show seriousness on fentanyl. Retrieved from Washingtontimes.com: https://amp.washingtontimes.com/news/2023/feb/22/rep-latta-us-must-empower-prosecutors-tighten-bord/

Justice News. (2020, 17 November). Retrieved from justice.gov: https://www.justice.gov/opa/pr/joint-statement-attorney-general-united-states-william-p-barr-and-fiscal-general-mexico.

News Drug Lab Shut Down. (2006, June 06). Retrieved from Chicagotribune.com: https://www.chicagotribune.com/news/ct-xpm-2006-06-06-0606060306-story.html.

Operation Log Jam Press Conference. (2012, July 26). Retrieved from DEA.gov: https://www.dea.gov/sites/default/files/pr/speeches-testimony/2012-2009/120726_op-log- jam.pdf.

Palmer, A. (2019, Oct 16). The China Connection: How One D.E.A. Agent Cracked a Global Fentanyl Ring.

Retrieved from NYTIMES.com: https://www.nytimes.com/2019/10/16/magazine/china-fentanyl-drug-ring.html.

Paxton Signs Multistate Letter Urging Joe Biden to Declare Fentanyl a Weapon of Mass Destruction. (2022, Sep 16). Retrieved from texasattorneygeneral.gov: https://www.texasattorneygeneral.gov/news/releases/paxton-signs-multistate-letter-urging- joe-biden-declare-fentanyl-weapon-mass-destruction.

Press Release First in the Nation Criminal Indictment of a Chinese National for Manufacturing and Distributing Fentanyl and Other Opiates. (2017, Oct 19). Retrieved from Justice.gov: https://www.justice.gov/usao-sdms/pr/first-nation-criminal-indictment-chinese-national- manufacturing-and-distributing.

Press Release Top China-Based Global Designer Drug Trafficker Arrested In U.S. (2015, May 28).

Retrieved from DEA.gov: https://www.dea.gov/press-releases/2015/05/28/top-china-based-global-designer-drug-trafficker-arrested-us

Seidel, F. M. (2021, April 30). Chinese money-laundering rings in Chicago, New York cleaning Mexican drug cartel cash. Retrieved from chicago.suntimes.com: https://chicago.suntimes.com/2021/4/30/22408448/chinese-money-laundering-mexican-drug- cartel-mirror-swap-trade-based-money-laundering-xianbing-gan.

Snipes, A. (2022, Oct 25). 'Enough to kill population': Massive amount of fentanyl seized in York Co. Retrieved from Foxcarolina.com: https://www.foxcarolina.com/2022/10/25/enough-kill- population-massive-amount-fentanyl-seized-york-co/.

Steven Rich, S. H. (2020, Jan 14). INVESTIGATIONS More than 100 billion pain pills saturated the nation over nine years. Retrieved from Wahingtonpost.com: https://www.washingtonpost.com/investigations/more-than-100-billion-pain-pills-saturated-the-nation-over-nine-years/2020/01/14/fde320ba-db13-11e9-a688-303693fb4b0b_story.html.

Swaby, N. (2023, Jan 21). Health. Retrieved from KING5.com: https://www.king5.com/article/news/health/35-fentanyl-related-overdose-deaths-king-county- one-month/281-3cfb149e-c94b-4ca3-89af-c1d1b92406e5.

The Changing Faces of Fentanyl Deaths. (2023, Jan 12). Retrieved from familiesagainstfentanyl.com:

https://www.familiesagainstfentanyl.org/research/fentanyl-by-age-and-cause-report
US Customs and Border Protection. (2023, Feb 22). Drug Seizure Statistics. Retrieved from CBP.com:https://www.cbp.gov/newsroom/stats/drug-seizure-statistics.

Walters, K. (2023, Jan 24). Increasing overdose deaths stress King County morgue. Retrieved from know.org: https://www.kuow.org/stories/lack-of-morgue-space-a-grim-indicator-of-opioid-crisis-impacts.

Wes Wilson, L. A. (2022, Dec 5). Local news Nueces County traffic stop turns into largest liquid fentanyl drug bust in US history. Retrieved from kiitv.com: https://www.kiiitv.com/article/news/local/nueces-county-traffic-stop-turns-into-largest-liquid-fentanyl-drug-bust-in-us-history/503-80e7b86d-0f82-420f-bb0b-f1c8d244aebc.

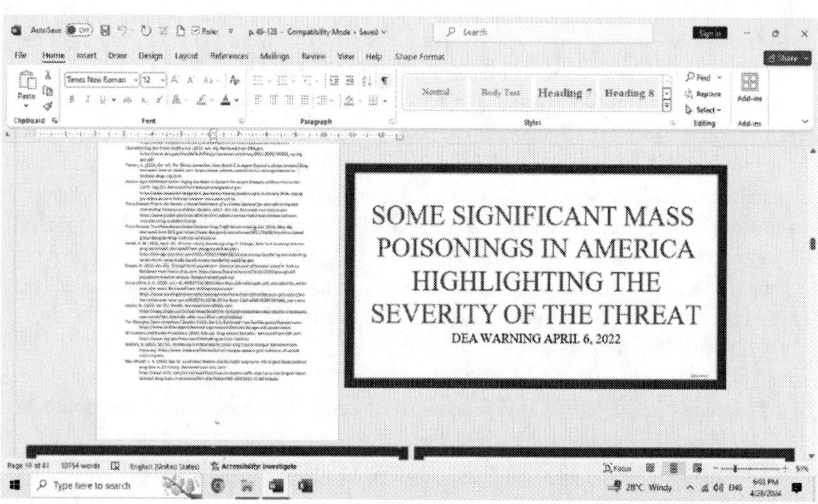

April 06, 2022
Contact: Media Relations
Phone Number: (571) 776-2508

For Immediate Release

DEA Warns of Increase in Mass-Overdose Events Involving Deadly Fentanyl

WASHINGTON – Today, the Drug Enforcement Administration sent a letter to federal, state, and local law enforcement partners warning of a nationwide spike in fentanyl-related mass-overdose events. Administrator Anne Milgram outlined the current threat and offered DEA support to law enforcement officers responding to these tragic incidents.

"Fentanyl is killing Americans at an unprecedented rate," said DEA Administrator Anne Milgram. "Already this year, numerous mass-overdose events have resulted in dozens of overdoses and deaths. Drug traffickers are driving addiction, and increasing their profits, by mixing fentanyl with other illicit drugs. Tragically, many overdose victims have no idea they are ingesting deadly fentanyl, until it's too late."

Fentanyl-related mass-overdose events, characterized as three or more overdoses occurring close in time and at the same location, have happened in at least seven American cities in recent months, resulting in 58 overdoses and 29 deaths. Cities impacted include Wilton Manors, Florida; Austin, Texas; Cortez, Colorado; Commerce City, Colorado; Omaha, Nebraska; St. Louis, Missouri; and Washington, D.C.

Tragic events like these are being driven by fentanyl. Fentanyl is highly-addictive, found in all 50 states, and drug traffickers are increasingly mixing it with other illicit drugs — in powder and pill form — in an effort to drive addiction and attract repeat buyers. These mass-overdose events typically occur in one of the following recurring scenarios: when drug dealers sell their product as "cocaine," when it actually contains fentanyl; or when drug dealers sell pills designed to appear nearly identical to legitimate prescriptions, but are actually fake prescription pills containing fentanyl. This is creating a frightening nationwide trend where many overdose victims are dying after unknowingly ingesting fentanyl.

Police say 10 people died in fatal fentanyl overdoses in Northeast D.C.

Authorities have tied lethal drugs to a single batch sold in Trinidad and Ivy City

By Peter Hermann

The Washington Post

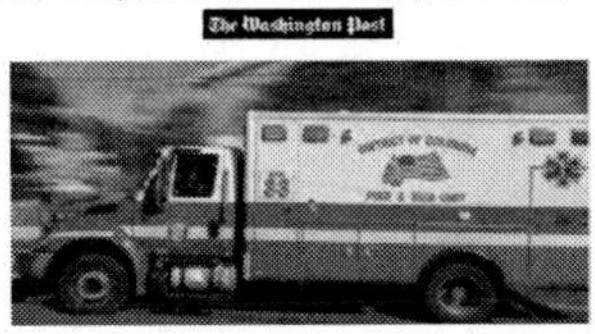

Ten people in two neighborhoods in Northeast Washington have now died from a lethal batch of fentanyl, police said, the second mass-casualty incident involving the deadly opioid in the District this year.

Police said at least 17 people overdosed on cocaine laced with fentanyl in Trinidad and Ivy City from Saturday morning through Monday evening, and seven of them survived.

In January, nine people died after taking a similar concoction in a neighborhood near Nationals Park.

On March 10, 2022, 6 individuals overdosed at a rental property in Wilton Manors, Florida after being exposed to a substance that they believed was cocaine, but contained fentanyl.

On March 4, 2022, 21 individuals overdosed, 3 of whom died, at a homeless shelter in downtown Austin, Texas after ingesting crack-cocaine and methamphetamine laced with fentanyl.

On March 3, 2022, 3 individuals overdosed and died in a hotel room in Cortez, Colorado after ingesting what that they believed were 30mg oxycodone pills, but which were in fact fake prescription pills containing fentanyl.

On February 20, 2022, 6 individuals overdosed, 5 of whom died, in the same apartment in Commerce City, Colorado after ingesting a substance that they believed was pure cocaine but was in fact pure fentanyl.

On February 6, 2022, 4 individuals overdosed, 2 of whom died, in the same apartment complex in Omaha, Nebraska after ingesting a substance that they believed was cocaine, but contained fentanyl.

Between February 5-7, 2022, 8 individuals overdosed, 7 of whom died, at an apartment complex in St. Louis, Missouri after ingesting crack-cocaine laced with fentanyl.

On January 28, 2022, 10 individuals overdosed, 9 of whom died, within the same city block in Washington, D.C. after ingesting crack-cocaine laced with fentanyl.

People

May 06, 2022

Ohio State Issues Warning About 'Fake Adderall' Pills Laced with Fentanyl After 2 Students Die

"While we strongly discourage any kind of drug misuse, if you, or someone you know, may choose to experiment with drugs," the OSU statement continued, "...consider confidentially picking up a free Naloxone kit or fentanyl test strips..."

abc 7 KVIA.COM

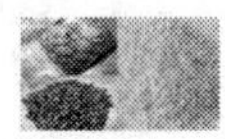

El Paso DEA warns of an opioid epidemic after 9 overdoses in 36 hours a total of nine patients were taken to local hospitals after they experienced signs of drug overdose. Additionally, El Paso Police officials said two people died of an accidental overdose.

May 30, 2022

FENTANYL WARNING FENTANYL WARNING FENTANYL WARNING FENTANYL WARNING FENTANYL WARNING FENTANYL WARNING

FOX9

June 9, 2022

Police warn public after 9 opioid overdoses in St. Paul over 24 hours

Police are warning members of the public after they've responded to nine suspected opioid overdoses over the course of the past 24 hours.

The St. Paul Police Department issued an "OD Alert" due to the incidents. Officers say all nine recent overdose patients survived. However, over the past five days, the city has reported five overdose deaths.

The alert is a reminder of the dangers of using street drugs. If you have access to naloxone, the opioid antidote, police say you should carry it with you.

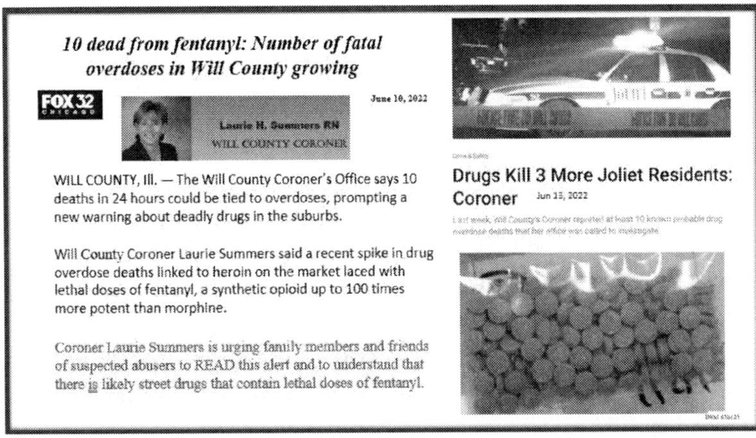
10 dead from fentanyl: Number of fatal overdoses in Will County growing
FOX 32 CHICAGO
June 10, 2022
Laurie H. Summers RN
WILL COUNTY CORONER
WILL COUNTY, Ill. — The Will County Coroner's Office says 10 deaths in 24 hours could be tied to overdoses, prompting a new warning about deadly drugs in the suburbs.
Will County Coroner Laurie Summers said a recent spike in drug overdose deaths linked to heroin on the market laced with lethal doses of fentanyl, a synthetic opioid up to 100 times more potent than morphine.
Coroner Laurie Summers is urging family members and friends of suspected abusers to READ this alert and to understand that there is likely street drugs that contain lethal doses of fentanyl.
Drugs Kill 3 More Joliet Residents: Coroner
Jun 13, 2022

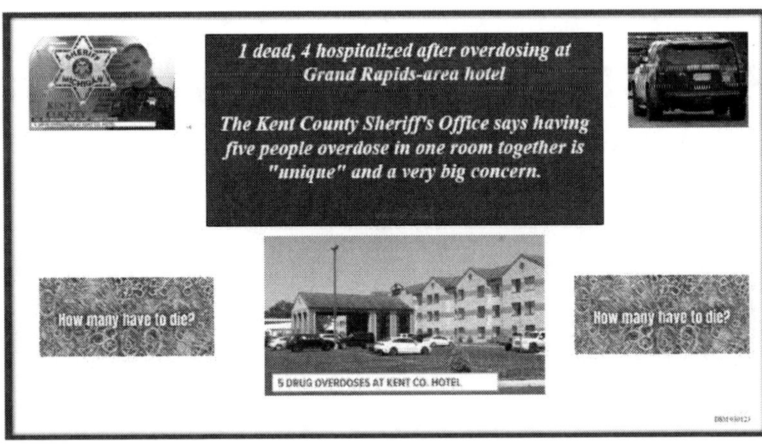
1 dead, 4 hospitalized after overdosing at Grand Rapids-area hotel
The Kent County Sheriff's Office says having five people overdose in one room together is "unique" and a very big concern.
How many have to die?
5 DRUG OVERDOSES AT KENT CO. HOTEL
How many have to die?

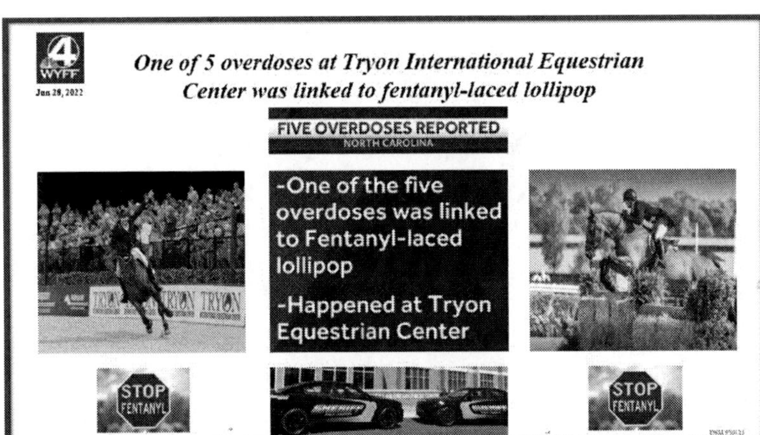
WYFF 4
Jun 28, 2022
One of 5 overdoses at Tryon International Equestrian Center was linked to fentanyl-laced lollipop
FIVE OVERDOSES REPORTED
NORTH CAROLINA
-One of the five overdoses was linked to Fentanyl-laced lollipop
-Happened at Tryon Equestrian Center
STOP FENTANYL
STOP FENTANYL

Gadsden County sees a deadly spike in fentanyl overdoses
WCTV.tv
Jul. 4, 2022
Death toll climbs to 9 from drug overdoses in Gadsden County
"We suspect that this was due to some type of opioid poisoning such as Fentanyl,"
Sheriff Morris Young.
Drug Enforcement Administration
ANNE MILGRAM
#DEA
Preliminary findings suggest the deaths are due to drugs like cocaine and marijuana being laced with fentanyl, according to investigators.

7 people found unresponsive after taking bad drugs laced with Fentanyl, Tampa police say
FOX 13
July 13, 2022
Seven people have been hospitalized due to consuming drugs laced with Fentanyl
When officers arrived, they found six people on the ground, all of whom were having a difficult time breathing.
Several were unresponsive, police said.
Several of the victims needed to be revived with Narcan.
ARRESTED
ALBERT WYCHE

WSB-TV 2
July 18, 2022
41 overdoses in 18 days: Metro Atlanta county is warning of a sudden overdose spike
Gwinnett County Police are warning of an overdose spike
GWINNETT COUNTY POLICE
POLICE
FENTANYL WARNING
Alpharetta
Marietta
Atlanta
FENTANYL WARNING

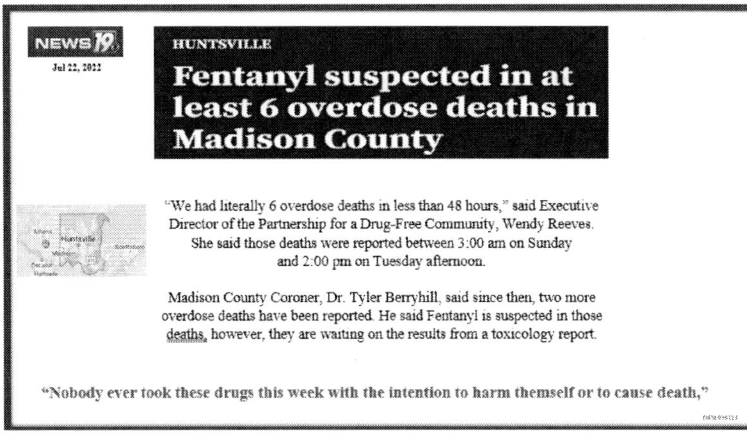
NEWS 19
Jul 22, 2022
HUNTSVILLE
Fentanyl suspected in at least 6 overdose deaths in Madison County
"We had literally 6 overdose deaths in less than 48 hours," said Executive Director of the Partnership for a Drug-Free Community, Wendy Reeves. She said those deaths were reported between 3:00 am on Sunday and 2:00 pm on Tuesday afternoon.
Madison County Coroner, Dr. Tyler Berryhill, said since then, two more overdose deaths have been reported. He said Fentanyl is suspected in those deaths, however, they are waiting on the results from a toxicology report.
"Nobody ever took these drugs this week with the intention to harm themself or to cause death,"

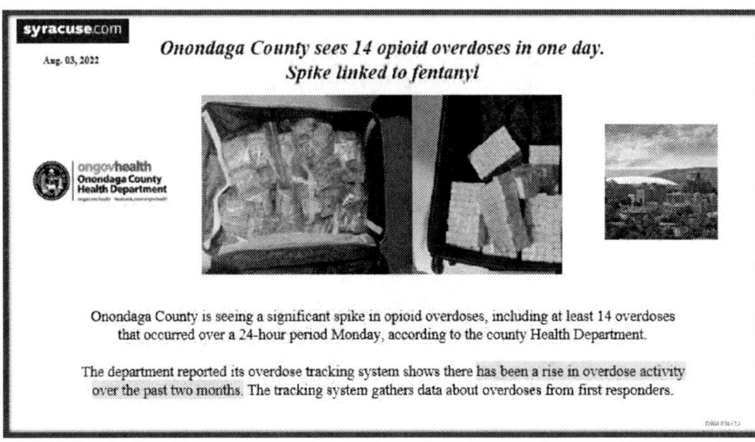
syracuse.com
Aug. 03, 2022
Onondaga County sees 14 opioid overdoses in one day. Spike linked to fentanyl
ongovhealth
Onondaga County Health Department
Onondaga County is seeing a significant spike in opioid overdoses, including at least 14 overdoses that occurred over a 24-hour period Monday, according to the county Health Department.
The department reported its overdose tracking system shows there has been a rise in overdose activity over the past two months. The tracking system gathers data about overdoses from first responders.

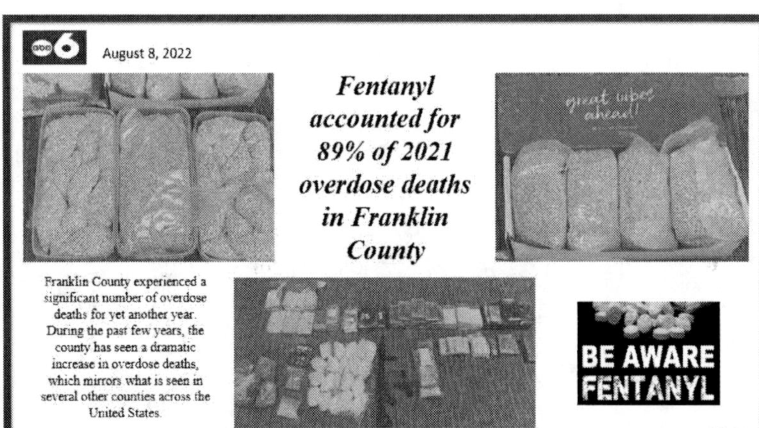
6
August 8, 2022
Fentanyl accounted for 89% of 2021 overdose deaths in Franklin County
Franklin County experienced a significant number of overdose deaths for yet another year. During the past few years, the county has seen a dramatic increase in overdose deaths, which mirrors what is seen in several other counties across the United States.
BE AWARE FENTANYL

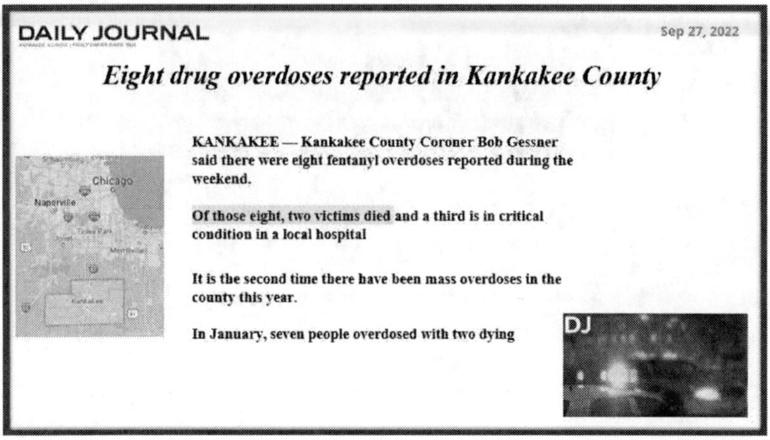
DAILY JOURNAL
Sep 27, 2022
Eight drug overdoses reported in Kankakee County
Chicago
KANKAKEE — Kankakee County Coroner Bob Gessner said there were eight fentanyl overdoses reported during the weekend.
Of those eight, two victims died and a third is in critical condition in a local hospital
It is the second time there have been mass overdoses in the county this year.
In January, seven people overdosed with two dying
DJ

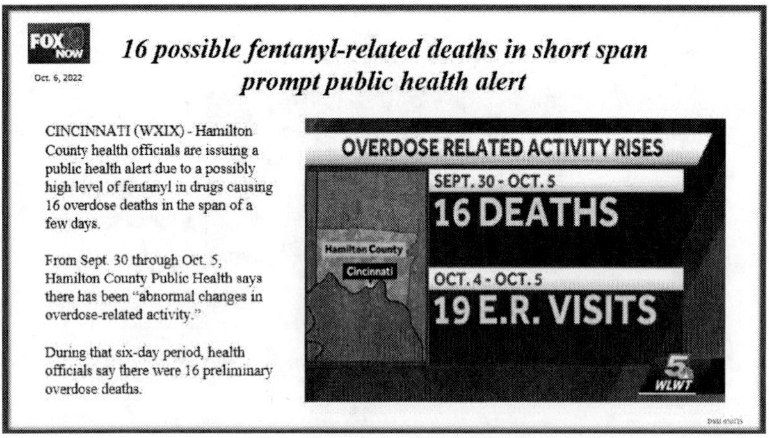
FOX NOW
Oct. 6, 2022
16 possible fentanyl-related deaths in short span prompt public health alert
CINCINNATI (WXIX) - Hamilton County health officials are issuing a public health alert due to a possibly high level of fentanyl in drugs causing 16 overdose deaths in the span of a few days.
From Sept. 30 through Oct. 5, Hamilton County Public Health says there has been "abnormal changes in overdose-related activity."
During that six-day period, health officials say there were 16 preliminary overdose deaths.
OVERDOSE RELATED ACTIVITY RISES
SEPT. 30 - OCT. 5
16 DEATHS
OCT. 4 - OCT. 5
19 E.R. VISITS
Hamilton County
Cincinnati
WLWT

3 dead from apparent fentanyl overdose in Stamford
Oct 13, 2022

Oct. 23, 2022

THE WALL STREET JOURNAL.

Three New Yorkers Ordered Cocaine From the Same Delivery Service. All Died From Fentanyl. Cocaine, long popular among New York professionals, is now often tainted with fentanyl, catching users unprepared and driving drug fatalities

9NEWS

November 1, 2022

3 men who died in suspected drug overdose in Denver were brothers

DENVER — The three men who were found dead in Denver on Sunday after a suspected drug overdose were related, according to family.

Police were called to an apartment on Kittredge Street in northeast Denver around 5:30 p.m. Sunday. On Tuesday, the coroner's office identified the three men who died there as 28-year-old Darren King Jr., 30-year-old Terrance King and 31-year-old Jairon Jackson.

CBS8

November 10, 2022

2 dead, 2 hospitalized in possible overdose in University Heights

First responders revived two of them with Narcan -- a drug used to counteract the effects of fentanyl -- and transported them to a hospital, SDPD said.

First responders revived two of them with Narcan -- a drug used to counteract the effects of fentanyl -- and transported them to a hospital, SDPD said.

San Diego Police Chief David Nisleit told CBS 8 that a man and a woman in their 30s were found dead in the home after someone called 911 about their roommates not waking up. He also said drugs were found in the home.

During a joint news conference Thursday with Mayor Todd Gloria on the fight against fentanyl, Chief Nisleit spoke about the overdose.

5 possible overdose victims rushed to hospital in Granada Hills

NOVEMBER 13, 2022

NEWS19

November 17, 2022

Four overdose deaths in 24 hours in Kershaw County

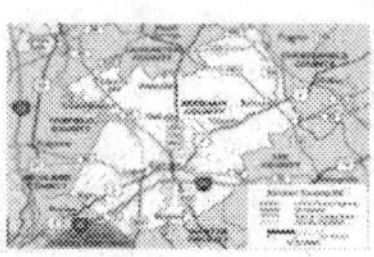

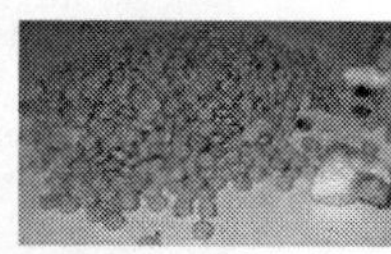

KERSHAW COUNTY, S.C. — Kershaw County Sheriff Lee Boan says his county is on pace to have the worst year on record of drug overdose deaths.

On Thursday the department posted an update that in a 24 hour stretch, 11 overdoses were called in, with four resulting in deaths.

FOX26

2 students possibly overdose at Dekaney High School in Harris Co., officials say

HARRIS COUNTY, TEXAS - On Thursday, FOX 26 received reports about a drug overdose at a local high school, videos circulating on social media show two students passed out at Dekaney High School

The scare happened on Thursday morning when two female students passed out in the cafeteria, one video shows school personnel and EMTs giving them CPR.

FOX CAROLINA

Nov. 20, 2022

Coroner: Investigation underway after 2 dead, 2 hurt in Anderson County following overdose

ANDERSON, S.C. (FOX Carolina) - The Anderson County Sheriff's Office is investigating after two people were found dead and one person was injured on Jones Street.

The Anderson County Coroner's Office said officials responded at around 2 a.m. on Sunday, Nov. 20 to a report of drug overdose. Deputies said at that time one person was taken to AnMed for treatment.

At around 6:44 a.m., the coroner said another call came and once on scene officials found two individuals were found dead outside a house and one person was found inside suffering from an overdose.

Montgomery County issues alert after 14 overdose deaths in week

Dayton Daily News

November 21, 2022

An overdose surge alert was issued Monday by Public Health - Dayton & Montgomery County after 14 people died in one week by suspected accidental overdoses.

The deaths occurred between Nov. 13 and Nov. 19, health department spokesman Dan Suffoletto said.

"Fourteen deaths in one week is a huge number, even taking into consideration what we've been through over the last couple of years," said Dawn Schwartz, project manager for the Montgomery County Community Overdose Action Team.

"You have to think about if we have that many deaths, think about how many overdoses we had both reported and not reported that didn't result in death in that same week. It's important for us to get out into the community that apparently there is some really, really bad stuff going on."

Broome overdose spike: 7 deaths in 11 days

BINGHAMTON homepage

Dec 9, 2022

BROOME COUNTY, NY – Broome County is once again experiencing a significant spike in drug overdose deaths.

According to the Broome County Health Department, there have been a suspected **7 deaths over the course of the past 11 days.**

The total number of deaths this year is already 75 compared to 54 last year.

BAY AREA

Six people treated in possible mass overdose on Christmas Day

by: Tori Gaines
Posted: Dec 26, 2022 / 12:56 PM PST
Updated: Dec 26, 2022 / 01:20 PM PST

SAN FRANCISCO (KRON) — Six people were treated for possible drug overdoses on Christmas Day, according to the San Francisco Fire Department. At 2:30 p.m., fire crews responded to the 1700 block of Post Street where they found six adult patients suffering from possible drug overdoses inside of a residence.

KRON 4

Onondaga County reports 25 fentanyl-related overdoses in last 24 hours

CNY CENTRAL

by Emma Misiaszek | Thursday, January 12th 2023

SYRACUSE, N.Y. — The Onondaga County Health Department reported at 4:30 p.m. Thursday that in the last 24 hours, approximately 25 overdoses have been reported in Onondaga County.

Initial information is showing a possible link to fentanyl-laced spike/spice, an illegal synthetic drug. Other substances that can potentially be laced with fentanyl include cocaine, molly, MDMA and other illicit drugs.

Crime & Safety

Onondaga County reporting 14 fentanyl overdoses in just 36 hours

Updated: Dec. 22, 2022, 5:50 p.m. | Published: Dec. 22, 2022, 1:35 p.m.

6 hospitalized after fentanyl overdoses at Mount Greenwood bar in Chicago

CBS NEWS CHICAGO

BY CBS CHICAGO TEAM
UPDATED ON: JANUARY 24, 2023 / 8:20 AM / CBS CHICAGO

CHICAGO (CBS) -- **Six people** were hospitalized after overdosing on fentanyl at a bar in Chicago's Mount Greenwood neighborhood.

The Chicago Fire Department was called to Lawlor's Bar in the 3600 block of West 111th Street Sunday afternoon.

According to CFD, two victims were transported to Advocate Christ Medical Center where they were stabilized. Three others were transported to Little Company of Mary Medical Center, where they were also stabilized.

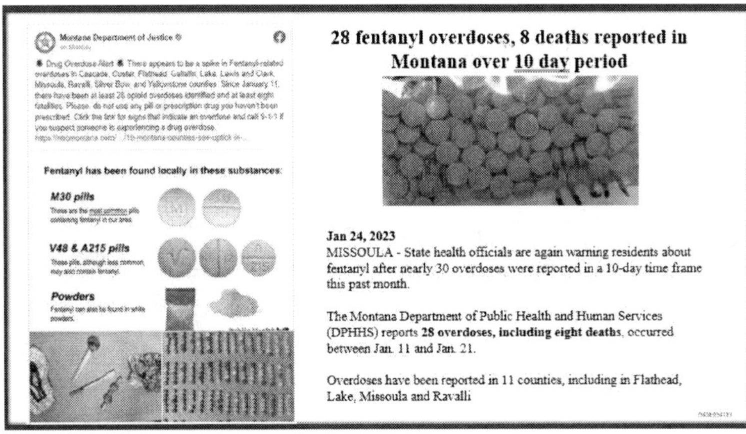

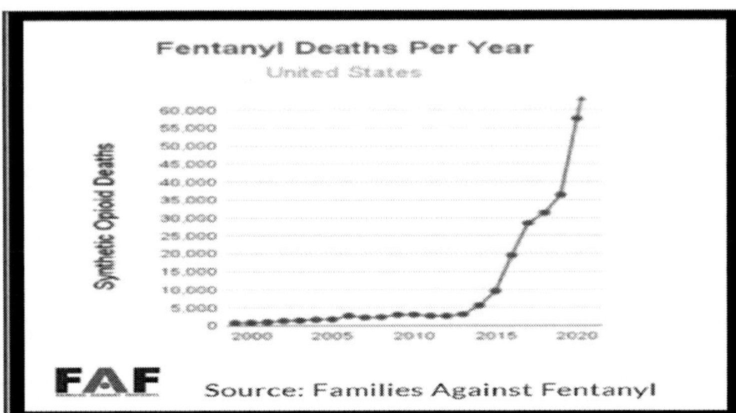

SOME SIGNIFICANT DRUG SEIZURES IN AMERICA HIGHLIGHTING THE SEVERITY OF THE THREAT

FOR IMMEDIATE RELEASE
Friday, November 19, 2021
Federal Charges Filed following Record-breaking Seizure of Fentanyl and Meth
NEWS RELEASE SUMMARY - November 19, 2021
SAN DIEGO – Acting U.S. Attorney Randy Grossman announced federal drug charges today against Carlos Martin Quintana-Arias of Mexico, following the seizure yesterday of 17,584 pounds of methamphetamine and 388.93 pounds of fentanyl from a commercial trailer attempting entry at the Otay Mesa, California, Commercial Port of Entry. U.S. Customs and Border Protection (CBP) confirmed that both drug seizures would be the largest in each drug category, for both this year and last year, in the entire United States.
The Complaint alleges that on November 18, 2021, at approximately 8:18 p.m., Quintana-Arias, a Mexican citizen, applied for entry into the U.S. as the driver and sole occupant of a 2009 Kenworth Tractor pulling a 1996 Stoug trailer. Quintana-Arias' manifest reflected the trailer contained automotive body parts. However, according to the Complaint, an X-Ray machine detected anomalies inside the trailer and a drug detection dog alerted to the rear door of the trailer.
Further inspection of the trailer's contents revealed a few automotive body parts among 6,266 packages of drugs. Of the total drug packages, 6,106 packages contained a substance that field-tested positive for methamphetamine; these packages together weighed approximately 7,976.2 kilograms (17,584.33 pounds). The other 160 packages contained a substance that field-tested positive for fentanyl and weighed approximately 176.40 kilograms (388.93 pounds).
"This is a staggering seizure that demonstrates the extent of our current fight against mass production of methamphetamine and fentanyl. But for the vigilance of our law enforcement partners, this record-breaking deluge of drugs would have caused incredible damage in our communities," said Acting U.S. Attorney Randy Grossman. "We commend our partner agencies for their tireless work and dedication to preventing these dangerous and deadly drugs from entering our country."
Record-breaking amounts of meth and fentanyl seized in San Diego
More than 17,500 lbs of meth and 389 lbs of fentanyl were seized from a tractor-trailer at the Otay Mesa Port last Thursday
Trucker arrested in record-breaking drug seizure at border

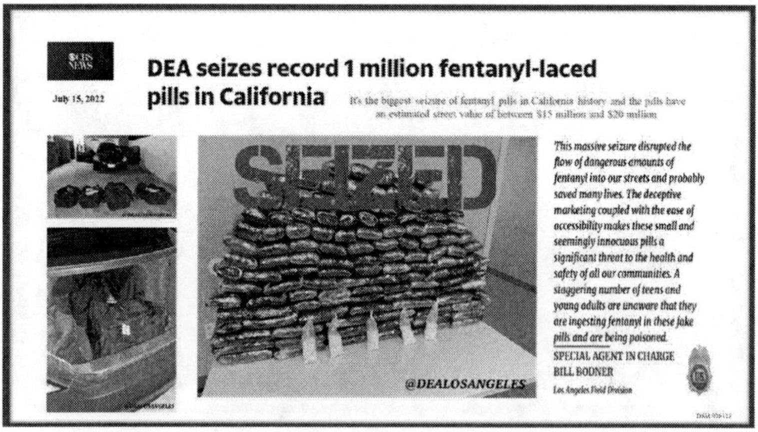
CBS NEWS
July 15, 2022
DEA seizes record 1 million fentanyl-laced pills in California
It's the biggest seizure of fentanyl pills in California history and the pills have an estimated street value of between $15 million and $20 million
This massive seizure disrupted the flow of dangerous amounts of fentanyl into our streets and probably saved many lives. The deceptive marketing coupled with the ease of accessibility makes these small and seemingly innocuous pills a significant threat to the health and safety of all our communities. A staggering number of teens and young adults are unaware that they are ingesting fentanyl in these fake pills and are being poisoned.
SPECIAL AGENT IN CHARGE
BILL BODNER
Los Angeles Field Division
@DEALOSANGELES

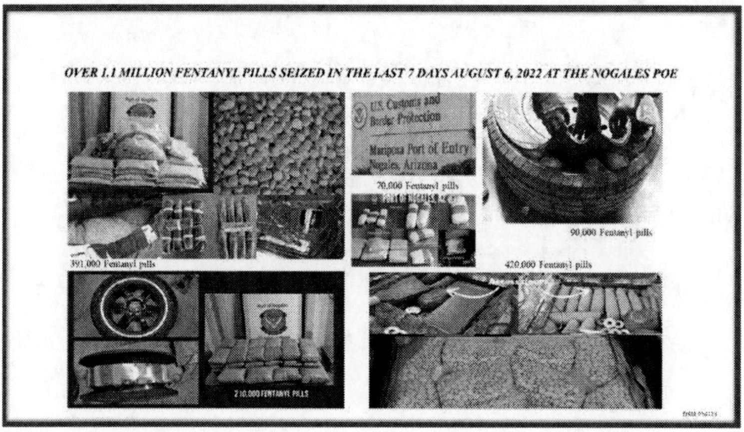
OVER 1.1 MILLION FENTANYL PILLS SEIZED IN THE LAST 7 DAYS AUGUST 6, 2022 AT THE NOGALES POE
U.S. Customs and Border Protection
Mariposa Port of Entry
Nogales, Arizona
70,000 Fentanyl pills
90,000 Fentanyl pills
391,000 Fentanyl pills
420,000 Fentanyl pills
210,000 FENTANYL PILLS

PARENTS BEWARE: "The Mexican Cartels are the Enemy of the Children"
SweeTARTS Original
Skittles
Nerds
This Distribution Tactic and Marketing Brings a New Level of Danger for American Kids

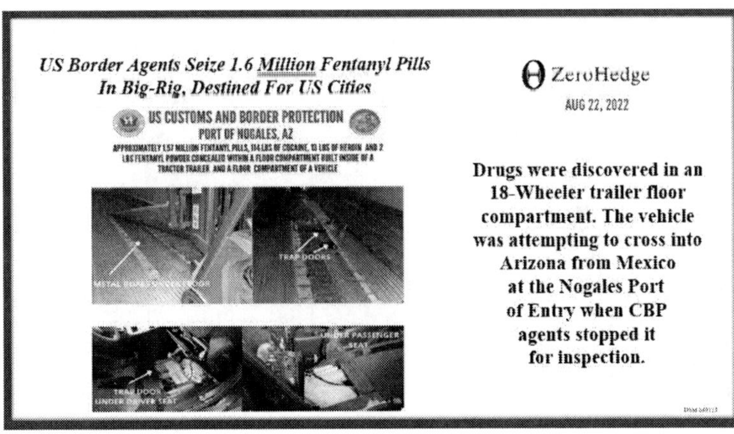
US Border Agents Seize 1.6 Million Fentanyl Pills In Big-Rig, Destined For US Cities
US CUSTOMS AND BORDER PROTECTION
PORT OF NOGALES, AZ
APPROXIMATELY 1.57 MILLION FENTANYL PILLS, 114 LBS OF COCAINE, 13 LBS OF HEROIN AND 2 LBS FENTANYL POWDER CONCEALED WITHIN A FLOOR COMPARTMENT BUILT INSIDE OF A TRACTOR TRAILER AND A FLOOR COMPARTMENT OF A VEHICLE
METAL BEAMS UNDER FLOOR
TRAP DOORS
TRAP DOOR UNDER DRIVER SEAT
UNDER PASSENGER SEAT
ZeroHedge
AUG 22, 2022
Drugs were discovered in an 18-Wheeler trailer floor compartment. The vehicle was attempting to cross into Arizona from Mexico at the Nogales Port of Entry when CBP agents stopped it for inspection.

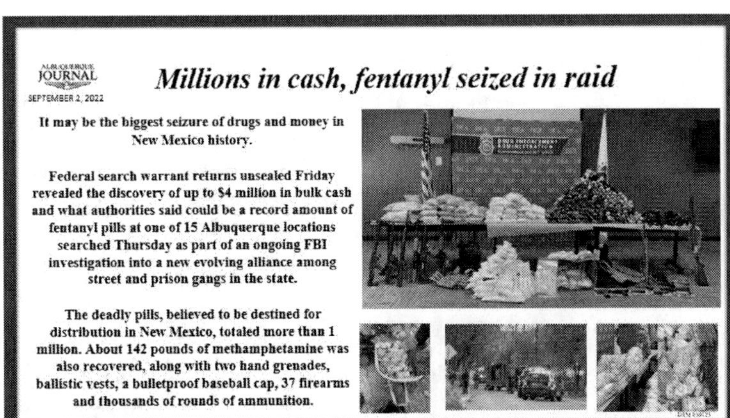
ALBUQUERQUE JOURNAL
SEPTEMBER 2, 2022
Millions in cash, fentanyl seized in raid
It may be the biggest seizure of drugs and money in New Mexico history.
Federal search warrant returns unsealed Friday revealed the discovery of up to $4 million in bulk cash and what authorities said could be a record amount of fentanyl pills at one of 15 Albuquerque locations searched Thursday as part of an ongoing FBI investigation into a new evolving alliance among street and prison gangs in the state.
The deadly pills, believed to be destined for distribution in New Mexico, totaled more than 1 million. About 142 pounds of methamphetamine was also recovered, along with two hand grenades, ballistic vests, a bulletproof baseball cap, 37 firearms and thousands of rounds of ammunition.

Over 1 million fentanyl pills seized by officers; single largest bust in Phoenix Police's history
Sep 23, 2022

News 13
Oct 25, 2022
South Carolina deputies seize 30,000 grams of fentanyl, arrest 6
WAR ON FENTANYL
YORK COUNTY
CN2
During the execution of one search warrant on Golden Pond Dr in Clover, investigators said they seized around 30,531 grams of fentanyl, 2869 grams of cocaine, 704 grams of methamphetamine, 454 grams of marijuana, four firearms and seven pill presses used to manufacture illegal pills.
MASSIVE AMOUNT OF FENTANYL SEIZED

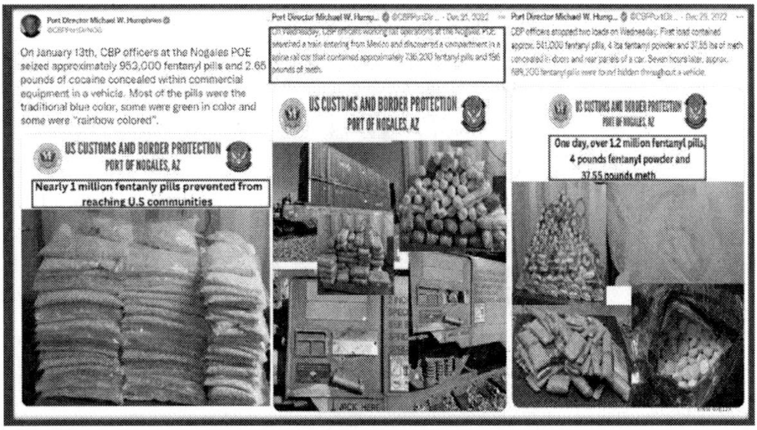
Port Director Michael W. Humphries
On January 13th, CBP officers at the Nogales POE seized approximately 953,000 fentanyl pills and 2.65 pounds of cocaine concealed within commercial equipment in a vehicle. Most of the pills were the traditional blue color, some were green in color and some were "rainbow colored".
US CUSTOMS AND BORDER PROTECTION
PORT OF NOGALES, AZ
Nearly 1 million fentanly pills prevented from reaching U.S communities
Port Director Michael W. Hump... · Dec 25, 2022
US CUSTOMS AND BORDER PROTECTION
PORT OF NOGALES, AZ
Port Director Michael W. Hump... · Dec 29, 2022
CBP officers stopped two loads on Wednesday. First load contained approx. 541,000 fentanyl pills, 4 lbs fentanyl powder and 37.55 lbs of meth concealed in doors and rear panels of a car. Seven hours later, approx. 689,200 fentanyl pills were found hidden throughout a vehicle.
US CUSTOMS AND BORDER PROTECTION
PORT OF NOGALES, AZ
One day, over 1.2 million fentanyl pills, 4 pounds fentanyl powder and 37.55 pounds meth

In the first 3 months of FY23, the Nogales POE has already surpassed the total amount of fentanyl seized throughout all of FY22, which was already a record year.

Fentanyl seized by CBP at the port of entry in Nogales, AZ.
More than 40,000 fentanyl pills found in a vehicle's modified battery
More than 10,000 fentanyl pills found in a body shaping garment worn by a woman.
July 10, 2022
Duralast

CNN
July 20, 2022
Man arrested in California for allegedly smuggling nearly $3.7 million of fentanyl in his car tire and gas tank
US Border Patrol agents arrested a man allegedly attempting to smuggle approximately 250 pounds of fentanyl in his truck's spare tire and gas tank

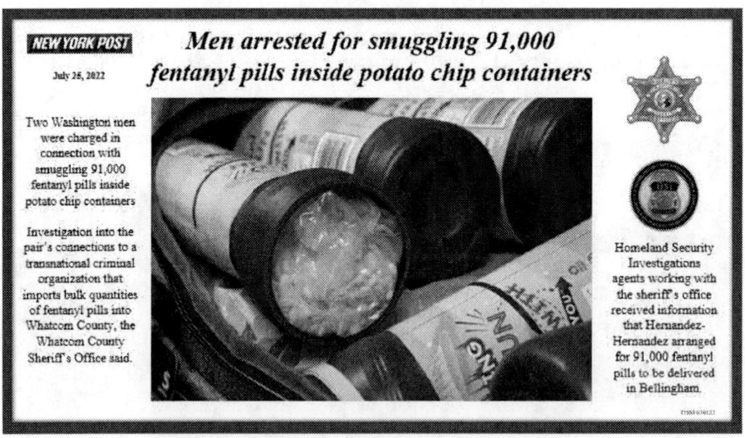
NEW YORK POST
July 25, 2022
Men arrested for smuggling 91,000 fentanyl pills inside potato chip containers
Two Washington men were charged in connection with smuggling 91,000 fentanyl pills inside potato chip containers
Investigation into the pair's connections to a transnational criminal organization that imports bulk quantities of fentanyl pills into Whatcom County, the Whatcom County Sheriff's Office said.
Homeland Security Investigations agents working with the sheriff's office received information that Hernandez-Hernandez arranged for 91,000 fentanyl pills to be delivered in Bellingham.

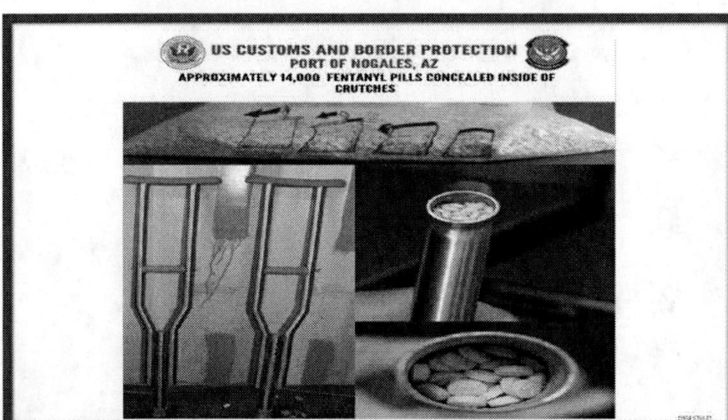
US CUSTOMS AND BORDER PROTECTION
PORT OF NOGALES, AZ
APPROXIMATELY 14,000 FENTANYL PILLS CONCEALED INSIDE OF CRUTCHES

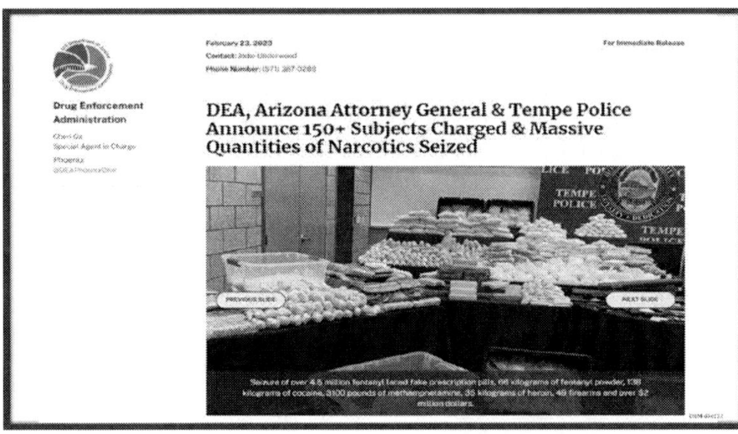

NEW DRUGS EMERGING AROUND THE COUNTRY ALSO HIGHLIGHTING THE SEVERITY OF THE THREAT

NITAZENES

Newsweek

7/22/22

New Drug About 10 Times Stronger Than Fentanyl Circulating in Colorado

Pyro, the street name of a new drug that is stronger than the high-risk narcotic fentanyl, has been circulating in Colorado and recently reportedly killed at least one person in Denver.

The N-pyrrolidino Etonitazene drug is a high-potency synthetic opioid that is between 1,000 and 1,500 times stronger than morphine, while fentanyl is only around 100 times stronger than morphine, local news station KKCO reported on Thursday.

Florida leads the nation in overdose deaths related to new synthetic drug, CDC data shows

FLORIDA OVERDOSE CRISIS

News4JAX

August 13, 2022

Florida is leading the nation in overdose deaths with a new synthetic drug called eutylone.

Eutylone is a synthetic psychoactive bath salt. Just last year it was listed as the seventh most identified drug detected
in over 8,000 cases.

Detroit DEA warns of animal tranquilizer street drug 'Tranq' where Narcan has no effect → FOX 2 January 17, 2023

A new trend the agency is monitoring closely is the rise in use of a relatively easy-to-get animal tranquilizer called xylazine. It is known on the streets – as Tranq. We are hiring technologists now for the fintech of tomorrow. "We have seen xylazine within our field division, so Ohio and Detroit," said Special Agent in Charge Orville Greene of the Detroit DEA

Flesh-eating drug 'tranq' meant for animals now linked to thousands of heroin, fentanyl ODs

NEW YORK POST September 25, 2022

The flesh-eating animal tranquilizer xylazine has been linked to thousands of drug overdoses across the country as it inundates heroin and fentanyl supplies in places such as Philadelphia, Delaware and Michigan, reports say.

Known on the street as "tranq," the sedative is now found in 91% of Philly's heroin and fentanyl supplies, according to a report earlier this month in the peer-reviewed journal Science Direct.

La Crosse police investigating 9 recent fatal drug overdoses

yesterday

January 25, 2023

Click to copy

RELATED TOPICS

Health
Addiction and treatment
La Crosse
Opioids

LA CROSSE, Wis. (AP) — La Crosse police are investigating nine recent drug overdose deaths amid concerns that a powerful animal tranquilizer may be present in the local illicit opioid supply.

The La Crosse Police Department, the city's mayor, Gundersen Health System and Tri-State Ambulance warned the community Tuesday about the high number of fatal overdoses during 2023's first three weeks.

Toxicology reports on those overdose deaths are pending, and it may take weeks to complete, the La Crosse Tribune reported.

But the deaths have raised concerns that the animal tranquilizer xylazine, known as "tranq," may have entered local illicit supplies of fentanyl, heroin and cocaine. The tranquilizer can leave users in an hours-long stupor, and it also causes slowed breathing that interferes with the effectiveness of naloxone, a medication used to reverse opioid overdoses.

"We want those who are struggling with substance abuse to know there is possibly a dangerous mix here in our community," said Jason Melby, La Crosse's assistant chief of police.

The ineffectiveness of naloxone in treating the recent overdoses highlights the importance of emergency care, such as supportive breathing, that can keep overdose patients alive even if the medication fails, said Dr. Chris Eberlein with emergency medicine at Gundersen Health System.

SEIZURES OF FENTANYL REPORTED IN MEXICO HIGHLIGHTING THE SEVERITY OF THE THREAT

Mexican police find 660 pounds of fentanyl in coconuts

Prosecutors in Mexico say police found 660 pounds (300 kilograms) of fentanyl pills packed into coconuts

By The Associated Press
December 2, 2022 3:33 PM

MEXICO CITY -- Prosecutors in Mexico say police found 660 pounds (300 kilograms) of fentanyl pills packed into coconuts.

The coconuts were found in a truck traveling on a highway in the northern border state of Sonora.

Prosecutors said the truck was detected Thursday on a road that runs along the Gulf of California, also known as the Sea of Cortez.

According to photos of the bust, the coconut husks had been neatly split in half, and re-assembled with plastic bags of fentanyl pills inside. The road eventually leads to the border town of Sonoyta, across the border from Lukeville, Arizona.

Mexico produces most of the fentanyl that reaches the United States, using chemical precursors imported from China and elsewhere.

Fentanyl is blamed for tens of thousands of U.S. overdose deaths each year, because the extremely powerful synthetic opioid is pressed into counterfeit pills often made to look like Xanax, oxycodone or Percocet. Many people who take them do not know they are taking fentanyl.

DEVASTATING IMPACT TO FAMILIES AND THE FUTURE GENERATION IN AMERICA FROM DEADLY DRUGS IMPORTED INTO THE USA

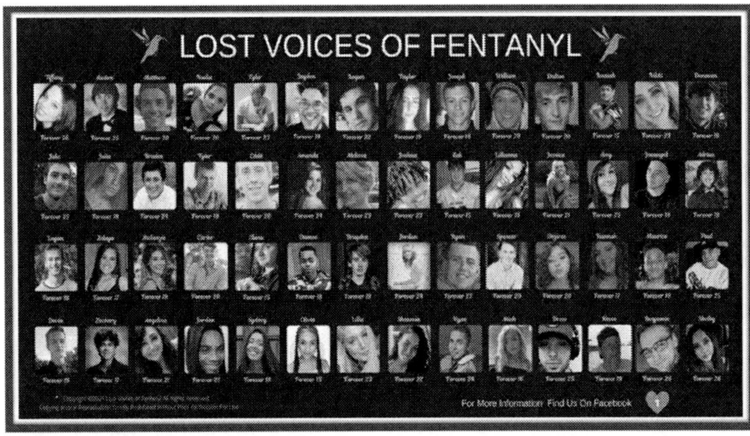
LOST VOICES OF FENTANYL
For More Information Find Us On Facebook

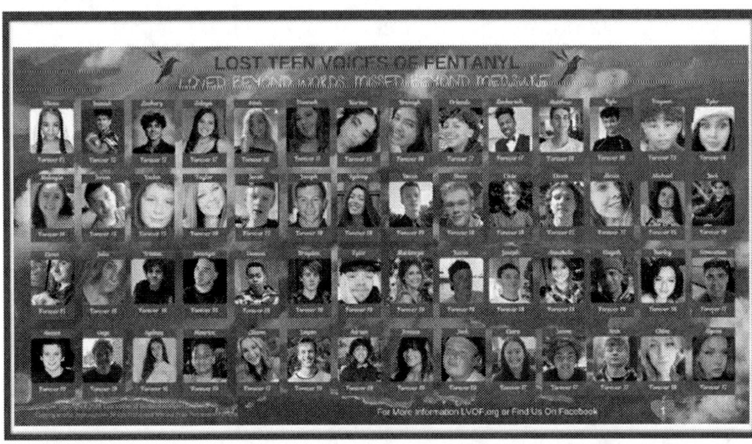
LOST TEEN VOICES OF FENTANYL
For More Information LVOF.org or Find Us On Facebook

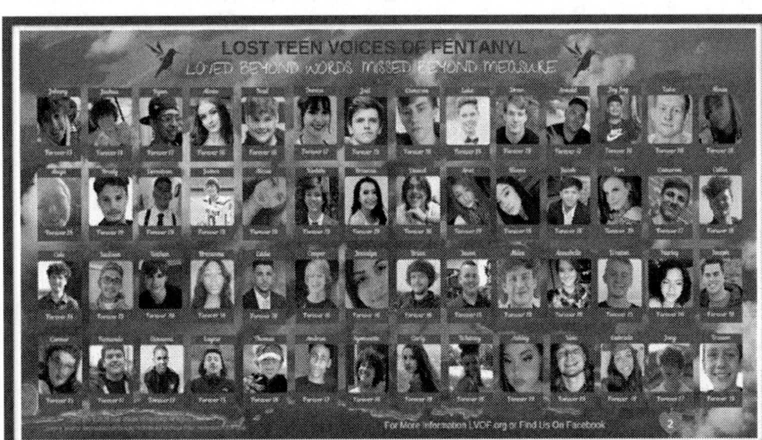
LOST TEEN VOICES OF FENTANYL
For More Information LVOF.org or Find Us On Facebook

Mr. BIGGS. Thank you, Mr. Maltz.

Now, we will proceed with the five-minute rule for questioning. I will recognize the gentleman from Texas, Mr. Nehls.

Mr. NEHLS. Thank you, Mr. Chair.

Dr. Singer, in your testimony you State, quote, Fentanyl is just the latest manifestation of what drug policy analysts calls "the iron law of prohibition."

"The harder the law enforcement, the harder the law." Enforcing prohibition incentivizes those who market prohibited substances to develop more potent forms that are easier to smuggle.

Doctor, I was a law enforcement officer; served in it for 30 years. I was the sheriff of Fort Bend County for eight years, a large agency.

I can tell you, sir, in my humble opinion, you, sir, are wrong. This here is Jose Alvarez. He is out of Mexico. Roadside investigation, Highway 59 North in my county, Hamilton, Texas, one of my officers located 10 bundles containing 10,000 tablets of fentanyl.

I want to explain something: That law enforcement across this country, we save lives. Two milligrams of fentanyl, one lethal dose. Five milligrams—look at the chart.

Are you telling me, sir, that we should not have saved those 25,000 lives that this fentanyl would have killed?

Dr. SINGER. I'm telling you that there's another 25,000 lethal doses right behind that one—

Mr. NEHLS. I want to show you another example. This is Mr. Luis Garza. Garza was followed by my officers, Beasley, Texas, Highway 59 North. During this investigation, my officers located five containers of 10,000 Xanax tablets—Xanax tablets that were discovered to contain fentanyl.

Should law enforcement not have protected 25,000 lives that these tablets would have killed?

Dr. SINGER. I must say—

Mr. NEHLS. Just say yes or no.

Dr. SINGER. Yes, they should have.

Mr. NEHLS. In your testimony, you State, quote, "Threatening drug dealers with life imprisonment or the death penalty is also unlikely to deter the drug trade," end quote.

Mr. Nadler was up here just a few minutes ago. I'm paraphrasing him. He says: We can't incarcerate ourselves out of this problem.

I'm agreeing with you. I realize that individuals, these drug cartels, drug dealers, they are risking their lives being involved in this business. I understand that.

I support President Trump and his recent comments related to making the sale and distribution of fentanyl a capital crime and the use of the death penalty. I believe this strategy will address this serious problem. Maybe it won't solve the problem, but I believe that, if you start strapping a few of these ruthless bastards to a gurney and start filling them with the same drug they were selling to kill Americans, it would me bring a great deal of satisfaction.

I want to thank those that are here. Ms. Rachwal, for Logan, I am so sorry.

I had dinner with a gentleman last night who lost his 27-year- old son—lost his 27-year-old son. He was shaking when I was having a conversation with him. I told him I'm going to be here today; I'm sorry for your loss.

I will do everything in my power to secure our southern border, to support our law enforcement, to make America first, to make America great again, and stop this deadly drug from making its way into our communities.

Thank you. I yield back. Oh, I yield my time.

Mr. BIGGS. Thank you for yielding and thank you for your questioning.

I want to make this point because I think it needs to be made, based on some of the statements from my friends about this issue, who I think are sincerely concerned as well.

The movement of illegal aliens across our southern border is unbelievably—I mean, we are talking over two million encounters last year, not to mention a million known gotaways.

The Border Patrol is distracted by dealing with those individuals that are surrendering. A million people, as I showed in the video earlier, coming across in camo and backpacks. They are not coming on holiday. They are coming to poison our children and our citizens.

The Border Patrol vacancy that occurs because we have—I know some of you are very familiar with Arizona, the Tohono O'odham Reservation, 62 linear miles on the border—62 linear miles. Basically, times where no one is there to patrol because they are dealing with the surrenders and gotaways.

Please remember that. This is coming and pouring across our southern border.

With that, the time is expired, and I will yield to the gentlelady, the Ranking Member from Texas, Ms. Jackson Lee.

Ms. JACKSON LEE. I will always say that we need to do this in a fully bipartisan-embracing way.

Ms. Rachwal, I want to, as I listened to you, and as well in the other room, and as well read your statement, I think we should put on the record Logan was kind, caring, smart, and creative. He loved animals. The plight that he faced really should be something that we can find common ground. As I indicated, I am interested in the manufacturing, online, where it gets directly in the hands of a beautiful, young man like Logan.

So, you listened to Mr. Maltz, and I understand that you are a clinical therapist. What about the videos, the involvement of education, professionals? What about just getting on the airwaves and making a major campaign? Can that help?

Ms. RACHWAL. I believe that everything needs to be done to help this problem. Yes, we have to hit it at all angles. Absolutely education.

I spoke in front of about 120 young kids yesterday morning, and over half of the room had never even heard about fentanyl. Probably 95 percent never heard about Narcan or naloxone.

So, education is huge. It's important, just important as this and the border. I believe it has to be hit from all angles.

Ms. JACKSON LEE. Well, we need to take you up on the offer, and let me also offer my sympathy to your husband as well. We need to take up the loud megaphone, and I think that is what I hear you saying.

Dr. Singer, we need to do this in the right way. So, I need you to be as focused and precise on this question about dealing with fentanyl in a manner that is going to be effective.

The question of research and the medical use, can you explain how important? That is, even this scourge of the epidemic of attacking our Nation in terms of addiction and death. How do you interject the fentanyl research, so that we can be common-sensefocused to save lives, but to deal with the research that medicine needs to do?

Dr. SINGER. Thank you, Representative Jackson Lee.

Yes, actually, as we know from past experience, classifying a particular category of a fentanyl analog as Schedule I, meaning no accepted medical use, basically, cuts off any opportunity to do research on the drug going forward. I think nobody can ever know that there's not going to be something good discovered.

We cutoff psychedelics 50 years ago for research, and just now we're starting to realize them in many useful—there are many lives that could have been saved over the last 50 years, but research was completely suppressed. The FDA is about to finally legalize MDMA maybe this year.

Marijuana is still Schedule I. Could anybody with a straight face that it has no accepted medical use?

Just as a matter of principle, to completely block research into a certain area because you've decided in advance that it's not going to lead to anything positive, I don't know how anybody could ever know that. They probably laughed at people who suggested you can get penicillin from a bread mold, but we did.

I think it's a distraction to focus on permanently outlawing FRSs because, as Dr. Westlake himself admitted, it did nothing to lower the overdose crisis. We're here to be focused on why people are dying from fentanyl overdoses, and this is sort of like a little shiny object on the side.

So, we get rid of FRSs. Meanwhile, I think the next thing we're going to be dealing with is nitazenes or tranq. We're already hearing in the East Coast cities, we're hearing horrible stories about xylazine making its way into, into fentanyl and the other products.

Ms. JACKSON LEE. Let me pose some other questions.

Dr. Westlake indicated that the creation of new fentanyl-related substance had ground to a halt internationally. Do you agree with that proposition?

Dr. SINGER. I really don't know you could say that. Just like it's been said on this Committee that we don't know how many smugglers have smuggled in—

Ms. JACKSON LEE. Then, my last point is the drugs that provide the adverse reaction, I'll call it, and other drugs, how important it is that our communities have access to that—schools, police, et cetera?

Dr. SINGER. Are you talking about reversal?

Ms. JACKSON LEE. Yes.

Mr. BIGGS. The gentlelady's time has expired, but you can answer the question.

Ms. JACKSON LEE. Thank you, Mr. Chair.

Dr. SINGER. I think it's very important that drugs that block or are antidotes to the opioid-related overdose deaths are made readily available. Naloxone has been around since the 1960's. There's good reason to believe from recent reports from the Food and Drug Administration they may actually make it available over the counter this coming month of March. So, let's hope they do.

Ms. JACKSON LEE. I will engage with you on that. Thank you so very much. I think it is very important.

Mr. BIGGS. Thank you.

The gentlelady's time has expired, but I am going to recognize her for a point of personal privilege to introduce a guest she has.

Ms. JACKSON LEE. I am delighted. I know that she will take this information and we will collaborate together. I am delighted to have Councilmember Carolyn Evans-Shabazz, who represents what we call District D, for destination, in Houston, Texas, who is here to advocate for children, for economic involvement or investment, and to represent the city of Houston. Thank you so very much for being here. Mr. BIGGS. Thank you and welcome. [Applause.]

We are glad to have you with us today.

The Chair recognizes the gentleman from Alabama, Mr. Moore.

Mr. MOORE. Thank you, Mr. Chair.

Certainly, I appreciate all the witnesses being here today.

Ms. Rachwal, we are certainly—our condolences to you and your family for the loss of Logan.

Thank you all for being here.

It takes a lot of courage to do what you did today, but I think, more than anything, that is an opportunity from a person standpoint to reach so many children in this country who need to hear that story coming from a mom's mouth and telling it like it is out there. So, thank you again for being here and we appreciate that. Mr. Maltz, I have been to the border a couple or three times. The one thing that I think that the Biden border policies have done, they have created—we have an invasion on the southern border, five million people since he has been in office, encounters.

The one thing that I noticed, and it kind of concerned me—I don't know if you have heard this—but there is a price now for human beings to be shipped across our southern border. They are dealing with the cartels. So, the prices we heard were about—well, this is a few years ago—but last week, the testimony in Yuma, Arizona, it is now $6,000 a head, if you want to come into the U.S. from Mexico or Guatemala, any of the Triangle Nations. If you are coming from Russia, it is up to $19,000. A hundred countries, I think 106 countries come through Yuma.

The thing now, you know, we talk about securing those points of entry on the border. I assume we are spending some money and doing that wisely, but the thing is the porous border between those ports of entry, the cartels have figured this out.

So, I was told—and I don't know if you have heard us, and maybe you can help shed some light—but many of these people don't have the money to come to the U.S. So, they cut a deal with the cartel, and there is one of two options. They either are going to be indentured servants or slaves; they are going to make payments to the cartel. The other option was backpacking heroin, cocaine, or fentanyl across the U.S. southern border.

Have you heard of any of those stories? We are just trying to get to the bottom of what these policies are doing and (1) why we are seeing such an influx of people, and (2) drugs.

Mr. MALTZ. Thank you for the question.

I mean, the cartels run a multibillion-dollar enterprise. As you pointed out, there are some experts that suggest they're making more money from the migrant smuggling now than drug smuggling.

They are doing whatever it takes to get their poisonous drugs into this country because they want to drive addiction, and they also want to make as much money as they can.

So, I have talked to Homeland Security experts that, obviously, are very concerned for the national security of the country, because we've never seen anything like this in the history of the country. I just want to make it clear to everyone in the room: This is nothing we've ever seen.

So, there are so many migrants coming in, and it's just unknown. We don't know what we don't know. That's why I get a kick out of this POE concept, because there's more deaths in America than we've ever seen. There are more seizures at the POE and the border that we've ever seen. There's more seizures throughout America by law enforcement than we've ever seen.

So, obviously, yes, putting some more X-ray machines at the POE is really awesome. I appreciate that. That's not going to stop the tsunami of deadly drugs coming into this country. That's why we've got to destroy those production labs and can't rely on Mexico to do it.

Mr. MOORE. That is a very valid point.

Richard Nixon, 50 years ago, he started the war on drugs with just over 6,000 deaths in this country. We had 107,000 people die last year from fentanyl poisoning. Unfortunately, many of them are young and they are getting younger, 18–45, I think.

So, you talk about they will stop at nothing. We actually at one spot on the border—do you all remember the two little girls they dropped over the border, the 3-year-old and the 5-year-old? They climbed up a ladder at the top of that wall—I don't know, it is 14– 15 feet—and the cartel dropped those two children.

As the Border Agents—we went to that spot—as the Border Agents ran to that spot, there was an opening one mile away where they were shipping their drugs through. So, they used those children as decoys.

That is what they are doing with these migrants. They will send them in waves across the southern border. As the CBP, we are now—the CBP is now nothing more than a concierge service. They can't focus on stopping the drugs because they are too busy trying to process people in and get them to the points of entry, or wherever they have got to take them to get them shipped in a bus to somewhere in our country.

Anyway, I want to thank you for being here, sir; all of you for being here.

Mr. Chair, I will yield the remainder of my time to you.

Mr. BIGGS. Thank you, Mr. Moore.

So, we heard about that U.S. citizens are driving and bringing fentanyl up. They are coming through the ports of entry. Now, why is that? Because the cartels are hiring U.S. citizens, because it is easier for a U.S. citizen to actually drive through a port of entry than a foreign national.

It is the cartel that is controlling it. Even our testimony last week said there is nobody that enters the U.S. without the cartel controlling it.

I will give you an example. We went out in this ridiculous caravan the other night to go to the border. As I got in that caravan, I said, "Nobody's coming because the cartel would see 30 cars coming and they're not going to allow anybody to come." Nobody came—not until everybody had gone, and then, they started to flow again.

Ladies and gentlemen, we don't even control our own southern border.

I regret to tell you that we have been called for votes on the floor.

I would ask our witnesses to please—you may take a recess. We will probably be back here in about 45 minutes. We are going to be in a recess for 45 minutes, and then, we will continue the hearing. Thank you.

We are in recess. [Recess.]

Mr. BIGGS. Subcommittee is called to order.

Thank you for being back here. Our recess lasted a little bit longer than we anticipated due to votes.

I now yield five minutes to the gentleman from Florida, Mr. Gaetz.

Mr. GAETZ. Dr. Singer, in your testimony you talked about the market demand for fentanyl, for drugs generally, but specifically for fentanyl. I guess I wanted to assess the utility of that analysis in the context of a drug that is often spliced into other things that people are using.

Did your son seek out fentanyl? Was he part of the market demand for fentanyl?

Dr. SINGER. Absolutely not. He bought a pill on Snapchat, a blue perc 30, and it had fentanyl in it.

Mr. GAETZ. Mr. Maltz, in your extensive experience at DEA, do you find that fentanyl is being laced into what people believe to be Percocet?

Mr. MALTZ. A hundred percent, yes.

Mr. GAETZ. Xanax as well?

Mr. MALTZ. Yes, sir.

Mr. GAETZ. And marijuana?

Mr. MALTZ. There are cases of marijuana. Don't know the extent of that. There have been fatalities reported with fentanyl in marijuana, yes.

Mr. GAETZ. MDMA and ecstasy, do you see—

Mr. MALTZ. Not sure about too much of that. Definitely in heroin, cocaine, and methamphetamines. More importantly, it is the pure fentanyl that is in the pills and the powder.

They are making these pills, millions of them every day. There are pill press locations.

Mr. GAETZ. I get if someone, I get that you would think about something as an overdose if someone was seeking out fentanyl, they believed they were taking a certain amount of it. They end up taking more and they end up overdosing.

If someone thinks that they are using a different substance, that doesn't strike me as an overdose, that strikes me as a poisoning.

Mr. MALTZ. Yes.

Mr. GAETZ. Dr. Singer, I would love your thoughts on it because—

Dr. SINGER. Yes.

Mr. GAETZ. —probably on the Republican side I am the easiest to concur that the war on drugs is one that has been won by drugs.

Dr. SINGER. Yes. Well, Congressman Gaetz, maybe you misunderstood me. There is, there are some people who actually want fentanyl. For the most part it is prohibition and the black market that it created that is responsible for this. Because as I mentioned about the iron law of prohibition, that is what incentivizes the cartels to come up with more potent forms.

So, initially, around 2012 or so we were seeing fentanyl appear as a mixture with heroin to increase, to boost its potency so that they could smuggle it in smaller amounts and sell it into more units.

Then it really got accelerated when the cartels realized it is easier to synthesize. You don't have to rely on the opium poppy being shipped. The reason why we are seeing so many innocent people who are, for example, buying a Percocet they think, even Prince, Prince he liked to use vicodin. His dealer, he thought his dealer got him vicodin but the toxicology reports showed he died of a fentanyl overdose.

It wasn't in those cases that people were seeking fentanyl, it is that this is what happens when you have a black market.

Mr. GAETZ. Sure.

Dr. SINGER. So, is that—

Mr. GAETZ. I wanted to ask you a little bit about those relationships between the dealers and the users. I found a tweet of yours from back in 2019 where you say when people cross political borders, they are not violating anyone's rights, given that they are simply exercising their natural God given rights of freedom of travel, economic liberty, freedom of contract, and freedom of association.

When you say freedom of contract are you talking about the contract between the drug traffickers and the users?

Dr. SINGER. No. I'm talking about a contract, for example, between a farmer and somebody who has, is offering to work on their farm and help pick crops, for example.

Mr. GAETZ. I am glad you mentioned the farmer, because we were just in Yuma, Arizona, and we met with a lot of the growers. These are, like, third, fifth generation growers. What they tell us about their freedoms and their property rights, property rights that I think Cato cares deeply about, is that they get violated by migrants who defecate in their fields, who create contamination for the food supply.

These are not insurable losses. So, they just have to eat these losses.

Does the violation of the property rights of the farmers you mention concern you?

Dr. SINGER. Of course, that would be trespassing on private property, so.

Mr. GAETZ. Right. Don't you think that the open borders policies that you have advocated for increase the frequency of that violation of people's property rights?

Dr. SINGER. People have no right to come on someone else's property without their permission.

I am not here as an immigration expert, but I can tell you as a libertarian, the overarching principle is that our fundamental, inalienable rights are not limited to people in the United States. It is a human phenomenon, all humans. All humans have the right to freedom of movement.

Mr. GAETZ. Not across somebody else's property; right?

Dr. SINGER. I beg your pardon?

Mr. GAETZ. Not across somebody's private property.

Dr. SINGER. Not private property, no.

Mr. GAETZ. Do you believe that everybody in the world has freedom of movement across our border?

Dr. SINGER. Unfortunately, no.

Mr. GAETZ. You would like that to be the case?

Dr. SINGER. Well, I think borders are for governments and not for people.

Mr. GAETZ. I don't know, Doctor.

Dr. SINGER. Borders define where—

Mr. GAETZ. See, I would observe that governments have to govern the conduct of people, and that the role of our government is to secure our border. That if it is open, it is the property rights we are concerned about and the life and health of our fellow Americans that continues to degrade.

I appreciate the colloquy and appreciate all the witnesses being here. I yield back.

Mr. BIGGS. The gentleman's time has expired.

I call upon and recognize the gentlelady from Pennsylvania, Ms. Dean.

Ms. DEAN. Thank you, Mr. Chair.

I want to thank all our witnesses for testifying today for this important discussion. First, let me extend my sincere sympathies to the Rachwal family for your indescribable loss of Logan, to you and your husband, and your son, I am very sorry for the loss of your beautiful boy.

You have lived a nightmare that many parents fear. My family faced the diabolical opioid crisis ravaging this country because our middle son was addicted to opioids. We went through an awful lot of trauma around that, and misunderstanding, misunderstanding him and what was affecting him. He is now 10 years in recovery. I think it is really only but for timing, perhaps, that we didn't lose him to fentanyl, because 10 years ago it was not so prevalent. So, God bless you, and God bless Logan. I want you to know that we have a bipartisan new caucus, and it is bipartisan, to work in a bipartisan way. It is called the Bipartisan Fentanyl Prevention Caucus. So, I am delighted to join Rep. Issa, Rep. Neguse, as well as Rep. Calvert to work on this issue to save lives.

During both the Trump and Biden Administrations the Federal Government noted increasing numbers of overdose deaths. People have said it here today, 108,000 in 2021, 70 percent of those involving fentanyl poisoning.

So, treating fentanyl and related substances with severity, as the Biden Administration and the Trump Administration did, is one step. Just last year, Congress authorized $60 million for additional CDP officers, and $70 million for inspection technologies. All those things are what we must do. We know that much of these substances is coming through legal ports of entry.

The result of that investment was an additional 13,000 pounds of fentanyl seized.

So, I wanted to just ask you, Ms. Rachwal, if you would like to say just a little bit about Logan. Then I was going to ask Dr. Singer for some public health recommendations.

Ms. RACHWAL. Well, obviously Logan, thank you, Logan was very young when he passed. He was 19. So, he was our second, our oldest son. He was a real good kid. He was a vulnerable kid. We sort of felt like we, obviously, lost out on so much of his life.

Logan the night he passed he was upset, he was distraught. He was extremely upset. His girlfriend and him were fighting. He was on Facetime and took the pill while his girlfriend, was on Facetime with her.

He sought out the pill on social media. That is how he passed.

Ms. DEAN. I am very, very sorry. This Committee has heard from other parents who have lost the indescribable, heart-crushing loss. Dr. Singer, in your testimony you talked about the natural, sadly, natural progression of this drug crisis. This one began with pharmaceuticals, evolved to heroin, then fentanyl, now synthetics. Now we're even talking about tranq and some other horrific substances.

What are the right public health solutions?

I really believe we have to think outside the box. We can't be afraid to embrace that this, that people, not just addicts, but those who are addicted and those who are just experimenting are at grave risk of death.

So, what are the public health things we should be doing?

Dr. SINGER. Thank you for that question.

In fact, what we need to do is instead of just focusing on the supply side, we need to focus on protecting people who are using drugs from the dangers of fentanyl and other even more deadly contaminants.

I have a chapter, actually, in the Cato Handbook for Policy Makers that was just released that dealt with this. Among the things that this Committee could do is, for example, our drug paraphernalia laws, make it illegal for a person to hand out a fentanyl test strip. Or now they make xylazine test strips for tranq because that is considered drug paraphernalia as testing equipment.

Many States are changing their laws to allow that, both Red and Blue States. South Dakota did last week. Arizona did a year ago. There are also Federal paraphernalia laws.

Another very important thing in my opinion is for this Committee to consider even repealing or amending 21 U.S.C. 856, also called the "Crack House Statute." I have a policy brief that came out yesterday about this.

Overdose prevention centers have existed throughout the developed world since 1986 when they first started in Switzerland. They are in 16 countries.

There are 147 of them in 91 locations. We are an outlier. Thirty-eight are in Canada, 25 are in Germany, 14 in Switzerland. We are an outlier because our Federal law prohibits people from helping their neighbors by setting up centers, so they can be brought inside and use in a safe environment, and have people standing by with naloxone.

Ms. DEAN. I see my time has expired. I thank you both for the conversation.

I couldn't agree with you more. I have said to people in my district—

Mr. BIGGS. The gentlelady's time has expired.

Ms. DEAN. I agree with your recommendations. Thank you.

Mr. BIGGS. Thank you.

The Chair recognizes the gentleman from Wisconsin, Mr. Tiffany.

Mr. TIFFANY. Thank you very much.

Ms. Rachwal, you make all of us Wisconsoners proud.

Do you know the statistics from 2019–2021, there was nearly a doubling of the number of deaths in Wisconsin from fentanyl. Is any State exempt from this in your travels?

Ms. RACHWAL. I agree with you, Mr. Tiffany, what I believe in those two years, Wisconsin's percentage was about 97 percent increase. In my opinion, with the experience that we have, which I feel is probably early in its stages because Logan it has been very recent, but I think every single State is experiencing an increase. Our kids are at risk. Every single kid is at risk. Even if there are kids that we are not seeing, some kids are not dying but they are dealing with addiction issues as well very young because these cartels, these pills are, they are being made to drive addiction.

That is what they want, they want these kids to be addicted. It is a business.

So, but I do believe it is everywhere.

Mr. TIFFANY. Is this why you said everything has to be done to try to get this under control?

Ms. RACHWAL. Absolutely. If we miss one little loophole, that is why we are seeing numbers go up. There is some things being done, but everything has to be done. It has to be done at every angle.

Mr. TIFFANY. Dr. Westlake, it is also good to have you from the great State of Wisconsin here also. I want to thank you.

I voted for the Hope agenda in Wisconsin which you helped put together which was really groundbreaking, wasn't it in America?

Dr. WESTLAKE. Yes.

Mr. TIFFANY. First of its kind.

Dr. WESTLAKE. Yes.

Mr. TIFFANY. What does, you are an emergency room doctor, what does death look like from fentanyl?

Dr. WESTLAKE. Right. So, opioids just cause respiratory suppression, so it just, people just stop breathing, and then they pass out, and then they turn blue, and then they die if not resuscitated.

Mr. TIFFANY. So, it is almost like they are being smothered?

Dr. WESTLAKE. Or, right, or the same thing as an execution. It can be the same thing as a chemical execution.

Mr. TIFFANY. So, it is similar to a chemical?

Dr. WESTLAKE. Right.

Mr. TIFFANY. Many of the critics of FRS scheduling, Dr. Westlake, cite concerns with mandatory minimums and sentencing guidelines, insisting that this criminal justice framework will do nothing to prevent FRS market saturation.

Could you briefly explain why it is important to permanently keep this on Schedule I with the associated criminal penalties?

Dr. WESTLAKE. Great. Yes, thanks for the question.

So, this, so criminal penalties do not stop use of drugs. Drug users are going to use drugs. People with substance abuse disorder are going to use drugs.

Traffickers, as Dr. Singer said, are going to traffic drugs regardless of the penalties.

What this does and what—I know this is novel, and where I think this is not some shiny object that is distracting from the purpose—this closes up the spigot of fentanyl-related substances. So, this targets the legal chemical companies in China from stopping creating fentanyl-related substances.

According to the GAO report in 2021, it has accomplished that. There are relatively no new fentanyl-related substances being created.

So, you have this big, this big faucet of illicit fentanyl, which is a huge problem. Right now, the spigot for fentanyl-related substances is turned off, but it could reopen. I think the 2,500 people that died in Florida from fentanyl-related substances that were legal in 2016–2017 would disagree that fentanyl-related substances are a shiny object.

Mr. TIFFANY. Mr. Maltz, what we basically heard from the other side is that immigration is not a problem. We didn't hear that in the testimony from Sheriff Dannels, Cochise County, Arizona, and the sheriff from Yuma County over the last month.

Do you agree with the sheriffs that immigration has fostered this increase in fentanyl coming across the border?

Mr. MALTZ. A hundred percent. The country is being invaded. There are migrants coming from all over 160 countries. They are looking to get here for a better life, many of them. OK. We also have terrorists, we have rapists, we have sexual predators, we have criminals coming over that border every day. There over a million got-aways coming into the country.

Here is the problem, Congressman: The people in this town don't listen to the experts that know what they are talking about, that have been there on the border.

Chair Biggs goes down there, like many of you go down there, and talk to the experts, not reading it in the Washington Post.

Mr. TIFFANY. Sir, I just need my final 15 seconds here. Thank you for that.

If for no other reason, let's set aside the human trafficking, and the largest human trafficking network that has been set up in the history of the world. Set it aside.

We have the greatest number of people on the Terror Watch List come across our border, correct?

Mr. MALTZ. Yes.

Mr. TIFFANY. Set that aside. If for no other reason, for fentanyl we should be securing the border.

I yield back.

Mr. BIGGS. The gentleman's time has expired.

The Chair recognizes the gentleman from Tennessee, Mr. Cohen.

Mr. COHEN. Thank you, Mr. Chair.

First, is it Rachwal? Ms. Rachwal, I was here when you testified and was very sorry about your son and his circumstances, your husband as well.

Did the University of Wisconsin, Milwaukee, after your son's overdose do anything to start to inform students about drugs and have some type of a public interest program there, public information?

Ms. RACHWAL. Did we? I am sorry, did we do?

Mr. COHEN. Did Wisconsin, Milwaukee, do anything?

Ms. RACHWAL. The university?

Mr. COHEN. Yes. Yes, ma'am.

Ms. RACHWAL. They did after we respectfully pushed them and continued to push them. We were able to get naloxone boxes installed across the campus for safety. Then we were also able to have them instill a freshman program so that the students were aware of what to do, and the signs, had posters up, all those kind of things.

Mr. COHEN. Well, thank you for what you did.

Do you know if that has been done in other, other colleges?

Ms. RACHWAL. In Wisconsin specifically, 90 percent of the University of Wisconsin system does have the naloxone boxes and they are following suit with that, but every school is different.

Mr. COHEN. Right.

Ms. RACHWAL. So, it is there is not a uniform approach at this point.

Mr. COHEN. As far as they have an orientation, they tell them about drugs and warn them?

Ms. RACHWAL. Correct.

Mr. COHEN. Who do they have to do that, do you know? Is it a policeperson, or is it a community person, an athlete, or what?

Ms. RACHWAL. Not an athlete. The police are involved. In fact, actually as we speak today here right now, there is a program at the university today that we were supposed to speak at that our board is actually presenting for us. So, there are speaking events that we are involved in, being involved in, but also the substance department of the school and the police.

Mr. COHEN. Thank you. Thank you.

I don't know who to ask the question to. Maybe Mr. Maltz, we can go over the top with your problems, but whatever.

What works? Dr. Singer, you can answer this, too, or Dr. Westlake. What has proven to work to reduce?

Dr. Singer, you have an answer. Please.

Dr. SINGER. Well, in many other countries they don't have our overdoes problem, even though there is a drug problem in a lot of Europe. So, for example, in Switzerland, Germany, Portugal, France, Spain, and Canada they put much more of an emphasis on harm reduction.

Harm reduction, the concept of harm reduction is to non- judgmentally do things for people that can make whatever choices they are making less dangerous. That comes natural to doctors because in this country, and in most of those countries, that is largely what they do. When I have a—

Mr. COHEN. How do you do that? Having Narcan around?

Dr. SINGER. When it comes to drugs, you can, again, make it easier for people to get the overdose naloxone. Allow people to get test strips to test to see if what they purchased on the black market is what they think it is, to see if that's fentanyl or xylazine. Also, allow—there are many groups in this country that want to set up these overdose prevention centers, which have been proven.

There has not been one overdose taking place.

There are two that are right now, in defiance of Federal law, operating in New York City. They started November 2021. By April 2022 they had already reversed 230 overdose deaths. Those are 230 people who would have been dead.

So, but they are not allowed to do that because it violates—

Mr. COHEN. That is the only place they have it is in New York City?

Dr. SINGER. I beg your pardon?

Mr. COHEN. The only place that has that program is in New York?

Dr. SINGER. Well, they, in November 2021, the mayor of New York, in defiance of 21 U.S.C. 856, permitted a nonprofit private harm reduction organization to operate two overdose prevention centers. They have been functioning. So far, the Justice Department hasn't acted on it.

Mr. COHEN. OK, thank you.

You know, I think all of us would like to see this reduced, eliminated if possible. Mr. Maltz, I appreciate your work in the past.

I don't know if the idea of the death penalty is a good idea because the reality is—and this is just, my guess—I don't think people who buy the fentanyl think they are going to overdose. So, they buy it. So, they have heard it is a fun trip, or a good trip, or whatever.

I suspect that the people that deal it don't think they are going to get caught. Even if you have the death penalty, they don't think I'm going to get caught. So, I don't know if that is the answer.

I think we have busted a lot of the cartels, have we not? I don't know their names. Is it Pablo Escobar or somebody we got and put away?

Mr. MALTZ. Sir, first, I apologize for yelling and screaming but, you know what, I have been dealing with the families for many years, and there is no action going on in this town.

I will tell you this—

Mr. COHEN. There will be action.

Mr. MALTZ. I will tell you this—

Mr. COHEN. There will be action.

Mr. MALTZ. Let me answer, let me answer the question.

First, I would appreciate it if you stop calling it an overdose. It is a poisoning, and it is a war against our kids. So, stop with the overdosing.

That is part of the problem. The American public thinks it is a substance that people want to take.

Mr. COHEN. My time is expired. I yield back.

Mr. BIGGS. Your time has expired.

Mr. GAETZ. Mr. Chair.

Mr. BIGGS. Are you finished answering the question, Mr. Maltz?

Mr. MALTZ. Yes, sir.

Mr. GAETZ. Mr. Chair.

Mr. BIGGS. Mr. Gaetz.

Mr. GAETZ. Mr. Chair, I move or I seek unanimous consent that Mr. Issa be permitted to sit on the panel for the purpose of accepting and yielding of time.

Mr. BIGGS. Without objection.

Ms. JACKSON LEE. Without objection I am ready to allow Mr. Issa to be on.

Mr. Issa, I am joining the caucus that you will be speaking of. So, hopefully, you and Congressman Dean will add me to that caucus. Thank you.

Mr. BIGGS. Thank you.

Now, I recognize Mr. Jordan.

Chair Jordan. Mr. Chair, I yield to Mr. Issa.

Mr. BIGGS. Mr. Issa.

Mr. ISSA. Thank you. Thank you, Mr. Chair. Thank you, Chair. The title of this hearing should be, "Inaction Is No Longer an Option."

So, one of the questions that, you had said was you are tired of nothing happening in this town. That is because we have had inaction as we have gone from 0–108,000 deaths a year with fentanyl. In San Diego we have a locker that has 147,000 pounds of deadly drug; a third of it is fentanyl. Ten years ago, zero was fentanyl and it was mostly marijuana and meth.

So, when we look at what we need to do, and I will just be brief and say what, what would you have us do on a bipartisan basis that would be the most effective single item?

We will start on the left.

Mr. MALTZ. So, Congressman, thanks for the question.

First, we have to declare this a public health and national security emergency from the White House, because it all starts at the top.

Then we have to get celebrities, and professional athletes, role models, to start making video reels to get to the kids on social media. Because right now on social media that is what they are doing all day, and that is why they are dying, because they are buying this stuff on social media.

By the way, sextortion is also very big on social media.

So, why are the social media companies allowed to facilitate the death and destruction of our communities?

Mr. ISSA. OK. I appreciate that because that is one of the areas that information simply has—certainly, is not equal to the 108,000 deaths.

From a standpoint of—and I will ask this, I will start at the far right here now—when someone knowingly produces a pill that looks like one kind of drug, but is, in fact, fentanyl, in California they have had the novel attempt to, in fact, have, when someone dies of it, have it be considered murder because it is a knowing act. Would you support a Federal law that made it, in fact, by definition, murder to produce deadly fentanyl pill that appears to be something else?

Ms. RACHWAL. Congressman, yes, absolutely.

If I took a drink and I got something poisoned in the drink and died, that would be murder. Correct?

Mr. ISSA. Correct.

So, those are two areas.

Third, of course, is we have two partners in this. We are the third partner because we are the buyer. Certainly, we have to do our part. This is where information and getting beyond just ignoring it is important.

Let me just ask you two questions: Mexico is currently enjoying a gain success of billions of dollars that is corroding the very ability of their government to manage their country, because the cartels have more money than the government. That is coming out of China where the precursors come out.

So, the question I have for all of you is, as we are advertising, as we are increasing the crimes, what actions should be taken to stem the flow from China through Mexico? Yes?

Dr. WESTLAKE. Again, so when you look at the spigot of elicit fentanyl, that is a huge issue. I am not here to really focus on that. I am focusing on fentanyl-related substances. One thing Congress can do tomorrow is permanently close that loophole.

Mr. ISSA. Yes, sir?

Dr. SINGER. Congressman Issa, we have been doing the same thing over and over again for 50 years, since President Nixon declared war on drugs, and expecting a different result each time. Doing it even harder and causing even more people to be imprisoned, and damaging relationships with even more countries is still not going to work. I guarantee you, because we will probably be here in a couple years talking about the nitazene crisis.

I think we should put the emphasis and focus on making it safer for the people who are going to continue to go to the black market and use drugs by getting the Government out of the way of groups that want to employ arm reduction strategies that save lives.

Mr. ISSA. I appreciate your view on that. I respectfully disagree. The countries that have tried it mostly have had other problems.

I do agree with one thing, which is that we have been fighting the fight for a long time. We have seen the drugs change.

Ma'am, I am going to close by saying I meet regularly with one after another parent, or sibling, or spouse of someone who has died from the, and whether they call it an overdose or a deadly poison, most of the time it is an amount that is deadly in a single pill.

That is not true of other drugs. It is true of fentanyl today. So, you have my deepest sympathies for your loss. We will, I promise, we will have action, not inaction.

Mr. Chair, thank you very much. Yield back.

Mr. BIGGS. Thank you, Mr. Issa.

The Chair recognizes Mr. Kiley. Mr. KILEY. Thank you, Mr. Chair.

I would like to followup on a point raised just now by Mr. Issa.

First, I wanted to also say I thank you, Ms. Rachwal, for being here and sharing your story. I know how difficult it is and how much courage it takes.

I have had the chance to work with parents who, like yourself, have found themselves in an unthinkable situation, including two parents, Chris and Laura Didier, who were my guests at the State of the Union a couple weeks ago.

I think it is because of the power of your voice and the voices of people like the Didiers, and other parents who have had that courage that the President did at least acknowledge the scale of this problem in his State of the Union address, the largest platform that he has as President.

Mr. Chair, we heard from the Ranking Member that this is not a crime problem. I would have to take issue with that statement. After all, we are talking about a poison that largely originates with dedicated criminal organizations, and that is peddled in our communities by dealers to unsuspecting young people, under false pretenses, using social media or any other means at their disposal.

So, yes, there are multiple dimensions to this problem, first and foremost securing the border, raising awareness. Holding criminals accountable is a very important dimension.

In that respect, we actually have some very recent news out of my district. In the last two days there has been a preliminary hearing for a defendant, the drug dealer Carson Schewe. His victim was a 20-year-old soon-to-be-father named Cade Webb who died of fentanyl poisoning after consuming a fake pill. Some may actually have heard about his story because he is the cousin of Logan Webb, who is the star pitcher for the San Francisco Giants who, after the tragedy, used his position to share the story to raise awareness. Then other Major League baseball players did so as well.

So, yesterday the preliminary hearing concluded. This happened to take place in Placer County where the D.A.'s office, led by District Attorney Morgan Gire, has been very committed to using every tool at their disposal to get a handle on the fentanyl crisis. They have been part of public awareness campaigns like One Pill Can Kill. They have been very aggressive in using the criminal laws to hold dealers accountable, under the belief that anyone who sells this lethal substance and doesn't care whether their customer lives or dies, is guilty of murder.

So, in the death of Cade Webb, and in prosecuting the dealer Carson Schewe, they decided to charge him with murder, because that is what this is.

Yesterday, there was a holding order in the case. It is now going to go to trial. This drug dealer will face murder charges for selling this lethal substance to this young man in our community.

So, I would just encourage prosecutors across the country to take a look at what the District Attorney's Office is doing under the leadership of Morgan Gire in Placer County because, yes, I think we need stiffer penalties. That does need to be legislated. There is a lot we can do under existing criminal laws.

Since Placer County started being more aggressive in prosecuting dealers, law enforcement is hearing about results on the street that dealers are now wary of selling in our community.

So, I would just ask the question to Mr. Maltz, we have heard that this isn't a crime problem. We have heard that having stiffer penalties for the dealers isn't going to really do anything.

Does that perspective resonate more with your experience, or does the perspective of the law enforcement in my district that this actually is serving as a real deterrent sound more realistic to you?

Mr. MALTZ. Well, there is leadership in California. I know in San Diego they have Task Force 10 with the DEA and Homeland Security, other agencies, and they are prosecuting defendants for the death of these kids that are dying.

I will tell you this: I talk to DEA agents every day. You know why they are upset right now? Because the Department of Justice is putting out more guidance, and more restrictions, and more requirements to charge minimum mandatory sentences for people that are killing our kids.

Like, it doesn't get any simpler: If they are killing our kids, they need to feel the pain and go to jail. It is not going to stop the problem because there are so many kids addicted. Because right now in America there is a lot of anxiety and social depression. COVID caused a lot of this. So, these kids are turning to these pills. They have no idea what they are getting.

My thing is, they have to be told that the pills will kill you. They don't know that because they are not getting the messages.

They are not watching this hearing. They are not watching mainstream media and cable news. That is why the athletes and celebrities have to be called to the White House and they have to participate. They have got to put China aside because of the big money they make, and they have to go, and they educate the kids and save lives.

Mr. BIGGS. The time of the gentleman is expired.

Mr. KILEY. Thank you, Mr. Maltz.

I yield back.

Mr. BIGGS. Thank you.

I would now recognize the gentlelady from Georgia, Ms. McBath.

Ms. MCBATH. Thank you, Mr. Chair.

First, I want to give my deepest condolences to the Rachwal family. I am so sorry for your loss.

I, too, have lost a child. It is just so heartbreaking because it is not the natural order of things. So, I do give you my deepest condolences.

For many across America this epidemic is a symptom of neglect. We have heard how far reaching and fast growing this public health crisis has become. What started as a plan by big pharmaceutical companies to profit on the pain of millions, a plan to shroud the addictiveness of these drugs in sales tactics and consultant speak, has changed the course of our country and the Americans who live in it.

We know the facts. They have been spouted all day. We have heard many of them here today. Millions of Americans addicted to opioids led us into an era of millions of Americans addicted to heroin, fentanyl, a drug up to 50 times stronger than heroin, pushed on our people by cartels most often supplied by the PRC, and it has only increased these deaths of despair.

We know the facts. We don't always know what goes on in the homes. When we go into a home and we see family, we see parents that are shattered by a loved one lost in the grips of a drug that has consumed them.

We see the wife in West Virginia whose husband came home in pain every night from work, that left them battered and bruised. The over-prescribed opioid that was supposed to be a cure for the pain became the cause of it. As addiction took hold, opioids were replaced with heroin, heroin laced with fentanyl. How two children are growing up without a father, supported now by a single mother who just saw the love of their life descend into darkness.

We see the father in Florida who just dropped his son off in his freshman dorm room. Since he was a little boy, he had always followed the rules. A quarterback on his high school team, he had always been the calm and quiet type. A concussion followed him to college.

Now, he was a child away from home, surrounded by his peers. He spent a night with his friends doing what many college kids do. It took one pill to overdose. Now, the father, who spent 18 years raising a son he could never be more proud of, would never see his boy again.

We see the daughter in Georgia bullied in her high school for being too fat 1 day, and too thin the next: For trying too hard in school, and not hard enough on her looks. When her friend promised an escape from the terror in her head and the pain in her heart, she accepts gratefully. Until the drug had a hold on her. Until the painkillers decided what she was doing and when she would do it. Her overdose on heroin was called a death of despair. That only scratched the surface.

Her mother and father are now forced to celebrate her birthday at her gravesite.

There is a heartbreak only reserved for those who question whether they have done, whether they had done more as a parent to save their child, a spouse, a child. When you focus in on a community, when you enter a home filled with that heartbreak, which I do understand, we can only begin to understand the human cost of this crisis.

These drugs have profited on pain and left only death and despair in their wake. This isn't a future for us as Americans. This isn't time for politics. This is a time for progress. What we do here must help to solve this crisis, not score political points.

So, please, Dr. Singer, what can we do right now that will give us the best chance of saving American lives, ending this epidemic, and keeping our families together?

Dr. SINGER. Well, Congresswoman McBath, thank you for that question.

As I said previously, and this is under the purview of this Committee, I think we should focus on trying to make the black market less dangerous for people who are going to go into the black market to purchase drugs by allowing them to be able to use, for example, test strips to test to see if they think they are buying a Percocet and it turns out it is fentanyl, we can help them by letting them know that and may avoid taking it.

Also, we should remove section, 21 U.S.C. 856 so that harm reduction organizations around the country could set up overdose prevention centers to prevent people from overdosing. Also, in those centers they would test their drugs before they use them and use them with clean needles and syringes which they have to return. It is outside of the public use, so people don't have to watch people use drugs.

So, these are things that this Committee could address.

Also, in many countries, Canada, U.K., Australia, since the Sixties primary care physicians have been able to prescribe take home methadone. In this country, we have this very burdensome process where to use methadone, which is a great and a very effective treatment for addiction, you have to go to a special clinic. You sometimes have to travel miles. You have to take it in the presence of a clinic staff because you are stigmatized as somebody who can't be trusted.

Whereas if you were able to—during the pandemic, actually, they allowed take home medication and saw no evidence of diversion or misuse of the methadone.

If we allowed primary care practitioners to prescribe methadone to treat substance use disorder, then there would be many more avenues where people can access methadone treatment.

Ms. MCBATH. Thank you. I yield my time.

Mr. BIGGS. Thank you.

The Chair recognizes now the gentleman from South Carolina, Mr. Fry.

Mr. FRY. Thank you, Mr. Chair. Thank you for holding this hearing. I appreciate your leadership in bringing attention of this.

To the panel, thank you for being here.

Ms. Rachwal, thank you. It is incredibly brave for you to address this Committee, to share that story.

When I was in the South Carolina General Assembly I chaired the House Opioid Abuse Prevention Study Committee. We had 18 bills, record funding, a lot of great things. We always started every field hearing with people who were in who were recovering, who had lost family members. To hear their stories, to hear your story today reminds me of that and how important it is to hear that story, that we start from the human element, and that we remember the families back home who have suffered the most.

The rise in fentanyl, I think the frustration that I have, at least up here, to the panel is that States have really, States and local governments have really tried to address this from an education campaign, to prevention, to treatment, and to law enforcement. That was not immune to the State of South Carolina either as we tried to pass legislation to address it.

The frustration that I have is that we can't actually deal, the States can't, as inventive as they are, and colleges and local government, they cannot actually deal with the problem until we deal with the source, which is fentanyl, which is China, which is the cartels.

To me, to look at the numbers in South Carolina, and of course this mirrors the country, in 2017 South Carolina saw a 312 percent increase in fentanyl-related overdoses. From 2019–2021 it was 178 percent. Nearly 69 percent, according to a South Carolina Department of Health and Environmental Control, 69 percent of all overdoses are related to fentanyl. Those numbers back up. Those have been increasing dramatically. Whereas in 2017 only 36 percent of overdose deaths were related to fentanyl.

So, we have seen this problem exacerbated. We we just visited Yuma, Arizona, for a field hearing where we talked to hospital systems, and ranchers, and residents. They are seeing it in their communities.

Of course, as we know, we are, every State, every local government, every community is a border town at this point given the amount of fentanyl overdoses that are taking place.

Mr. Chair, at this point I would like to seek unanimous consent to put the South Carolina Department of Health and Environmental Control Overdose Report into the record.

Mr. BIGGS. Without objection.

Mr. FRY. Thank you, Mr. Chair.

I think from the perspective of the DEA, Mr. Maltz, what are some of the firsthand experiences that you have seen or heard of, of your agents, or the agents of the DEA dealing with drug smugglers? What are some of the experiences that they have had in the field?

Mr. MALTZ. Well, they are very frustrated for the lack of the support. Like I said, the Department of Justice putting added requirements to put people in jail that are killing our kids.

The real frustration that I have seen is kind of highlighted in the recent trial in New York and the conviction of Genaro Garcia Luna. He was the FBI equivalent in Mexico. The corruption is so systemic in Mexico that the cartels run the country. Now with the migrant smuggling, it is just overwhelming the resources on the border and throughout America.

So, the reality is if you have a water leak in your house, the plumber comes, he shuts the main valve down. We have a fentanyl disaster in America flooding the streets. We have got to shut down the valve in Mexico.

How do we do it? The best and brightest patriots in America, like some Congressmen have already said, and offer support to the Mexican Government to use technology to destroy these chemical production labs. Then we will see a disruption in the supply to this country.

The frustration is that law enforcement is out there putting their lives on the line. They don't get the proper support. More importantly is that it is just getting worse because the cartels are operating with impunity, working with China, that want to destroy America forever.

Mr. FRY. Thank you, Mr. Chair.

I yield the remaining balance of my time to you, sir.

Mr. BIGGS. Thank you.

So, some of the things that have been talked about today make me think of deterrence. What deters someone from taking a drug that has been laced with fentanyl?

What deters someone from producing and distributing fentanyl into this country?

Mr. Maltz, some people have said, that was an early talker, "cannot incarcerate our way out of this." Then they said but we need to have tough penalties, including incarceration for those who deal the drugs.

Is that a tacit admission that there is a way to deter dealers, and that would include sentencing to incarceration?

Mr. MALTZ. Absolutely. You want to put these people in jail for the longest amount of time that are killing our kids.

We are not talking about putting couriers that are just moving product, they don't even know what they are moving. You have to deal with each case separately. For the organization that is destroying our country, they have to feel the pain.

Now, I will tell you this: You asked a question about the frustration. Right now, we have hundreds lined up in Mexico for extradition. The Administrator of DEA testified. We can't get them out. We want to hold them responsible for what they are doing. That is going to be a deterrent.

We saw that in Colombia for years when we went after the Norte del Valle Cartel, the Medellin Cartel, and everyone. So, we have to have these strong punishments.

Mr. BIGGS. Thanks. Thanks, Mr. Maltz. I now recognize Ms. Lee from Florida.

Ms. LEE. Thank you, Mr. Chair.

Thank you to our witnesses for being here today.

Today's hearing has allowed us all an opportunity to see how the crisis of fentanyl is affecting every community in America. In my own community in Florida we recently seized, authorities seized more than 11 pounds of fentanyl. This amount alone was enough to kill 2.7 million people.

Agent Maltz, I would like to return to your testimony. As a former Federal prosecutor, I recognize the critical work that DEA agents are doing every day across America to fight the cartels and to keep America safe. One thing, a distinction that you have made here today that I think is important, I would like for you to share with us a bit about how this problem has grown in its scope, and the difference between organized crime and what you would categorize as narcoterrorists?

Tell us, what is a narcoterrorist? What has led you to that conclusion?

Mr. MALTZ. Great question. I really appreciate that because I lived this nightmare for many years, over 10 years.

When I was the head of the Special Operations Division I wasn't reading in the local newspapers, I was living it with my counterparts around the world. So, China started the synthetic bombing campaign around 2008–2009 with K2 spice and bath salts. Please go read about and you will see all the capacities in the country for no synthetic drugs.

Then around 2012 they started with the fentanyl analogs in the mail services, through the internet websites.

Then they diverted, started sending pure fentanyl to Mexico. They also started, of course, for years they have been sending precursor chemicals to make methamphetamine. That is why we have tons of methamphetamine in the country. We didn't even talk about that today. That is another whole hearing.

Now, in Mexico they are using all that money, they are building up capabilities. They are buying weapons systems. They are dropping C4 explosives on their adversaries.

I went down to the border and there were 9,000 drones coming into America surveilling our brave men and women in Border Patrol. This is unacceptable. We are at war with the cartels, but we are still treating it like they are drug traffickers.

They are not drug cartels. Please stop saying drug cartels. They are narcoterrorists like we have never seen. They run the country of Mexico, they intimidate, they corrupt, they are slaughtering people, chopping off heads, dismembering bodies. They have arsenals. They have weapons that we don't even have in certain countries around the world.

So, they have evolved. Everything is evolving. The problem is the Government is still using old talking points. This is not grandpa's opioid crisis. OK? The pills, that is years ago. Yes, kids got addicted because of big pharma. Somebody said that. Big pharma never got held accountable because it is all about the money.

Now, the cartels and China are the focus of our problem, so we need to deal with them.

Ms. LEE. So, Agent Maltz, in light of that changing landscape, in light of the escalation of the severity of this type of organization, how does that change what you need and what we should be doing here in Congress to equip DEA and our, and your law enforcement partners to fight this fight?

Mr. MALTZ. DEA needs resources, but so does all the agencies as far as manpower. You know why? A lot of them are quitting. They are running away. They are getting jobs in the private sector because they are sick and tired of lack of action.

The boss of the DEA right now, she is running around with a One Pill Can Kill campaign, spreading awareness like we have never seen.

I go back to this Committee can ask the Department of Education, what are they doing? Why is CDC not putting out timely and accurate stats on the greatest crisis to the history of this country? What is the answer to that? Because as a taxpayer, I would like to see the CDC director, because she has already fell on the sword on the lack of reporting on COVID, and the inaccuracies. How is that acceptable with all the technology we have?

There is no consistency across the country. The guy in King County, Washington, talked about no cooler space. They are not trained. They don't have the technologies.

So, there is a lot of accountabilities that needs to be brought to the table in this town. The DEA, they are going to continue to fight, just like Homeland Security, FBI, ATF, the Marshals, because they get paid to save lives.

The problem is it is much bigger than DEA and the law enforcement now. That is why we need to consider other options with the great patriots that work behind the scenes that could do some real good devastation. They could decimate the production labs.

Why is that a bad thing, decimate chemical production labs? I wish there were more people over here that would listen to this, but they are not interested. They are out there doing something else. I don't know what is more important than the death of our kids.

Ms. LEE. Agent Maltz, another question. Can you tell us what it means when a substance is classified as Schedule I, Schedule II? How is that important? What would it mean to you all in terms of the work that you are going to try to combat this problem?

Mr. MALTZ. Well, a third grader can understand that you don't want to put deadly substances on the street. You want to at least categorize them as Schedule I drugs.

Fentanyl, the pharmaceutical grade fentanyl, is a Schedule II and needs to remain a Schedule II. The elicit fentanyl substances that are out there, it is like Whack-A-Mole. The DEA and all the agencies they can't keep up with the way these guys are changing the difficult chemical compounds. It is, like, it is just so common, you just need common sense to understand that argument, they are killing our kids. We need to classify fentanyl-related substances as Schedule I.

That is not going to solve this problem, but it is something that will help.

Ms. LEE. Thank you, Agent Maltz. Mr. Chair, I yield back.

Mr. BIGGS. Thank you.

I yield five minutes to myself.

I appreciate all of you being here telling your story, and also bringing different perspectives on this very, very critical, I view it as a national security and national health issue.

When we look at this, we had several of my colleagues across the aisle talk about they gave $60 million here and $70 million there. When I go to the border and talk to Border Patrol agents, who are so concerned about this problem, they say, we don't need more money, we need to be able to enforce the law. We are being denied the capacity to enforce the law.

That includes and is because they are being overrun. So, we will go their whole shifts with entire CDP agency that is supposed to be watching our border are actually working as processors at a detention facility, where they won't be detained, Dr. Singer. They are not getting detained, they are being, they are being transported to wherever they want to be in the country, to the tune of over five million encounters, millions over the last two years.

Then you have over a million, about a million two known gotaways between the ports of entry. Anybody who watches will tell you it is at least one-to-one on the unknown got-aways. When we showed you the video earlier today these are young men and women bringing—dressed in camo. They don't want to be caught. They are port, transporting this drug across the border.

Comes up, I can tell you where it comes up from the Tohono O'odham, across the Tohono O'odham Reservation, goes up to I–8. There are load-up places there. Then from your crows, you're a crow's fly about 30 miles south of Phoenix.

From there it is going throughout the country. It is finding its way into the hands of college students who really they don't know anything about fentanyl because it has not been made a big deal.

We know about it because we talk about it.

So, when I hear people say 90 percent of it is interdicted through the port of entry; no. Ninety percent of what you catch may be in the port of entry. Of course, that data is old and out of touch. It is coming through between the ports of entry and being dissemi- nated widely in this country.

Now, we have very little deterrence. Because I am going to tell you that if these people are caught; they are caught in the Tucson Sector. They have a backpack of fentanyl. All you have to do is take that backpack off and walk a step away and the Deputy Attorney General there, the U.S. Attorney there is not going to prosecute that case.

There is no deterrence whatsoever. Why are they not going to? They are going to say we need, for instance, if it is marijuana, they say we have to have 400 pounds of marijuana on the person. Well, nobody can carry 400 pounds of marijuana.

Same thing goes with fentanyl. Most of it is now coming in pills. It is coming in pill form because Americans want pills. They are pressing them down south of the border, and they are disguised as pain medication, Percocet, Perc 30, whatever it is.

So, that is the reality of what is happening. I appreciate, Dr. Singer, you said we want to make the black market less dangerous. One way you make this less dangerous for the black market is to make it more dangerous for the people who are producing and distributing this drug.

So, you may not be able to incarcerate yourself, your way out of this, but you better do something to either destroy the facilities, destroy the economic capacity of this group, or they are going to keep going.

I will just tell you that right now it is a multi-billion dollar per month industry. We need to, we need to call them what it is: They are terrorists. We need to declare them terrorists so we can get at their money stream. Because if we can get at their money stream, we will impede them and we will slow this down.

That is some of what needs to happen here.

As we wrap up this hearing, I hope that across the aisle we have found some comity on where we can go to start interdicting this horrific problem. That has to happen.

I just, again, thank you, our witnesses, for being here today. You have some documents you want to put in?

Ms. JACKSON LEE. If you don't mind, yes. Mr. BIGGS. Please, please.

Ms. JACKSON LEE. When you have had your concluding remarks.

Mr. BIGGS. Well, she wants to, not for concluding remarks, but I will recognize you for putting documents into the record.

Ms. JACKSON LEE. Thank you.

If I might, Mr. Chair, just make one or two points to answer you. Which is, that is the direction of the legislation that I hope you will look at that enhances and responds to the manufacturers and the distributors.

Obviously, our jurisdiction is here in the United States and, hence, penalties, and for those who wind up killing people because of the drug use. Their actions wind up killing people.

I just want to conclude on, Mr. Maltz, your patriotism and your enthusiasm. I work with DEA agents all the time, those based on Houston. Know their work, as I do the FBI, the ATF. So, let me just say that you have been heard loudly and clearly.

Ms. Rachwal and husband have been heard very loudly and clearly.

So, legislation that I hope the Chair will look at answers all these questions, particularly your outreach, your focus, major campaign, the social media, and the megaphone. You want the megaphone while you are doing your work, you want the megaphone.

I do know that the DEA does some very dangerous work, particularly, those who are undercover. We want to appreciate them as well.

Dr. Singer, we need your voice. We thank you for that. We thank Dr. Westlake for being here as well.

So, I hope the Chair and I will have an opportunity to engage. I want to put into the record, ask unanimous consent, a letter from the Law Enforcement Action Partnership, signed by a coalition of current and former law enforcement officers, judges, and public safety professionals.

The statement of Jason Pye, Director, Rule of Law Initiative, Due Process Institute.

A letter from Jillian E. Snider, Policy Director of Criminal Justice and Civil Liberties at the R Street Institute.

A letter from Mazen Saleh, Policy Director of Integrated Harm Reduction at the R Street Institute.

A letter from a coalition of organizations in support of the Test Act. (ph.)

I want to thank Mr. Cohen, and Ms. McBath, and Ms. Dean for their presence here today.

Ask unanimous consent to place these in the record. Mr. BIGGS. Without objection.

Ms. JACKSON LEE. Thank you, Mr. Chair. Mr. BIGGS. Thank you.

Again, thanks to all the Members who attended. Thanks to those in the audience who came.

I appreciate each one of you, again, on the panel. You were heard. You are important. We are going to now thank you by adjourning.

We are adjourned.

[Whereupon, at 12:27 p.m., the Subcommittee was adjourned.]

All materials submitted for the record by Members of the Select Subcommittee on the Weaponization of the Federal Government can be found at: https://docs.house.gov/Committee/Calendar/ByEvent.aspx?EventID=115371.

Chapter 2

Protecting the U.S. Homeland: Fighting the Flow of Fentanyl from the Southwest Border*

Committee on Homeland Security

U.S. HOUSE OF REPRESENTATIVES, COMMITTEE ON HOMELAND SECURITY, SUBCOMMITTEE ON BORDER SECURITY AND ENFORCEMENT,

Washington, DC.

The subcommittee met, pursuant to notice, at 2:21 p.m., in room 310, Cannon House Office Building, Hon. Clay Higgins (Chairman of the subcommittee) presiding.

Present: Representatives Higgins, Gonzales, Luttrell, Brecheen, Correa, Jackson Lee, Thanedar, Garcia, and Ramirez.

Also present: Representatives D'Esposito, Ivey, and Goldman.

Mr. HIGGINS. The Committee on Homeland Security Subcommittee on Border Security and Enforcement will come to order. Without objection, the subcommittee may recess at any point.

The purpose of this hearing is to receive testimony from Government experts on the elaborate drug operations conducted by the transnational

* This is an edited, reformatted and augmented version of Hearing Before the Subcommittee on Border Security and Enforcement of The Committee on Homeland Security, House of Representatives, Serial No. 118–21, Dated July 12, 2023.

In: Understanding the Fentanyl Crisis
Editor: Michael K. Reyes
ISBN: 979-8-89113-830-8

criminal organizations along the United States-Mexico border which threaten the safety and security of American communities.

From the importation of precursor chemicals for production from China to the distribution of fentanyl in the United States, transnational criminal organizations are wreaking havoc on American communities, and the Committee on Homeland Security seeks answers.

I now recognize myself for an opening statement.

Good afternoon, gentlemen. Thank you for being here, and welcome to the Subcommittee on Border Security and Enforcement hearing on fighting the flow of fentanyl from the Southwest Border. The purpose of today's hearing is to examine the Biden administration's failures and perhaps to examine some areas of shared success with previous administrations.

We welcome our witnesses from the Office of the National Drug Control Policy, the Department of Homeland Security, the Drug Enforcement Administration, and I thank you all for being here today.

I'd like to begin by thanking our Customs and Border Protection frontline agents and officers who work tirelessly every day to protect our country despite the negligent policies that they're subject to and the lack of support that they have reported from the Biden administration.

Every day, transnational criminal organizations use America's complex highway systems to smuggle illicit drugs, such as deadly fentanyl, and human beings into our country. These criminal organizations pose an enormous threat to the United States, as they undermine our public safety and flood our streets with drugs.

The Centers for Disease Control and Prevention, the CDC, cites drug poisoning as the leading cause of mortality due to injury in the United States. Over 150 people die in our Nation every day from overdoses related to synthetic opioids like fentanyl.

Fentanyl has poured across our borders and into the streets of America while the Biden administration continues to implement policies that have, in fact, emboldened and enriched these transnational criminal organizations.

It would be impossible to discuss the free flow of fentanyl at our borders without mentioning China's significant role in the shipping of precursor chemicals to the Mexican cartels. The cartels and China have a complicated money- and drug-laundering operation. This operation kills Americans every day. In fact, according to the CDC, fentanyl is the leading cause of death of Americans age 18 to 45.

As the flow of illegal immigrants continues to overwhelm Customs and Border Protection, it's inevitable that more and more drugs will slip through our defenses and into our country. As long as the Biden administration continues to fail enforcement of our immigration laws, the cartels will continue to reap the benefits.

Secretary Mayorkas has been derelict in his duties and has failed this country. He's continuously refused to enforce immigration law. He refused to prosecute illegal entries and refused to utilize previous immigration tools that had been proven effective. These actions have increased the flow of illegal aliens into this country, enriched the Mexican cartels, and overwhelmed our front-line agents and officers, which has led, of course, to more and more drugs flowing into the United States.

There's quantifiable impact of this destruction on our country. As drugs have poured into the United States, overdose deaths have increased every year, from 92,000 in 2020 to 109,680 in 2022. These are our brothers, our sisters, our family, our friends and neighbors. The Biden administration must reconcile with this devastation, and it's our job in Congress to hold the administration accountable.

The cartels have quickly learned to outmaneuver the system we had in place. With the help of the Chinese Communist Party and the Biden administration's ineffectiveness, they've smuggled an unprecedented amount of fentanyl and trafficked these dangerous and deadly drugs into our country, have taken a record number of American lives, and brought in regular billion-dollar profits. They've torn countless scores of thousands of American families apart.

This subcommittee will not allow the Biden administration, nor Secretary Mayorkas, to sweep their failures under the rug.

Today, this hearing will expose the arterial bleed at our Southern Border and the ensuing fight against synthetic opioids that has made its way to the forefront of all of our lives.

I yield back the balance of my time, and I look forward to hearing from our witnesses [The statement of Chairman Higgins follows:]

Statement of Chairman Clay Higgins July 12, 2023

Good afternoon and welcome to the Subcommittee on Border Security and Enforcement hearing on fighting the flow of fentanyl from the Southwest Border. The purpose of today's hearing is to examine the Biden administration's haphazard fight to disrupt the flow of fentanyl into the United States. I would like to welcome our witnesses from the Office of National

Drug Control Policy, Department of Homeland Security, and the Drug Enforcement Administration for being here today.

Most recently, I was appointed by Speaker McCarthy to serve on the Task Force to Combat Mexican Drug Cartels. The purpose of the task force is to examine cartel operations, educate the American people on the impacts of cartel violence, provide legislative recommendations, and most importantly help save lives. I look forward to working with my colleagues in this crucial endeavor.

Every day, Transnational Criminal Organizations uses America's complex highway systems to smuggle illicit drugs, such as deadly fentanyl, and humans into our country. These criminal organizations pose an enormous threat to the United States as they undermine our public safety and flood our streets with drugs.

The Centers for Disease Control and Prevention (CDC) cites drug poisoning as the leading cause of mortality due to injury in the United States. Of the more than 105,000 drug poisoning overdose deaths in 2022, more than 75 percent involved opioids including fentanyl.

Under the Biden administration, America has been suffering from wave upon wave of misery flooding across our Southwest Border. Fentanyl has poured across our borders and into the streets of America while the Biden administration continues to implement policies that embolden and enrich these Transnational Criminal Organizations.

Mexican cartels rely on China for the precursor chemicals used to make synthetic opioids. The Sinaloa and Cártel de Jalisco Nueva Generación (CJNG) are the two biggest importers of synthetic opioids into the United States, and both rely on a complex system with partners in China to import fentanyl precursors. The precursors are then processed in labs in Mexico and then smuggled into the United States. We would be mistaken not to mention China's significant role in the shipping of precursors and laundering of money. It is vital that the Biden administration recognize China's role in providing the vital ingredients used in illicit products that are killing United States youth. In fact, according to the CDC, fentanyl is the leading cause of death of Americans ages 18–45.

As the flow of illegal immigrants continues to overwhelm Customs and Border Protection, it is inevitable that more and more drugs will slip through our defenses and into our country.

Secretary Mayorkas has been derelict in his duties to this country and has continuously refused to enforce immigration law, refused to prosecute illegal entries, and refused to utilize previous immigration tools at his disposal. These actions have increased the flow of illegal aliens into this country, enriched Mexican cartels, and overwhelmed our front-line agents and officers, which has led to more and more drugs flowing into the United States.

The reckless open-border policies set by President Biden and Mayorkas have greatly benefited the Mexican cartels. The cartels quickly learned to outmaneuver the system, and with the help of the Chinese Communist Party, they have smuggled an unprecedented amount of fentanyl, taken a record number of American lives, brought in billion-dollar profits, and have torn families apart.

Secretary Mayorkas' blatant disregard for the security and sanctity of the American people has wounded our great nation deeply. This subcommittee intends to hold Secretary Mayorkas and the Biden administration accountable for their actions.

With that, I yield back the balance of my time and look forward to hearing from our witnesses.

Mr. HIGGINS. Without objection, I'd like to waive on the gentleman from New York, Mr. D'Esposito.

Mr. D'Esposito will be permitted to sit on the dais for this subcommittee hearing and ask questions of the witnesses.

I recognize the Ranking Member.

Mr. CORREA. Thank you, Mr. Chairman.

Again, thank you very much for holding this most important hearing on transnational criminal organizations and, of course, fentanyl.

Mr. Chairman, I want to ask also unanimous consent that Mr. Ivey and Mr. Goldman be permitted to sit with the subcommittee and question today's witnesses.

Mr. HIGGINS. Without objection.

Mr. CORREA. Again, Mr. Chairman, thank you for holding this most important hearing.

We also need to dismantle fentanyl supply lines. The surging resources to conduct inbound inspections are badly needed. We need to work collaboratively to make sure that these seizures lead to arrests and prosecutions of those engaged in these illegal, dangerous businesses.

That's why I'm glad to hear about the Department's recent successes in operations like Blue Lotus, the Four Horsemen—both of these that have seized nearly 10,000 pounds of fentanyl that were destined to go to our communities. Of course, these operations also resulted in almost 300 arrests. I understand the Department has used the intel from these successes to move to the next phase, which is to target and prevent other fentanyl from entering the United States.

I hope our witnesses today will share about—a little bit of information about the two new operations being moved ahead, which are Operation Artemis and Operation Rolling Wave.

For today's witnesses from the White House, DEA, CBP, and Homeland Security Investigations, or HSI, I want to hear in your testimony about how the administration has been working to mitigate these threats to our country as well as to Main Street.

We know transnational criminal organizations and the illicit supply of fentanyl are not new challenges. In fact, the number of fentanyl seizures began to increase in the summer of 2020 under the previous administration. As you know, the threat of fentanyl does not begin or end at our Southern Border.

We need to also improve our public health care response to this crisis and address the addiction plaguing our communities, while providing support for those that are trying to recover from drug addiction.

Of course, to tackle transnational criminal organizations and fentanyl, we can't just focus on seizures alone. We also need to go after their profits and supply chains. Again, let me repeat: We also need to go after their profits and supply chains.

I'm glad to hear that, under this administration, Homeland Security Investigation has continued Operation Pelican Bones, which seeks to disrupt the financial tools used by transnational criminal organizations to launder money; as well as Operation Hydra that goes after the precursors needed to create fentanyl; and, of course, Operation Chain Breaker that targets the equipment needed to manufacture pills.

Initiatives like these, gentlemen, to dismantle illicit networks and limit TCOs' financial accesses are needed. Yet we also need to recognize that this is a global threat, a world-wide threat. Strong and collaborative partnerships with international partners are critical to dismantling transnational criminal organizations.

That's why this morning the Chairman and I introduced the bipartisan Cooperation on Combating Human Smuggling and Trafficking Act, which would direct Homeland Security Investigations to expand its Transnational Criminal Investigative Units. These vetted and trained units of foreign law enforcement work with HSI to investigate transnational criminal organizations. They need to stop human smuggling and the flow of dangerous drugs before they reach our borders.

I hope my colleagues across the aisle will continue to join me in calling for responsible action, like expanding these transnational criminal investigative units and putting more resources toward our ports of entry, instead of throwing around harmful rhetoric about invading Mexico, our second-largest trading partner and, of course, a critical partner in fighting transnational crime.

While I have focused primarily on the law enforcement action we can take to dismantle transnational criminal organizations, we must also recognize that this isn't the only border issue. It's also a public health care challenge. These criminals across the world seek to make record profits at the cost of lives—American lives on Main Street. There is wide-spread, untreated drug addiction in our streets, leading some individuals to consume dangerous substances that may be laced with fentanyl.

Hope our witnesses today from the Office of National Drug Control Policy can speak also to the administration's strategy to reduce the demand for illicit drugs on our streets.

Again, I want to thank the witnesses for taking time from your very busy schedules to talk to us today. I welcome your suggestions how we in Congress can help you better accomplish your job.

Thank you very much, and I now turn it back to Chairman Higgins for today's proceedings.

[The statement of Ranking Member Correa follows:]

Statement of Ranking Member J. Luis Correa July 12, 2023

I would like to start by thanking Chairman Higgins for holding today's hearing on transnational criminal organizations and fentanyl. For today's witnesses from the White House, DEA, CBP, and Homeland Security Investigations (HSI), I look forward to hearing your testimony about the administration's actions to mitigate these threats.

We know transnational criminal organizations and the illicit supply of fentanyl are not new challenges. In fact, the number of fentanyl seizures began to increase in the summer of 2020 under the previous administration. But the threat of fentanyl does not begin or end at the Southern Border.

We need to improve our public health response to this crisis and address the addiction plaguing our communities while providing support to those recovering. We also need to dismantle fentanyl supply chains, surging resources to conduct inbound inspections, and working to indict, arrest, and prosecute those engaged in this illegal business. That's why I was glad to hear about the Department's recent successes in Operations Blue Lotus and Four Horsemen, which seized nearly 10,000 pounds of fentanyl headed for our communities and resulted in 284 arrests.

I understand that the Department has used the insights gained from these two operations to launch the next phase of its campaign to target and prevent fentanyl from entering the United States. I hope our witnesses will share more about the two new operations, Operation Artemis and Operation Rolling Wave. To tackle transnational criminal organizations and fentanyl, we can't just focus on seizures. We also need to go after their profits and supply chains.

I am glad that, under this administration, Homeland Security Investigations has continued Operation Pelican Bones—which seeks to disrupt the financial tools used by transnational criminal organizations to launder money—as well as Operation Hydra, which goes after the precursor chemicals needed to create fentanyl, and Operation Chain Breaker, which targets the equipment needed to manufacture pills. Initiatives like these are critical to dismantle illicit networks and limit TCOs' financial access. But we also need to recognize that this is a global threat, and strong, collaborative partnerships with international partners are critical to dismantling transnational criminal organizations.

That's why this morning the Chairman and I introduced the bipartisan Cooperation on Combatting Human Smuggling and Trafficking Act, which would direct Homeland Security Investigations to expand its Transnational Criminal Investigative Units. These vetted and trained units of foreign law enforcement work with HSI to investigate transnational criminal organizations, aiming to stop human smuggling and the flow of dangerous drugs before they reach our borders.

I hope my colleagues across the aisle will continue to join me in calling for responsible action, like expanding these transnational criminal investigative units and putting more resources toward our ports of entry, instead of throwing around harmful rhetoric about invading Mexico—one of our closest trading partners and a critical partner in the fight against transnational crime.

While I have focused primarily on the law enforcement actions we can take to dismantle transnational criminal organizations, we must recognize that this isn't only a border security challenge or law enforcement challenge. It's a public health challenge, as transnational criminal organizations seek to make record profits at the cost of American lives. There is wide-spread untreated addiction for drugs, leading some individuals to consume dangerous substances that may be laced with fentanyl. I hope our witness from the Office of National Drug Control Policy can speak to the administration's strategy to reduce the demand for illicit drugs in our communities. Again, I appreciate all of witnesses' willingness to appear today to discuss how we can increase our efforts to combat this serious threat. I welcome any suggestions about how Congress can help you accomplish your missions.

Mr. HIGGINS. I thank Ranking Member Correa.

All the Members of the committee are reminded that opening statements may be submitted for the record.

[The statements of Ranking Member Thompson and Hon. Jackson Lee follow:]

Statement of Ranking Member Bennie G. Thompson
July 12, 2023

Let me start by saying that tackling the drug crisis is one of our most pressing national security, law enforcement, and public health challenges, and we must do more to protect American lives. Fentanyl presents the newest iteration of a drug problem that America has had for decades.

One way Congress can help protect Americans is to allocate resources to aggressively target the source of drug trafficking—Transnational Criminal Organizations or TCOs. We must understand that these organizations, including cartels south of our border, operate as a business. They are profit-driven. They are violent and criminal. But they are not political or ideological. Transnational criminal organizations profit from the demand for illicit drugs and at the expense of American lives. The Biden administration, through the agencies testifying today among others, are working tirelessly to combat the TCOs and drug traffickers. Rather than waste resources building a wall or using migrants as scapegoats, the Biden administration has made historic investments in border security and in fighting the scourge of fentanyl. The administration has directed resources to the places where the drugs are actually entering this country.

We know that about 90 percent of fentanyl is trafficked in cars and trucks through ports of entry, not between them. Even the fentanyl caught between ports of entry is mostly seized in vehicles at checkpoints or out at sea—not on the backs of migrants. In addition, it's important to recognize that U.S.

citizens, not undocumented migrants, represent more than 85 percent of convictions for fentanyl trafficking.

The Biden administration has invested in technology at the ports of entry to scan travelers, vehicles, and cargo entering the United States with the intent to distribute illicit drugs. With these investments, seizures are now at a record high. Unfortunately, CBP is only able to scan about 2 percent of passenger vehicles and just 15 percent of commercial vehicles. Imagine the amount of drugs we could stop from coming into the country if we invested as much in non-intrusive inspection technology as Republicans want to spend on more border wall.

This whole-of-Government approach led to the administration to establish Operations Blue Lotus and Four Horsemen this spring. Under these initiatives, CBP, HSI and State and local partners stopped nearly 10,000 pounds of fentanyl from entering our communities and conducted 284 arrests for fentanyl-related charges in just 2 months. These operations are just a couple measures in the Biden administration's multi-pronged strategy to combat TCOs and curtail the flow of illicit fentanyl. I want to commend Customs and Border Protection and other agencies for their coordinated efforts to increase the number of seizures and related investigations. I can't help but note that just a few years ago my Republican colleagues touted drug seizures as a measure of success under the Trump administration.

Now that the Biden administration has record seizures due to its investments and its commitment to detection and interdiction efforts, my Republican colleagues are criticizing the administration. This is the height of hypocrisy.

While I appreciate the administration's efforts to stop fentanyl and other drugs from entering our communities, it's important to recognize that this is just one part of the solution. Law enforcement and border security alone will never be enough. We must also tackle this crisis with treatment and recovery options to restore people's health and break the devastating cycle of addiction.

I urge my Republican colleagues to work together to provide the necessary resources to Federal agencies to combat TCOs and prevent fentanyl trafficking.

COMMITTEE ON HOMELAND SECURITY

Ranking Member Bennie G. Thompson

For Immediate Release

Hearing Statement of Border Security & Enforcement Subcommittee Ranking Member Lou Correa (D-CA)

Protecting the U.S. Homeland: Fighting the Flow of Fentanyl from the Southwest Border, July 12, 2023

I would like to start by thanking Chairman Higgins for holding today's hearing on transnational criminal organizations and fentanyl. For today's witnesses from the White House, DEA, CBP, and Homeland Security Investigations (HSI), I look forward to hearing your testimony about the Administration's actions to mitigate these threats.

We know transnational criminal organizations and the illicit supply of fentanyl are not new challenges. In fact, the number of fentanyl seizures began to increase in the summer of 2020 under the previous Administration. But the threat of fentanyl does not begin or end at the southern border.

We need to improve our public health response to this crisis and address the addiction plaguing our communities while providing support to those recovering. We also need to dismantle fentanyl supply chains, surging resources to conduct inbound inspections, and working to indict, arrest, and prosecute those engaged in this illegal business. That's why I was glad to hear about the Department's recent successes in Operations Blue Lotus and Four Horsemen, which seized nearly 10,000 pounds of fentanyl headed for our communities and resulted in 284 arrests.

I understand that the Department has used the insights gained from these two operations to launch the next phase of its campaign to target and prevent fentanyl from entering the United States. I hope our witnesses will share more about the two new operations, Operation Artemis and Operation Rolling Wave. To tackle transnational criminal organizations and fentanyl, we can't just focus on seizures. We also need to go after their profits and supply chains.

I am glad that, under this Administration, Homeland Security Investigations has continued Operation Pelican Bones—which seeks to disrupt the financial tools used by transnational criminal organizations to launder money— as well as Operation Hydra, which goes after the precursor chemicals needed to create fentanyl and Operation Chain Breaker, which targets the equipment needed to manufacture pills.

Initiatives like these are critical to dismantle illicit networks and limit TCOs' financial access. But we also need to recognize that this is a global threat, and strong, collaborative partnerships with international partners are critical to dismantling transnational criminal organizations.

That's why this morning the Chairman and I introduced the bipartisan Cooperation on Combatting Human Smuggling and Trafficking Act, which would direct Homeland Security Investigations to expand its Transnational Criminal Investigative Units. These vetted and trained units of foreign law enforcement work with HSI to investigate transnational criminal organizations, aiming to stop human smuggling and the flow of dangerous drugs before they reach our borders.

I hope my colleagues across the aisle will continue to join me in calling for responsible action, like expanding these transnational criminal investigative units and putting more resources towards our ports of entry, instead of throwing around harmful rhetoric about invading Mexico—one of our closest trading partners and a critical partner in the fight against transnational crime.

While I have focused primarily on the law enforcement actions we can take to dismantle transnational criminal organizations, we must recognize that this isn't only a border security challenge or law enforcement challenge. It's a public health challenge, as transnational criminal organizations seek to make record profits at the cost of American lives. There is widespread untreated addiction for drugs, leading some individuals to consume dangerous substances that may be laced with fentanyl. I hope our witness from the Office of National Drug Control Policy can speak to the Administration's strategy to reduce the demand for illicit drugs in our communities.

Again, I appreciate all of witnesses' willingness to appear today to discuss how we can increase our efforts to combat this serious threat. I welcome any suggestions about how Congress can help you accomplish your missions.

# # #

Media contact: Adam Comis at 202-225-9978

Statement of Honorable Sheila Jackson Lee July 12, 2023

Thank you, Chairman Higgins and Ranking Member Correa, for the opportunity to speak today and thank you to the witnesses who are here.

My thanks to our hearing witnesses:

- Mr. Kemp Chester, senior advisor of National Drug Control Policy
- Mr. Steven Cagen, assistant director of Homeland Security Investigations
- Mr. James Mandryck, deputy assistant commissioner, Office of Intelligence, CBP
- Mr. George Papadopoulos, acting chief of operations, DEA
- Mr. Tyrone Durham, director, Nation-State Threat Center.

As a member of the House Judiciary and Homeland Security Committees I have a unique view on the threat that fentanyl poses to our children, families, communities, and our Nation.

As the Ranking Member of the Judiciary Committee's Subcommittee on Crime and Federal Government Surveillance I introduced The Stop Fentanyl Now Act of 2023.

The Stop Fentanyl Now Act, a is important bill that will protect children and youth from fentanyl, fentanyl-related synthetics, and fentanyl-laced substances.

As illicit fentanyl floods our communities, fentanyl-related deaths continue to increase at a devastating rate—claiming nearly 200 lives each day in every corner of the country.

No community is safe from this public health crisis.

As illicit fentanyl floods our communities, fentanyl-related deaths continue to increase at a devastating rate—claiming nearly 200 lives each day in every corner of the country.

Texas Statistics

In my home State of Texas, fentanyl was linked to more than 1,600 fatal overdoses in 2021 while the CDC reports that there were more than 70,000 fentanyl-related deaths in the United States in that same year, including roughly 1,500 individuals under the age of 20.

In 2022, more than 2,000 people died from fentanyl in Texas, killing more than 5 Texans aged 18–45 per day.

I want to again reiterate unintentional fentanyl use, given that 97 percent of the 870 unintentional synthetic opioid deaths in Texas in 2022 were fentanyl-related.

National Statistics

Fentanyl is now the leading cause of accidental death for young Americans, killing more people than suicide, car accidents, or gun violence.

No community is safe from this public health crisis.

It is found in every part of the United States.

Every drug purchased on the internet, on the street, or from people can contain fentanyl regardless of the form (powders, capsules, pills, and more).

The U.S. Drug Enforcement Administration found that 1 in 3 counterfeit pills on the market contained a potentially lethal dose of fentanyl.

Kids of color have been the hardest hit by the fentanyl crisis, with the highest increase in deaths among Native American, Latinx, and Black youth.

More than 5,000 children and teens have died from overdoses involving fentanyl in the past two decades, according to data published in the Journal of American Medical Association (JAMA) Pediatrics (on May 8, 2023).

More than half of those deaths occurred in the first 2 years of the COVID–19 pandemic.

Fentanyl was involved in 1,557 adolescent deaths in 2021, a thirty-fold increase since 2013; when the wave of overdose deaths involving synthetic opioids started in the United States.

A surge that began in 2018 led to a nearly three-fold increase in deaths among older adolescents and a nearly six-fold increase among children younger than 5.

In 2021, 40 infants and 93 children ages 1 to 4 died from a fentanyl overdose. Specifically, fentanyl has been mistaken by children as candy and chalk.

According to the DEA, bright-colored fentanyl pills designed to hook children have been spotted in nearly two dozen States.

The DEA also suggested cartels are coloring blocks of the drug so that it resembles sidewalk chalk.

These fatal pediatric overdoses involving fentanyl mirror trends seen in adults.

In 2021, nearly 70,000 U.S. adults fatally overdosed on fentanyl, the biggest spike in overdose deaths in the country's history.

Since 1999, however, the vast majority of pediatric deaths from fentanyl have been among older teens ages 15 to 19 (89.6 percent).

Teen deaths from fentanyl have surged overthe past few years—tripling overall and increasing 5 times for Black teens—according to provisional data from the Centers for Disease Control.

In 2021, 77 percent of all teen overdose deaths involved fentanyl.

The FDA also recently warned of "rainbow fentanyl" manufactured to look like candy to appeal to children.

Experts agree the surge of fentanyl deaths is overwhelmingly traceable to social media, where children can easily buy prescription and other drugs, many of which are counterfeit and contain lethal doses of fentanyl.

For all ages, 43.8 percent of deaths occurred at home, and 87.5 percent were unintentional.

And the drug is now the primary agent noted in the pediatric opioid crisis.

In particular, accidental exposures to fentanyl patches continue to be deadly to children.

According tothe FDA, children can overdose on new and used fentanyl patches by putting them in their mouth or sticking the patches on their skin.

This can cause death by slowing the child's breathing and decreasing the levels of oxygen in their blood.

H.R. 4272, the Stop Fentanyl Now Act of 2023

The Stop Fentanyl Now Act of 2023 is a necessary response to the recent surge in overdoses and death that is claiming thousands of young lives each year.

My bill would:

- Provide training and resources to ensure schools and teachers can administer opioid overdose reversal drugs or devices;
- Stop the on-line sale of little pink pills and other brightly-colored pills that have been used to target and drive addiction among youth—and have contributed to the recent surge in fentanyl-related overdoses and deaths;
- Require HHS and DOJ to develop and implement a national strategy to educate the public about fentanyl, fentanyl-related synthetics, and fentanyl-laced substances;

- Provide grants to States to develop and implement treatment programs for individuals addicted to these substances;
- Decriminalize fentanyl test strips and provide grants to States that adopt similar legislation;
- Encourage DOJ to increase resources available to law enforcement agencies to combat the trafficking of these substances;
- Require DOJ to establish an interagency task force to coordinate Federal, State, and local efforts to combat the trafficking of these substances;
- Require HHS to conduct research to better understand the effects of these substances, develop new treatments for individuals addicted to them, and determine best practices for prevention; and
- Enhance penalties for offenses involving the distribution or manufacture of adulterated or misbranded drugs, doing so with the intent to defraud or mislead, as well as promotion or sale of adulterated or misbranded drugs on-line. The Stop Fentanyl Now Act of 2023 is comprehensive legislation that broadly covers distribution of fentanyl-related synthetics and fentanyl-laced substances by seeking to break the supply chain that is now on-line and more available to our youth while punishing those who are criminally engaged in such activity that is aimed at destroying young Americans.

The bill also addresses demand for these drugs by educating the public, including parents, teachers, and teens, and providing treatment to those who suffer from substance use disorders.

The Stop Fentanyl Now Act of 2023 rejects the urge to criminalize drug usage in order to address the problems caused by fentanyl and recognizes that non-illicit fentanyl has medical uses.

And while we must stop the criminal production and distribution of fentanyl and fentanyl-related synthetics, we must also recognize that mass criminalization and incarceration will never solve the problems associated with drugs of any kind.

We cannot incarcerate our way out of the country's latest epidemic of drug abuse, especially when they involve mandatory minimum sentencing schemes that fall hardest on low-level offenders and do nothing to promote public safety or get drugs off the street.

While we must be committed to securing our border, if we want to protect our children and stop the senseless loss of life caused by fentanyl, fentanyl-related substances, and fentanyl-laced substances, the Federal response must focus on prevention and education, treatment, interdiction, and enforcement.

We must pass this legislation to truly protect Americans from the scourge of fentanyl-related deaths.

This multi-disciplinary, whole-of-Government approach is doable and should be done.

Failure to do so could be the cost of saving more lives. Thank you, I yield back the remainder of my time.

Attachment.—DEA Trafficker-Quantities of "Rainbow Fentanyl" Arrive in New York

October 04, 2022
https://www.dea.gov/press-releases/2022/10/04/trafficker-quantities-rainbow- fentanyl-arrive-new-york

One person was arrested and approximately 15,000 fentanyl pills were seized as part of an ongoing investigation into a fentanyl trafficking organization. The fentanyl pills, in various colors, were destined for distribution throughout New York City and had been concealed in a LEGO box to deter law enforcement attention. The fentanyl pills were also imprinted with "M" and "30" to resemble "30 M," Oxycodone Hydrochloride 30 mg pills.

This significant seizure, the largest to date in New York City, signals more wide- spread distribution of these dangerous colorful pills. The case highlights Mexican cartels' most recent tactics to attract the public while deceiving them about the lethal drugs. The Sinaloa Cartel and Jalisco New Generation Cartel are mass-producing fentanyl pills in rainbow colors to not only brand their products, but use colors and dyes to mimic candy and/or legitimate prescription drugs.

Frank A. Tarentino III, Special Agent in Charge of the U.S. Drug Enforcement Administration's New York Division, Bridget G. Brennan, New York City's Special Narcotics Prosecutor, New York City Police Commissioner Keechant L. Sewell and New York State Police Superintendent Kevin P. Bruen announced the seizure and arrest following the arraignment of Latesha Bush.

"Rainbow fentanyl is a clear and present danger, and it is here in New York City," said DEA Special Agent in Charge Frank Tarentino. "Approximately forty percent of the pills we analyze in our lab contain a lethal dose; and in a recent 15-week enforcement operation, DEA New York seized half a million lethal pills. These staggering statistics underscore the importance of reminding the public that just one pill can kill; and this operation alone removed the equivalent of 500,000 lethal doses of fentanyl from circulation in the Empire State. In the same reporting period, DEA seized the equivalent of over 36 million lethal doses nationally."

NYC Special Narcotics Prosecutor Bridget G. Brennan said, "Using happy colors to make a deadly drug seem fun and harmless is a new low, even for the Mexican cartels. Fentanyl is already involved in more than 80 percent of overdose deaths in the city. If you take any drug sold on the street or through the internet, regardless of its medicinal markings or festive appearance, you risk your life. My office and our partners are committed to intercepting lethal fentanyl and ensuring that these rainbow-colored pills don't lead more people down a sad path of substance use and overdose death."

"Disguising fentanyl as candy—and concealing it in children's toys—will never hide the fact that fentanyl is a deadly poison that harms our communities, our families, and our city," said Police Commissioner Keechant L. Sewell. "The criminal complaint unsealed today is another example of the NYPD's relentless commitment to never stop working to rid New York city of illegal drugs and I want to thank the Special Narcotics Prosecutor for the city of New York, the DEA New York Division, the New York State Police, and everyone else involved in this case for their exceptional work."

New York State Police Superintendent Kevin P. Bruen said, "I want to thank our members and law enforcement partners for their unwavering work in stopping the flow of illegal drugs throughout our State. The arrest of Latesha Bush and the seizure of these lethal drugs are the direct result of a commitment to aggressively target and pursue criminals who perpetuate the distribution of these narcotics. Together, we will continue to eliminate these operations and those who seek to destroy the quality of life within our communities."

A criminal complaint filed by the Office of the Special Narcotics Prosecutor (SNP) charges Bush, of Trenton, N.J., with Criminal Possession of a Controlled Substance in the First and Third Degrees.

Bush was arraigned in Manhattan Criminal Court on Friday, September 30, 2022. Bail was set at $25,000 cash/$150,000 insurance company bond/$100,000 partially secured surety bond.

The investigation was conducted by DEA's New York Drug Enforcement Task Force (NYDETF) Group T–12, which is comprised of agents and officers with DEA New York Division and the New York City Police Department. SNP's Investigators Unit assisted in the investigation.

On Wednesday, September 28, 2022, at approximately 7:11 p.m., members of NYDETF Group T–12 were conducting surveillance as part of an ongoing investigation into narcotics trafficking when they allegedly observed Bush carrying what-appeared to be a black tote bag wrapped around a large object as she entered a vehicle in front of 475 10th Avenue in Manhattan.

Upon stopping the vehicle, agents and officers allegedly found Bush in the rear seat, with two black tote bags and a yellow LEGO container also in the rear seat. Inside the LEGO container were several brick-shaped packages covered in black tape lying next to LEGO blocks. The black tape covering one of the packages had been partially opened, exposing multi-colored pills inside. A subsequent examination of the packages revealed they contained approximately 15,000 pills.

During the investigation, agents and officers learned that just prior to the arrest, Bush had travelled from New Jersey to the vicinity of 475 10th Avenue in a rental car. Agents and officers also learned that the multi-colored fentanyl pills allegedly originated in Mexico.

DEA laboratory analysis of the narcotics seized in New York is pending. Preliminary testing indicated the presence of fentanyl.

Last week the DEA announced the results of the third phase of the One Pill Can Kill initiative focused on combatting the fake pill threat which led to the seizure of more than 10.2 million fentanyl pills and approximately 980 pounds of fentanyl powder during the period of May 23 through Sept. 8, 2022. The amount of fentanyl taken off the streets during this surge is equivalent to more than 36 million lethal doses removed from the illegal drug supply. Additionally, 338 weapons were seized, including rifles, shotguns, pistols, and hand grenades. There were 390 cases investigated during this period, 51 cases are linked to overdose poisonings and 35 cases link directly to one or both of the primary Mexican cartels responsible for the majority of fentanyl in the United States—the Sinaloa Cartel and the Jalisco New Generation Cartel (CJNG). In addition, 129 investigations are linked to social media platforms, including Snapchat, Facebook Messenger, Instagram, and TikTok.

Special Agent in Charge Frank A. Tarentino thanked the New York City Office of the Special Narcotics Prosecutor, the New York City Police Department, the New York State Police, SNP's Special Investigations Bureau and Investigators Unit and Group T–12 of the New York Drug Enforcement Task Force.

Mr. HIGGINS. I'm very pleased to have a distinguished panel of witnesses before us today on this very important topic, and I ask that our witnesses please rise and raise your right hands.

[Witnesses sworn.]

Mr. HIGGINS. Let the record reflect that the witnesses have answered in the affirmative.

Thank you, gentlemen. Please be seated.

I'd now like to formally introduce our witnesses.

Mr. Kemp Chester is a senior advisor to the director of National Drug Control Policy. Previously, Mr. Chester served for 27 years as a United States Army officer, serving in a number of command and staff positions within the United States and abroad. In his current role, Mr. Chester directs policy focused on addressing the production and trafficking of illicit drugs, including the United States counternarcotics relationships with China and India.

Our witness seated at the table next to Mr. Chester is Mr. Steven Cagen. He serves as the assistant director of the Countering Transnational Organized Crime Division for Homeland Security Investigations, where he leads a wide array of operations investigating TCOs and narcotics trafficking. Mr. Cagen comes with 25 years of Federal law enforcement experience, including combating drugs and arms trafficking in Mexico City and working his way through the ranks of Senior Executive Service.

Thank you for being here, sir.

Mr. James Mandryck is deputy assistant commissioner in the Office of Intelligence at the United States Customs and Border Protection. In his role, Mr. Mandryck supports the day-to-day operations of CBP's intelligence enterprise, including the tactical and operational analysis that drives law enforcement operational activities. Mr. Mandryck previously served as a senior executive overseeing the National Border Security Intelligence Watch.

Thank you for being here, good sir.

Our next witness is Mr. George S. Papadopoulos, who was most recently appointed as United States Drug Enforcement Administration's principal deputy administrator. That's quite a title. Prior to this role, Mr. Papadopoulos served as the agency's acting chief of operations, where he oversaw all operational and enforcement matters for the DEA.

Thank you for being here today, good sir.

Mr. Tyrone Durham is the acting director of the Nation-State Threat Center in the Office of Intelligence and Analysis at the Department of Homeland Security.

I thank you, Mr. Durham, for joining us today. I thank all the witnesses for joining us.

I now recognize Mr. Chester for 5 minutes to summarize his opening statement.

Statement of Kemp L. Chester, Senior Advisor to the Director of National Drug Control Policy, Office of National Drug Control Policy, Executive Office of the President

Mr. CHESTER. Chairman Higgins, Ranking Member Correa, and Members of the subcommittee, thank you for the opportunity to testify today on the very real challenge we confront from the pro duction and trafficking of deadly synthetic opioids across our borders and into our communities.

I know I don't need to remind anyone here that someone in America dies from a drug overdose or poisoning about every 5 minutes of every hour of every day. That is why the President made ending the opioid epidemic a key pillar in his unity agenda, challenging us to change the trajectory of this crisis and save American lives.

Not long ago, the dominant model of drug trafficking involved plant-based drugs like cocaine or heroin or methamphetamine made from crude chemicals, moved through a hierarchical drugtrafficking organization and eventually sold in a face-to-face cash transaction somewhere in the United States. While that structure still exists, it has been joined by a synthetic opioid production and supply chain that operates as a global business and exploits the structure of legitimate commerce to obtain precursor chemicals, move funds, and make internet-based sales of raw materials and finished drugs using both fiat and cryptocurrency.

Today, the ability of an American teenager to find illicit drugs is literally in the palm of their hand and as simple as opening a social media app.

We are in the midst of a strategic transition between two eras, where the cultivation and production of large volumes of plant-based drugs has not ended, but the era of small-volume, high-potency synthetic opioid production has clearly begun.

This problem does not start at our border and it will not end at our border. It is a national security and economic prosperity problem, as much as it is a law enforcement and public health one.

In April of this year, the administration announced its strategic approach to disrupt the global illicit fentanyl supply chain. We call this approach commercial disruption, which focuses and synchronizes all the tools of national power to simultaneously attack four key vulnerabilities in the supply chain: precursor chemicals; the pill presses, dye molds, and encapsulating machines used to create counterfeit pills; the commercial shipping that moves these items around the world; and the flow of financial benefits and operating capital to those involved in the illicit drug industry.

As part of this, we maintain close and mutually-beneficial partnerships with key countries, such as Mexico and India, who play a role in preventing the proliferation of these dangerous synthetic drugs and in advancing our efforts to disrupt their supply chain. So for an issue in which United States and PRC interests align, we are disappointed that they have chosen not to substantively engage with the United States on counternarcotics for more than a year. But this is a global problem, and the United States leadership is essential.

Under our leadership, the international community has scheduled nearly a dozen precursor chemicals, and we've raised global awareness of the illicit synthetic drug supply chain.

Last week, Director Gupta joined Secretary of State Blinken for the first meeting of the global coalition against synthetic drugs. More than 80 countries convened at the ministerial level to accelerate efforts against synthetic drugs.

Our efforts to reduce the presence of these drugs in our communities must be closely linked with our equally strong efforts to decrease their use. The administration is committing a historic level of resources to lower the demand for these drugs and keep Americans safe from their harms. The simple truth is it cannot be easier to get illicit drugs in America than it is to get treatment.

We are seeing some signs of progress. Just today, the CDC released new data on provisional drug overdose deaths, showing a continued flattening of drug overdose deaths through early 2023, halting a period of rapid increase from 2019 to 2021.

But that is not enough. Now is the time to redouble our efforts, accelerate our work, and move this Nation and the world beyond a crisis that has vexed us for the better part of a decade. People in the throes of addiction are in a fight every day, and they should expect nothing less from us as well.

On behalf of Dr. Gupta and the hard-working people at the Office of National Drug Control Policy, I would like to thank this subcommittee and your Congressional colleagues for your leadership and bipartisanship on this incredibly difficult issue. Ending the opioid and overdose epidemic demands the best efforts of us all, and we look forward to continuing our work with you.

Thank you, and I look forward to your questions. [The prepared statement of Mr. Chester follows:]

"Leading the Strategic Response to Disrupt the Flow of Illicit Fentanyl Across Our Borders"

Committee on Homeland Security Subcommittee on Border Security and Enforcement
Subcommittee on Counterterrorism, Law Enforcement, and Intelligence United States House of Representatives

Wednesday, July 12, 2023

Prepared Statement of Kemp L. Chester
Wednesday, July 12, 2023

Chairman Higgins, Chairman Pfluger, Ranking Member Correa, Ranking Member Magaziner and Members of the Subcommittees, thank you for the opportunity to testify today on the very real challenge we confront from the production and trafficking of deadly synthetic opioids across our borders and into our communities. I am honored to join my colleagues from the Departments of Homeland Security and Justice, who are vital partners in implementing the National Drug Control Strategy, and in keeping our country and our communities safe.

Introduction

I am sure I do not need to remind anyone in this room that over a 1-year period we have lost more than 109,000 Americans to a drug overdose or poisoning, more than 69 percent of which can be attributed to a synthetic opioid like illicit fentanyl and other substances that are structurally similar to fentanyl. That is someone in America dying from a drug overdose or poisoning about every 5 minutes, every hour, of every day.

Alongside those we have lost are those who have suffered a non-fatal overdose. It is estimated that for every fatal overdose there are 14 non-fatal overdoses—more than 1.5 million in 2022 alone. Additionally, 46 million people in America, almost 14 percent of the population, are currently suffering from substance use disorder. Too many Americans—those we have lost to overdoses, those who have overdosed but did not lose their lives, and those living with a substance use disorder—have either succumbed to drug use or carry the burden of it in some way.

This is why the President made ending the opioid and overdose epidemic a key pillar of his Unity Agenda, challenging us to reduce the number of drug overdose deaths, put quality public health services within reach for people with substance use disorder, and strengthen public safety by disrupting the drug production and trafficking pipeline that profits by harming Americans.

The Environment of Drug Production and Trafficking

There was a time, not very long ago, that drug production was limited to processing poppy, or harvesting coca, or manipulating over-the-counter pharmaceuticals with crude chemicals to make methamphetamine. Those finished drugs were moved through a hierarchical drug trafficking organization to a street-level retailer, and eventually sold in a face-to-face cash transaction on a street corner somewhere in the United States. That was the dominant model of drug trafficking we saw for decades.

While that drug production and trafficking structure still exists, it has been joined by a synthetic opioid production and supply chain that is, in essence, a global business enterprise that demonstrates access to huge capital resources, conducts routine collaboration among raw material suppliers across international borders, uses advanced technology to fund and conduct business, and possesses the capacity for product innovation and strategies to expand markets.

These synthetic opioid producers and traffickers operate as free-riders on the back of the 21st Century global economy that moves products, ideas, and money across borders with incredible speed, and they exploit that legitimate economic structure to sustain and enhance their illicit business. This includes key activities such as the provision of precursor chemicals, some of which are unregulated, and their finished products that can be shipped in plain sight around the world; physically dislocated payments that include the movement of funds across borders; and the internet-based sales of raw materials and finished drugs using both fiat and cryptocurrency. And these synthetic opioids—principally fentanyl and its analogues, though there are others—that are killing Americans are manufactured outside of the United States and brought across our borders and into our communities by a variety of means. Today, an American teenager can find illicit drugs in the palm of their hand, and simply by opening a social media app.

We find ourselves in the midst of a strategic transition between two eras, where the cultivation and production of large volumes of plant-based drugs like heroin and cocaine has not ended, but the era of small volume, high-potency, synthetic drug production has clearly begun.

While we need to address the on-going plant-based drug problem that continues to harm our citizens, we must simultaneously develop and implement the means necessary to confront the emerging synthetic opioid production and trafficking environment that is defined by complexity, dynamism, and resiliency. This requires increased effort, a more sophisticated approach, better use of the tools available to us, and the application of new tools we have not traditionally employed against the illicit drug problem. We cannot simply charge into the future by doing the exact same things we have been doing, but just trying to do them better, and we cannot address the most dynamic and complex drug production and trafficking environment in history with the same strategies that may have served us well in the past but are insufficient for the challenges we face today.

While the administration is aggressively pursuing investments in non-intrusive inspection equipment, artificial intelligence, machine learning, and more, to prevent these drugs from crossing our geographic borders, we must bear in mind that this problem does not start at our border and it will not end at our border. It starts with the illicit synthetic opioid production in another country and ends in an emergency department or morgue somewhere in America. For the United States, it is a national security and economic prosperity problem as much as it is a public safety and public health one, and we must face it head-on with the bold, comprehensive, and determined strategic approach it deserves.

Doing so requires strong leadership from the White House providing unity of both purpose and effort across the Federal Government; strong bilateral relationships with key countries that share responsibility to address the problem and must be part of the solution; and perhaps, most importantly, the United States' global leadership.

The Administration's Strategic Approach

The President has declared "that international drug trafficking, including the illicit production, global sale, and widespread distribution of illegal . . . fentanyl and other synthetic opioids . . . constitutes an unusual and extraordinary threat to the national security, foreign policy, and economy of the United States." In April of this year, the administration announced its Strengthened Approach to Crack Down on Illicit Fentanyl Supply Chains, a whole-of-Government approach to save lives by disrupting the trafficking of illicit fentanyl and its precursors into American communities. We call this approach Commercial Disruption, and it focuses and synchronizes our national security and public safety capabilities, including innovative approaches, against criminal facilitators and enablers, and attacks four key vulnerabilities in the illicit fentanyl supply chain to maximize our impact across the drug producers' and traffickers' spectrum of capabilities:

The precursor chemicals, including unregulated chemicals that can be used to create immediate precursors.

- The pill presses, die molds, and encapsulating machines used to create the pills that are killing far too many Americans.
- The drug producers' ability to move raw materials like precursors and manufacturing machinery around the world via commercial shipping.
- The flow of financial benefits and operating capital to individuals and groups directly and indirectly involved in the illicit drug industry.

Targeting those four critical elements will allow us to remove the advantages fentanyl producers and traffickers currently enjoy, disrupt their production and supply chains, and reduce the availability of these dangerous substances in America's communities.

As part of this approach, we are also working much more closely with our private-sector partners. The vast majority of the physical and virtual terrain on which drug traffickers operate such as the dark web, e-commerce sites, mail and express consignment shippers and freight forwarders, banks, cryptocurrency vendors, legitimate chemical suppliers, and pill press and die manufacturers, are private-sector entities. And some of them likely have no idea they are a constituent part of an illicit business enterprise.

We must raise a sophisticated awareness of this environment with the commercial sector around the world, and engage with them in a full partnership, so we can sift out the unwitting from the knowing and intentional actors here in the United States and abroad, and then focus our efforts on the latter in a more precise way.

Bilateral Relationships with Key Countries

A second significant aspect of addressing this challenge is maintaining close and mutually beneficial partnerships with key countries who not only play a role in preventing the global proliferation of these dangerous synthetic drugs, but will also play a role in advancing our global efforts to disrupt the global supply chain.

Mexico.—We have redoubled our efforts with the government of Mexico, working alongside it as it does more to address fentanyl production and trafficking. President Biden has stressed the importance he places on this issue with President Lopez Obrador, and our two governments are working more closely than ever on the fentanyl problem to establish tangible goals, assess progress, and follow-through on mutual commitments.

Given the combination of our shared border, our two-hundred-year bilateral relationship, and the negative effects that drug producers and traffickers in Mexico have on both sides of the border, it is vitally important that our bilateral relationship be characterized by mutual respect, and a sense of the shared responsibility we have to address the shared threat of drug trafficking and its associated criminality. Further, we have strengthened all of North America in our work with Mexico and Canada through the trilateral North American Drug Dialogue.

Just as the United States does not have to lose 109,000 people to drug overdoses or poisonings every year, the people of Mexico can have a future free from an expectation of unaccountable criminality and the scourge of drug production that corrupts their towns, victimizes their families, and pollutes their natural spaces.

The People's Republic of China.—As we are leading the global effort to disrupt the production and trafficking of these drugs, we look forward to the People's Republic of China (PRC) joining us in that effort.

However, no one should mistake our willingness to engage for an acceptance of the status quo, especially on an issue felt so acutely in the United States and when so many lives have been impacted. Years of seizure and law enforcement data show that unscrupulous elements within the PRC have been a major source for precursor chemical shipments, pill presses, and die molds entering the Western Hemisphere. This is also an issue in which the interests of the United States and China align, and our past engagement on the counternarcotics issue has brought some impressive results, including the domestic scheduling of fentanyl as a class, which had an immediate impact on reducing the flow of fentanyl and its analogues directly from the PRC. The

United States will work with the PRC whenever possible to fully address the grave and growing problem of illicit synthetic drug production and trafficking at the global level.

Given the gravity of this issue, it is disappointing that the PRC has chosen to not take substantive steps to counter illicit synthetic drug production and trafficking for more than a year. With leadership comes accountability, and while the PRC plays a major role in this global problem, it has thus far declined to play a constructive role in helping to solve it. Last week, as nearly 100 countries and international organizations gathered in a demonstration of deep concern and a desire for tangible solutions to the grave and growing problem of illicit synthetic drug production and trafficking, the PRC declined its invitation to participate in the virtual ministerial meeting to launch the Global Coalition to Address Synthetic Drugs. We sincerely hope that the PRC can find the political will to address this problem commensurate with its capability to do so.

India.—The United States and India have been growing our counternarcotics relationship since 2020 through a bilateral counternarcotics Working Group, addressing the law enforcement, multilateral, regulatory, and drug demand reduction dimensions of this problem with a focus on tangible results and mutually beneficial outcomes.

During Prime Minister Modi's recent visit to the White House, the two leaders committed to work toward a broader and deeper bilateral Drug Policy Framework for the 21st Century. Under this new framework, we will look to expand cooperation and collaboration to disrupt the illicit production and international trafficking of illicit drugs, including synthetic drugs, such as fentanyl and amphetamine-type stimulants, and the illicit diversion of their precursors within India's chemical industry. They also committed to a holistic public health partnership to prevent and treat illicit drug use, address workforce shortages and skilling requirements across both countries, and showcase a secure, resilient, reliable, and growing pharmaceutical supply chain as a model for the world.

The world's oldest democracy, working in close partnership with the world's largest, cannot only achieve tangible and positive results, but will model for the rest of the world how great nations can work together to counter threats, seize opportunities, and demonstrate sincere partnership in addressing one of the most significant global issues we face.

Strong United States Global Leadership

Finally, as important as our bilateral relationships are, this is a global problem, and global problems require global solutions. The United States has learned a great deal from its opioid epidemic, and no other country has the depth of experience, expertise, or political wherewithal to lead on this issue. And that leadership involves not only sharing every single lesson we have learned the hard way over the past several years with our partners, but also serving as an example of how we are navigating this complex problem with care for those suffering from the disease of addiction, while systematically dismantling the global infrastructure of those who continue to reap obscene profits through the suffering and death of Americans.

The international community has successfully scheduled nearly a dozen precursor chemicals with global partners through the United Nations Commission on Narcotic Drugs, including 5 fentanyl precursors at the request of the United States.

We have led in raising global awareness of the nature of the global illicit synthetic drug supply chain, and are working to make common-sense and responsible measures to disrupt the exploitation of legitimate commerce a global norm.

And we have led by example, by committing billions of dollars, more than half our Federal drug control budget, to public health measures to prevent our youth from falling into the cycle of drug use and addiction, reduce the harms caused by these drugs and save lives, extend treatment services to everyone who needs and wants them, and making our communities and workplaces recovery-ready.

It is an unfortunate fact that there are three kinds of countries in the world: those who have a synthetic opioid problem and are dealing with it; those who have the problem but do not yet know it; and those who will have a problem with fentanyl or another synthetic opioid in the coming years. Too much illicit fentanyl production occurs, generating too much money, and absent decisive action this illicit market will expand exponentially around the world. It is important for all nations to put into place, now, the protective measures that will prevent this expansion and protect their people.

On July 7, Director Gupta joined Secretary of State Blinken for the first meeting of the Global Coalition to Address Synthetic Drug Threats. This ministerial-level meeting, hosted by the United States, brought together nearly 100 countries and international organizations to accelerate efforts against illicit synthetic drugs by: (1) Preventing the illicit manufacture and trafficking of synthetic drugs, (2) detecting emerging drug threats and drug use patterns, and (3) promoting public health interventions and services to prevent and reduce drug use, overdose, and other related harms. This first-of-its-kind global coalition will develop concrete solutions, drive national actions, and leverage the collective effort of like-minded countries who agree that countering illicit synthetic drugs must be a global policy priority.

Complementing Our Public Safety Efforts with a Strong Public Health Response

Because there is a complex interplay between the availability of drugs in the United States and their use, our public safety efforts to reduce their presence in our communities must be closely linked with our equally strong public health efforts to reduce their use. Traffickers are not going to import products no one wants, and individuals cannot overdose on drugs that are not available for them to purchase.

Therefore, disrupting the flow of drugs into the United States is not only vital to keep drugs from harming our citizens, but is especially important as the means to relieve the pressure of the steady flow of drugs into our communities and to allow our historic investments in public health interventions to take hold. The simple truth is that if it is easier to get illicit drugs in America than it is to get treatment, we will never bend the curve.

The administration has been working to greatly expand access to addiction treatment, harm reduction interventions, youth substance use prevention programs, and recovery support services. Much of this work is being done in partnership with Congress, and I want to thank the Members of this committee and the Congress at large for your support of numerous pieces of legislation in helping to address this crisis. These include the bipartisan omnibus Government funding bill, which included key provisions to help lower barriers to treatment and deliver necessary tools and resources to our communities to address the overdose crisis, such as the bipartisan Mainstreaming Addiction Treatment Act and the Medication Access and Training Expansion Act. Thanks to these provisions, prescribers across the country will be able to treat their patients who have opioid use disorder with buprenorphine, a medication proven to help people achieve recovery, without obtaining additional Federal licensing.

The Office of National Drug Control Policy has also funded the development of a number of model State laws to help local jurisdictions across the country expand access to naloxone, improve treatment in jails and prisons, and deploy settlement funds from the various opioid lawsuits effectively, among others. Similarly, ONDCP has worked with its partners across the Government to make permanent the COVID–19-related flexibilities that expanded access to treatment, and support people in recovery.

We are seeing signs of progress. The latest report on 12-month rolling data shows the number of drug poisoning deaths in the United States flattened in 2022 after a period of sharp increase from 2019 to 2021, and the number of fatal drug overdoses has decreased from its peak of 110,378 projected for the 12-month period ending March 2022.

But that is not enough. Now is the time to redouble our efforts, accelerate our work, and move this Nation, and the world, beyond a crisis that has vexed us for the better part of a decade. People in the throes of addiction are in a fight every day, and they should expect nothing less from us as well.

Conclusion

The administration's leadership on this critical issue, the close collaboration among partners within the United States and around the world, and the work of the Members of this committee and your colleagues in Congress have kept this issue at the forefront of our national consciousness and are changing the trajectory of this particularly complex national security, public safety, and public health challenge. We have much work ahead of us, and your partnership will be as critical in the months ahead as it has been thus far.

On behalf of Dr. Gupta and the hard-working people at the Office of National Drug Control Policy, I would like to thank the committee and your Congressional colleagues for your foresight and leadership on this incredibly difficult issue. Ending the opioid and overdose epidemic demands the best efforts of us all: The entirety of the Federal Government; States, Tribes, and local communities; private-sector partners and stakeholders; and the Congress, which has time and again demonstrated a strong spirit of bipartisanship on this issue.

The Office of National Drug Control Policy looks forward to continuing its work with this committee, the Congress, and our other partners to disrupt the production and trafficking of these dangerous drugs, prevent drug overdoses and poisonings, and save American lives.

Mr. HIGGINS. Thank you, Mr. Chester.

I now recognize Mr. Cagen for 5 minutes to summarize his opening statement.

Statement of Steven W. Cagen, Assistant Director, Homeland Security Investigations, U.S. Immigration and Customs Enforcement, U.S. Department of Homeland Security Regarding a Hearing on Protecting the U.S. Homeland: Fighting the Flow of Fentanyl from the Southwest Border

Before the U.S. House of Representatives House Committee on Homeland Security
Subcommittee on Border Security and Enforcement

Mr. CAGEN. Thank you, Chairman

Chairman Higgins, Ranking Member Correa, and distinguished Members of the committee, thank you for the opportunity to be here today to discuss Homeland Security Investigations' efforts to disrupt and dismantle transnational criminal organizations and combat the flow of illicit fentanyl into the United States.

As a principal investigative component of Department of Homeland Security, HSI combats transnational criminal organizations at every critical location within an illicit supply chain: internationally, where TCOs operate and manufacture illicit narcotics; at our Nation's physical borders, where smugglers attempt to exploit America's legitimate trade, travel, and financial systems; and domestically, where the criminal organizations earn substantial profits from selling this poison to our friends, neighbors, and family members.

The threat posed by TCOs is pervasive. These organizations do not limit themselves to a single criminal enterprise and have evolved beyond narcotics smuggling into poly criminal organizations involved in weapons trafficking, cyber crime, human smuggling, money laundering, and more, all of which HSI investigates. HSI combats TCOs by using its unique, broad investigative authorities to enforce over 400 Federal laws and target TCOs from multiple investigative angles. Simply put, HSI attacks the entire illicit network.

Mexican cartels have taken over fentanyl production and operate on an industrial scale, where they obtain precursor chemicals from China and synthesize these chemicals in Mexico to produce the deadly poison.

Chinese criminal organizations further facilitate the trafficking and distribution of fentanyl pills through the sale of industrial pill press equipment to Mexican cartels.

The Mexican cartels' ability to traffic deadly fentanyl into the United States is greatly enhanced by Chinese money-laundering organizations. Chinese money-laundering organizations have developed sophisticated networks in the United States, Mexico, China, and throughout Asia to facilitate their money-laundering schemes. These organizations have a vast global infrastructure to clean illicit proceeds for various criminal organizations, mostly including Mexican cartels.

HSI's counter-TCO efforts begin abroad, where we have the largest international investigative presence within DHS, comprised of hundreds of HSI special agents, strategically assigned in 93 offices in 56 countries. This includes offices located in Mexico, where the vast majority of fentanyl is produced; and throughout the Asian-Pacific region, where the precursor chemicals originate.

HSI's international efforts are greatly enhanced by our Transnational Criminal Investigative Units, or TCIUs, comprised of vetted foreign law enforcement officials and prosecutors, who lead some of HSI's most significant and mutually beneficial extraterritorial investigations and prosecutions targeting TCOs.

At our Nation's physical borders, HSI works with our DHS partners to combat TCO movements of illicit goods. HSI's Border Enforcement Security Task Force, or BEST task forces, represent one of the agency's premiere tools for turning border seizures into TCO- toppling investigations.

HSI's partnerships, including task force officers from CBP and DEA, are integral to the whole-of-Government approach in countering TCOs that traffic narcotics that threaten public safety of the United States.

There are currently 90 BESTs comprised of law enforcement officers from more than 200 agencies and National Guard units.

HSI is simultaneously attacking the illicit narcotic supply chain through an intelligence-based counternarcotics operation that blends traditional investigative and analytical techniques with interagency collaboration, industry partners, and computer-based tools to disrupt and dismantle the chemical supply chain. The interdiction of precursor shipments plays a key role in disrupting the TCOs' ability to produce a finished product before it even gets to our borders.

HSI's Operation Hydra has seized or disrupted the delivery of more than 3 million pounds of precursor chemicals that were destined for narcotics production in labs in Mexico.

HSI has also launched a targeted enforcement campaign to combat fentanyl. This year, HSI and CBP initiated Operation Blue Lotus, which surge resources to key locations, both domestically and internationally, to target fentanyl and develop criminal cases along the Southwest Border. Operation Blue Lotus resulted in the seizure of more than 8,200 pounds of fentanyl, thereby decreasing the flow of illicit fentanyl smuggled into the United States from Mexico, while simultaneously illuminating TCO networks.

Working alongside our partners here today, HSI remains dedicated to stemming the flow of illicit narcotics at every critical location within the supply chain.

Thank you again for the opportunity to appear before you today and your continued support for HSI in our enduring effort to attack the flow of illicit fentanyl into the United States.

I look forward to your questions today.

[The prepared statement of Mr. Cagen follows:]

Prepared Statement of Steven W. Cagen Wednesday, July 12, 2023

Chairman Higgins, Ranking Member Correa, and distinguished Members: Thank you for the opportunity to appear before you today to discuss Homeland Security Investigations' (HSI) efforts to disrupt and dismantle transnational criminal organizations (TCOs) and combat the flow of illicit fentanyl into the United States. With more than 6,800 special agents located in hundreds of offices throughout the United States and the world, HSI investigates, disrupts, and dismantles terrorist, transnational, and other criminal organizations that threaten our Nation's security. My statement today will focus on the broad spectrum of illicit activities perpetrated by TCOs, HSI's collaborative efforts to combat TCOs, and the resources needed to ensure continued success in the disruption and dismantlement of TCOs domestically and internationally.

As the principal investigative component of the Department of Homeland Security (DHS), HSI is responsible for investigating transnational crime. In collaboration with its partners in the United States and abroad, HSI special agents develop evidence to identify and advance criminal cases against TCOs, terrorist networks and facilitators, and other criminal elements that threaten the homeland. HSI works with prosecutors to arrest and indict violators, execute criminal search warrants, seize criminally-derived money and assets, and take other actions with the goal of disrupting and dismantling TCOs operating throughout the world. These efforts help protect the national security and public safety of the United States.

TCOs flood the United States with deadly drugs, including illicit fentanyl and other opioids. HSI conducts Federal criminal investigations at every phase of the illicit drug supply chain: internationally, where TCOs operate and manufacture illicit drugs; at our Nation's borders and ports of entry (POEs), where smuggling cells attempt to exploit America's legitimate trade, travel, and transportation systems; and in communities throughout the United States. HSI combats TCOs through multiple avenues of criminal enforcement. Not only does HSI target the narcotics smuggling activities of the TCOs, it also targets the financial networks they utilize to fund and profit from their illegal activity. HSI also targets the various other illegal activities the TCOs employ to fuel their criminal organizations, including human smuggling and trafficking, cyber crime, intellectual property rights violations, and fraud.

Evolution of Transnational Criminal Organizations

Criminal organizations in the 21st Century do not limit themselves to a single criminal enterprise. These criminal organizations have expanded beyond narcotics smuggling and have morphed into poly criminal TCOs involved in the associated crimes of weapons trafficking, human trafficking, human smuggling, money laundering, and other crimes—all of which HSI investigates. Rather than narrowly focusing on a single element of the TCOs, HSI combats TCOs by using its unique and broad investigative authorities to enforce over 400 Federal laws. Investigative efforts must be broad in scope to fully dismantle enterprises that transcend borders. TCOs have also evolved beyond insular entities and have sought out partnerships with competing TCOs in furtherance of their criminal activities. For example, the illicit collaboration between Chinese TCOs and Mexican cartels has created a complex criminal ecosystem that is fueling money laundering and narcotics trafficking operations, specifically illicit fentanyl, into and within the United States. Chinese money-laundering organizations have developed sophisticated networks in the United States, Mexico, China, and throughout Asia to facilitate money-laundering schemes. These organizations utilize their vast global infrastructure to clean illicit proceeds for various criminal organizations, including Mexican cartels. Moreover, as Mexican cartels have taken over fentanyl production and operate on an industrial scale, they are obtaining precursor chemicals from China and synthesizing these chemicals in Mexico to produce fentanyl. Mexican cartels then smuggle the fentanyl into the United States in either powder or pill form for distribution. HSI is attacking this illicit narcotics supply chain through an intelligence-based counternarcotics operation that blends traditional investigative and analytical techniques with interagency collaboration, industry partnerships, and computer-based tools.

Chinese TCOs also facilitate the trafficking and distribution of illicit fentanyl pills by providing the Mexican cartels with the pill press equipment to make the fake oxycodone pills. They are made to look identical to prescription oxycodone but are laced with deadly fentanyl. These fake pills are the most common type of illicit fentanyl pill, and are responsible for thousands of overdose fatalities, as the user believes they are taking a real oxycodone pill. In order to manufacture these pills, Mexican cartels require industrial pill press equipment to turn powdered fentanyl into pill form. The Mexican cartels are purchasing these pill presses directly from Chinese manufacturers that are producing the equipment specifically for illicit activity. HSI is actively disrupting the pill press supply chain, and to date has seized over 1,500 pill presses and parts used to make deadly fentanyl-laced pills.

HSI International Efforts

HSI's efforts to combat TCOs and illicit fentanyl begin abroad. HSI has the largest international investigative presence within DHS, comprising hundreds of HSI special agents assigned to 93 offices in 56 countries. These include offices in Mexico, where the vast majority of illicit fentanyl is produced, and throughout the Asia-Pacific region, where synthetic drug precursor chemicals often originate.

HSI special agents abroad develop and foster relationships with host Government law enforcement partners to exchange information, coordinate and support investigations, and facilitate enforcement actions and prosecutions to disrupt and dismantle TCOs. HSI and its counterparts in other countries identify and disrupt sources of illicit drugs, transportation and smuggling networks, and money-laundering operations. These efforts by HSI and its partners aim to prevent dangerous narcotics and other illicit goods from reaching our borders and also stop illicit outbound flows of illegally derived currency and weapons.

Transnational Criminal Investigative Unit Program

The effectiveness of our international counternarcotics efforts is greatly enhanced by HSI's Transnational Criminal Investigative Unit (TCIU) Program. TCIUs are comprised of vetted foreign law enforcement officials and prosecutors who support some of HSI's most significant extraterritorial investigations and prosecutions targeting TCOs. HSI has established 15 TCIUs around the world. These consist of more than 600 vetted and trained law enforcement officers across North, Central, and South America, the Caribbean, the Middle East, and Asia. In fiscal year 2022, TCIU efforts world-wide resulted in 3,800 criminal arrests and the seizure of nearly $18.6 million and over 350,000 pounds of narcotics and precursor chemicals. Targeting the fentanyl precursor chemical supply chain is an integral element of HSI's approach to stopping the production of illicit drugs. HSI blends interagency and foreign collaboration, industry partnerships, financial intelligence, and computer-based tools to identify, target, and interdict precursor chemical shipments destined for Mexican cartels. Disruptions to the procurement phase can have an outsized impact on the narcotics production supply chain. Mexican cartels operate on an industrial scale when procuring precursor chemicals, and many interdiction efforts are led by investigators and prosecutors in the Mexican Attorney General's office who comprise the HSI Mexico City TCIU. In fiscal year 2022, efforts by the TCIU resulted in more than 120 criminal arrests and the seizure of approximately $1.1 million and 18,200 pounds of precursor chemicals. The TCIU also leads investigations targeting the labs where the chemicals are synthesized into illicit drugs.

National Targeting Center—Investigations

HSI's National Targeting Center—Investigations (NTC–I) was established in 2013 in collaboration with U.S. Customs and Border Protection's (CBP) National Targeting Center to further our shared border security mission. NTC–

I supports the entire border security continuum, from CBP interdictions and HSI investigations, to the joint exploitation of intelligence. Through NTC–I, HSI supports all of DHS's domestic and international offices by targeting illicit precursor chemical movements within the commercial air and maritime transportation systems.

The combination of NTC–I targeting and foreign action through HSI's TCIUs is critical to stopping the flow of illicit drugs and dismantling TCOs. Using these resources, HSI targets the supply chains responsible for foreign origin shipments of precursor chemicals destined for Mexico. Thus far, this methodology has resulted in the seizure of approximately 3.3 million pounds of dual-use precursor chemicals intended for making illicit fentanyl and methamphetamine.

HSI Domestic Efforts

HSI's ability to conduct complex large-scale investigations represents one of DHS's best weapons for dismantling TCOs. Part of HSI's mandate is to turn individual border seizures and arrests into multi-jurisdictional, multi-defendant investigations to disrupt, dismantle, and prosecute high-level members of TCOs. HSI special agents work every day with CBP officers and in coordination with other Federal, State, local, and Tribal law enforcement partners to identify and investigate drug-smuggling organizations attempting to introduce illicit contraband into the United States. CBP's expansion of non-intrusive inspection (NII) scanning at Southwest Border POEs is poised to increase the number of CBP-origin seizures, which HSI special agents are required to investigate. To keep pace, HSI will require additional staffing to support the investigation and prosecution of individuals associated with POE seizures. Recent HSI Congressional appropriations tied to NII expansion represent an important initial step. HSI is moving quickly to deploy these new resources to Southwest Border POEs receiving NII augmentation. Given the required NII expansion to all land border POEs, additional staffing will be essential to ensure HSI retains adequate personnel to respond to these seizures and to conduct the complex investigations intended to degrade and remove TCO threats to the homeland.

Border Enforcement Security Task Forces

The Jaime Zapata Border Enforcement Security Task Force (BEST) Act was signed into law in December 2012. The Act was named in honor of Jaime Zapata, an HSI special agent who, while working to combat violent drug cartels, was killed in the line of duty in Mexico. This law amended the Homeland Security Act of 2002 to formally establish the BEST program, with the primary mission of combating emerging and existing transnational organized crime by employing a threat-based/risk mitigation investigative task force model that recognizes the unique resources and capabilities of all participating law enforcement partners. In June 2022, the Bipartisan Safer Communities Act provided HSI with statutory authority to reimburse the salaries for State and local law enforcement task force officers who participate in BESTs.

BESTs eliminate the barriers between Federal and local investigations, close the gap with international partners in multinational criminal investigations, and create an environment that minimizes the vulnerabilities in our operations that TCOs have traditionally capitalized on to exploit our Nation's borders. There are currently 90 BESTs located across the United States, including Puerto Rico and the U.S. Virgin Islands, comprising approximately 1,000 law enforcement officers and personnel representing Federal, State, local, Tribal, and international law enforcement agencies, as well as National Guard units. In fiscal year 2022, BESTs initiated more than 5,300 investigations resulting in more than 6,000 criminal arrests and seizures of more than 317,000 pounds of narcotics, more than 480,000 pounds of precursor chemicals, and more than $206 million of illicit proceeds and assets.

Operation Blue Lotus

HSI has also launched targeted enforcement campaigns to combat illicit narcotics, particularly fentanyl. Between March 13, 2023 and May 10, 2023, CBP and HSI launched Operation Blue Lotus to facilitate and increase fentanyl interdictions at and between the POEs and develop criminal cases along the Southwest Border. Focusing operations at the ports of San Ysidro and Otay Mesa, California, and Nogales, Arizona, Operation Blue Lotus aimed to curtail the flow of illicit fentanyl smuggled into the United States from Mexico, while simultaneously illuminating TCOs networks. Operation

Blue Lotus successfully resulted in the combined seizures of over 8,200 pounds of fentanyl.

Building upon the success of Operation Blue Lotus, on June 12, 2023, HSI launched Operation Blue Lotus 2.0 to strategically leverage its administrative, civil, and criminal law enforcement authorities to attack fentanyl distribution. Operation Blue Lotus 2.0 focuses operations along the border and interior facilities, including express consignment and international mail locations, to combat fentanyl trafficking nodes and target the smuggling of fentanyl and other illicit narcotics in the United States.

Cyber-Related Efforts

TCOs have become increasingly tech-savvy. For example, many have adopted anonymous cryptocurrency transactions through darknet marketplaces. These transactions may involve foreign vendors, but the result is the shipment of illicit drugs to or within our country.

Cyber Crimes Center

To keep pace with rapidly-evolving criminal techniques, HSI created the Cyber Crimes Center (C3) to provide investigative assistance, training, and equipment to support domestic and international investigations of cyber-related crimes for DHS. C3 supports HSI's mission through the programmatic oversight and coordination of investigations of cyber-related criminal activity and provides a range of forensic, intelligence, and investigative support services across all HSI programmatic areas.

C3's cyber investigators and analysts support HSI on-line undercover investigations targeting market site operators, vendors, and prolific buyers of opioids and other contraband on the darknet. C3 also supports tracing and identifying illicit proceeds derived from criminal activity on the dark web and investigating the subsequent money-laundering activities. Digital forensics play an ever-increasing role in investigating complex multinational narcotics organizations, and C3's Computer Forensics Unit and the HSI Computer Forensic Program are critical tools in combating the flow of drugs into the United States. C3's Computer Forensics Unit also provides forensic training and support to our Federal, State, local, Tribal, and international law enforcement partners.

A top priority for HSI is to improve collective law enforcement capabilities by providing training to partner law enforcement agencies. For example, C3 developed a cyber-training curriculum with a focus on darknet investigations and illicit payment networks associated with opioid smuggling and distribution. Since 2017, HSI has delivered this training course to more than 12,000 Federal, State, local, and international law enforcement personnel in over 70 locations world-wide.

Illicit Finance—Following the Money

One of the most effective methods for dismantling TCOs engaged in narcotics trafficking is to attack the criminal financial networks that are the lifeblood of their operations. HSI special agents work to identify and seize the illicit proceeds and in strumentalities of crime and target financial networks that transport, launder, and hide such proceeds. As a customs agency with significant access to financial and trade data, HSI is uniquely positioned to identify TCO schemes to hide illicit drug proceeds within legitimate commerce. HSI's financial efforts in fiscal year 2022 resulted in 2,607 arrests, 1,600 criminal indictments, 1,028 convictions, and the seizure of more than $4.2 billion in illicit currency and other assets (as valued at the time of seizure).

National Bulk Cash Smuggling Center

Despite the rise of alternative stores of value, such as virtual assets, bulk cash smuggling remains a key mechanism for TCO repatriation of drug proceeds. Criminal actors often avoid traditional financial institutions, which must comply with Bank Secrecy Act reporting requirements—instead repatriating their illicit proceeds through conveyances such as commercial and private aircraft, passenger and commercial vehicles, and maritime vessels, as well as via pedestrian crossings at our land borders.

Established in 2009, HSI's National Bulk Cash Smuggling Center (BCSC) is a critical component of the agency's and overall U.S. Government's efforts to combat bulk cash smuggling by TCOs. The BCSC operates strategic programs that leverage advanced data analytics, interagency partnerships, and law enforcement technology systems to identify complex money-laundering networks and provide support for HSI financial investigations. The criminal intelligence functions of the BCSC provide operational analysis in support of HSI-led interdiction efforts, including port profiles highlighting cash-flow activity at targeted POEs and corridor analyses to assist in planning the timing, location, and strategy for interdiction operations. The BCSC also administers a targeted, investigation-focused license plate reader program to identify larger criminal networks and a warrant-based GPS tracking program that provides valuable intelligence on the behaviors of criminal groups engaged in bulk cash smuggling. Since its inception through fiscal year 2022, the BCSC has initiated or substantially contributed to the seizure of bulk cash totaling over $1.73 billion.

TCOs are increasingly augmenting bulk currency smuggling with use of alternate value platforms in response to financial regulations and law enforcement efforts to identify money-laundering networks. A single movement of TCO proceeds may involve bulk cash, stored value cards, money orders, cryptocurrency, wire transfers, funnel accounts, and trade-based money laundering (TBML). HSI adapts to evolving criminal methodologies by leveraging new law enforcement technologies to identify money-laundering activity through these emerging alternate value platforms and seize criminal assets.

Trade-Based Money Laundering

TBML is the process of disguising criminal proceeds through international trade to hide their illicit origins. As the U.S. Government's primary law enforcement agency that investigates TBML, HSI utilizes data resources—maintained by DHS encompassing trade, travel, and financial information—to identify TBML schemes. HSI has established several national initiatives that target specific TBML schemes and provides subject-matter expertise, analytical support, and enforcement-related support to HSI special agents. Specifically, HSI has the ability to intercept and interdict trade and individuals associated with TBML that have a nexus to the borders of the United States and provide the necessary information to initiate criminal investigations targeting this activity.

Integral to these efforts are HSI-established Trade Transparency Units (TTUs), which combat the growing threat of international money laundering by TCOs via trade-based money laundering. The TTUs accomplish this mission using partner country data-sharing programs and the Data Analysis & Research for Trade Transparency Systems program. Through established partnerships, the TTUs have access to foreign trade, travel, and financial information used to support on-going criminal investigations and to address TBML on a global scale. These partnerships are based on bilateral agreements between the United States and 19 partner countries for the sharing of trade and financial information. Through the TTUs, HSI field offices can request information pertaining to companies and individuals that would otherwise be unavailable without the bilateral agreements.

Cryptocurrency

Cryptocurrencies are increasingly used to facilitate domestic and cross-border crime. They can be exploited by any criminal organization, and this is especially true as it pertains to on-line distribution of fentanyl, methamphetamine, and other illicit drugs.

Cryptocurrencies are attractive to TCOs because they offer a relatively fast, inexpensive, and pseudonymous system of transactions. HSI investigations related to cryptocurrency have risen from one criminal investigation in 2011 to over 530 criminal investigations in fiscal year 2023 to date. In fiscal year 2022, HSI seized nearly $4 billion (valued at the time of seizure) in cryptocurrency. This substantial increase signifies growing confidence in cryptocurrency use by criminals and criminal networks.

Conclusion

Thank you again for the opportunity to appear before you today and for your continued support of HSI and our efforts to use our unique authorities and global footprint to dismantle TCOs and combat the flow of illicit fentanyl into the United States. I look forward to your questions.

Mr. HIGGINS. Thank you, Mr. Cagen.

I now recognize Mr. Mandryck for 5 minutes to summarize his opening statements.

Statement of James Mandryck, Deputy Assistant Commissioner, Office of Intelligence, U.S. Customs and Border Protection, U.S. Department of Homeland Security

Mr. MANDRYCK. Chairman Higgins, Ranking Member Correa, and distinguished Members of the subcommittee, thank you for the opportunity to testify here today about the fentanyl threat and CBP's intelligence and data-driven response and approach to combating this proliferation of this dangerous drug.

CBP uses multifaceted approaches to counter fentanyl. Our approach includes advanced detection capabilities, such as specialized canines and nonintrusive inspection equipment; intelligence collection; research and analysis; laboratory testing and scientific analysis; domestic and foreign partnerships; and most importantly, the experience, expertise, and dedication of the CBP work force.

This enforcement posture has led to record-level seizures, including over 22,000 pounds of fentanyl so far this fiscal year, the equivalent of over 90 million doses and over a billion dollars in cartel profits.

Today I'd like to provide a little more information about the composition of the fentanyl seized by CBP, current production and smuggling trends, and the significance of our enforcement efforts within this threat landscape.

When it comes to composition, this fiscal year, 88 percent of the fentanyl seized by CBP has been in pill form, continuing the trending shift away from powder. The concerning shift indicates an increased sophistication of the transnational criminal organizations to control production and mimic legitimate pharmaceuticals that ultimately target unsuspecting end-users.

Another growing trend we've witnessed is the expanded use of xylazine as an adulterant in fentanyl to extend the user's high. Xylazine, a central nervous system depressant, is not an opioid, so naloxone does not reverse its effects, making this dangerous synthetic combination even more deadly.

The production of illicit fentanyl entering the United States shifted back in 2020. At that time, fentanyl was produced as a finished product in China, then smuggled into Mexico, and then onward to the United States. Over the past 3 years, production has shifted to Mexico-based TCOs that infiltrate supply chains to import precursor and pre-precursor chemicals, primarily from China, and then recruit or coerce scientists to produce metric tons of finished fentanyl.

Through intelligence-led operations such as Operation Artemis, CBP has identified previously unknown logistical supply chains, some of whom that transship to the United States before arriving in Mexico, discoveries that have led to changes in cargo inspections and processing and resulted in significant seizures of precursors, pill presses, and dye molds, as well as the identification of unknown criminal actors.

Within Mexico, we continue to see elevated levels of violence between cartels along lucrative smuggling corridors, especially in Mexico's northern border states.

TCOs involved in trafficking synthetics have begun to expand from historic strongholds in western Mexico to access additional smuggling corridors in eastern Mexico through newfound alliances. These types of alliances have always been driven by monetary gain. What has changed is how profits from these illicit activities are transferred and distributed.

Historically, CBP saw a major portion of illicit proceeds depart the United States as bulk cash currency. However, TCOs are increasingly taking advantage of technologies like cryptocurrency and informal value transfer systems, such as the Chinese underground banking system, to reduce their risk of cross-border interdiction.

Exploitation of these systems allows for immediate transfers of illicit profits into the—from the United States to the TCO hierarchy in Mexico. In many cases, these money transfers are done cheaper than historic laundering options and, in most cases, with guaranteed success for the customer.

Furthermore, TCOs continue to seek opportunities to move their illicit profits from the United States without currency or monetary instruments, including trade-based money laundering and the acquisition of firearms in the United States that are smuggled into Mexico to help control those corridors.

The complex challenges require strong and deliberate partnerships across the Government at all levels, as well as with our international partners.

Exemplified by the success of recent intelligence and data-driven operations such as Operation Blue Lotus, Four Horsemen, Rolling Wave, and Operation Artemis are CBP's hand-in-hand work with our investigative partners becoming critical disrupting and dismantling the networks behind fentanyl synthesis. In just 2 months, Operation Blue Lotus and Operation Four Horsemen resulted in the seizure of nearly 10,000 pounds of fentanyl and almost 300 arrests. CBP is currently executing Operation Artemis and Operation Rolling Wave, which target the illicit procurement, manufacturing, and trafficking of fentanyl and precursor chemicals by leveraging investigative, prosecutorial, and regulatory resources, and enhancing law enforcement information sharing and coordination.

In addition to our close work with U.S. partners, CBP has strong relationships with foreign and industry partners across the globe to further detect, disrupt, and dismantle criminal organizations. The consistent evolution of technology and the adaptability of transnational criminal groups requires us to become more adaptable and combat these challenges.

I thank you for your continued support for CBP and the opportunity to testify in this important topic today. I look forward to your questions.

[The prepared statement of Mr. Mandryck follows:]

Prepared Statement of James Mandryck, July 12, 2023 for a Hearing Before United States House of Representatives Committee on Homeland Security, Subcommittee on Border Security and Enforcement on "Protecting the U.S. Homeland: Fighting the Flow of Fentanyl from the Southwest Border"

Introduction

Chairman Higgins, Ranking Member Correa, and distinguished Members of the subcommittee, thank you for the opportunity to discuss U.S. Customs and Border Protection's (CBP) efforts to combat the dynamic threat of transnational criminal organizations (TCOs) and prevent the entry of dangerous illicit drugs, including fentanyl, into the United States.

The reach and influence of TCOs continues to expand across and beyond the Southwest and Northern Borders. These criminal organizations are sophisticated and operate with immense capability, capacity, and nearly unlimited resources. TCOs increasingly demonstrate the intent and ability to produce and modify synthetic drugs, making detection and identification difficult. They also continually adjust their tactics, techniques, and operational procedures to circumvent detection and interdiction by law enforcement, including transporting smaller quantities of drugs and improving concealment techniques.

As others have testified,[1] synthetic opioids like fentanyl—a synthetic opioid that is 80–100 times stronger than morphine—and its analogues are produced using precursor chemicals made available by criminal elements, often in the People's Republic of China. The precursor chemicals are shipped to Mexico where TCOs use these precursors to finish production. This fentanyl is either sold in powder form or pressed into pills. These drugs are then smuggled across the Southwest Border, most often through ports of entry (POEs).[2]

Because there is no single tool or capability that can detect all suspected threats in all situations and environments, CBP uses a multifaceted, intelligence-driven approach that combines advance targeting, sophisticated detection capabilities, specialized canines, non-intrusive inspection technology (NII), laboratory testing, scientific analysis, domestic and foreign partnerships, and information sharing. Most importantly, we also have dedicated, highly-trained officers, agents, and intelligence research specialists whose experience and expertise are essential components of all CBP's efforts to combat transnational threats and prevent the entry of illegal drugs into U.S. communities.

Our enforcement approach enables the agency to nimbly shift resources and swiftly respond to emerging threats, such as the deadly threat posed by illicit fentanyl, fentanyl analogues, other synthetic opioids, and methamphetamine, as well as the precursors and other chemicals used in illicit drug production.

Drug Trends and Interdictions

As noted above, most illicit drugs, including fentanyl, enter the United States through our Southwest Border POEs, hidden in passenger vehicles or belongings, concealed in commercial trucks, a nd carried by pedestrians. In

[1] See, e.g., Written testimony, Kemp Chester, Senior Advisor, International Relations and Supply Reduction, Office of National Drug Control Policy, for a February 1, 2023, House Energy and Commerce Committee Hearing. https://d1dth6e84htgma.cloudfront.net/WitnesslTestimonylChesterlHEl02l01l2023l487130aade.pdf?updatedlat=2023-02-01T14:- 37:29.433Z.

[2] https://www.cbp.gov/newsroom/stats/drug-seizure-statistics.

fiscal year 2022, for example, nearly 66 percent of illicit drugs seized by weight by CBP at the Southwest Border were seized at POEs.[3]

CBP seizures of fentanyl have been escalating for several years.[4] In fiscal year 2022, CBP seized nearly 15,000 pounds of fentanyl Nation-wide, with the majority— 12,500 pounds—seized at POEs. We have already exceeded that amount this fiscal year. At our POEs alone, fentanyl seizures increased more than 200 percent in fiscal year 2022 compared to fiscal year 2019 and fiscal year 2020 totals combined. In fiscal year 2023 to date, CBP seizures at POEs already exceed more than 17,600 pounds of fentanyl.[5] These seizures permanently removed these drugs from the illicit supply chain, kept them out of our communities, and denied drug trafficking organizations profits and operating capital.

Marijuana, methamphetamine, heroin, and cocaine remain the top-seized drugs by weight but shifting trends over recent years produced significant increases in synthetic drugs like fentanyl. Fentanyl is the most frequently seized illicit synthetic opioid, but CBP has also encountered 31 substances that are chemically similar to fentanyl, as well as 44 unique synthetic opioids that are not from the fentanyl class.[6]

Although our statistics measure drug seizures by weight, CBP estimates it interdicted 1.1 billion potential doses of illicit fentanyl in fiscal year 2022. By the measure of potential doses, CBP fentanyl seizures were only second to methamphetamine, of which an estimated 16 billion doses in fiscal year 2022 were seized.[7] For reference, Earth's population is approximately 8 billion people.

CBP's enforcement efforts focus on detecting and interdicting suspected illicit drugs; quickly anticipating and adapting to changing tactics and techniques used by cartels, traffickers, smugglers, and their networks; enhancing collaboration among key partners; producing actionable

---

[3] Of the 288,287 pounds of drugs CBP seized at the Southwest Border in fiscal year 2022, 189,682 pounds were seized at POEs. Excluding marijuana, CBP seized 202,631 pounds of illicit drugs at the Southwest Border, of which 179,317 pounds (88.5 percent) were seized at POEs. https://www.cbp.gov/newsroom/stats/drug-seizure-statistics. CBP Air and Marine Operations also contributed to drug seizure events with other agencies. These operations resulted in the seizure of approximately 270,000 pounds of drugs in fiscal year 2022. https://www.cbp.gov/newsroom/stats/cbp-enforcement-statistics/air-and-marine-operations-statistics.

[4] https://www.cbp.gov/newsroom/stats/drug-seizure-statistics.

[5] As of May 31, 2023.

[6] A complete list can be made available by CBP Laboratories and Scientific Services.

[7] CBP would be happy to brief the Subcommittee on its illicit drug dose estimation tool and how it derived these estimates.

intelligence to target the illicit opioid supply chain; and protecting our personnel from exposure to opioids.

Detection and Inspection

CBP, with the support of Congress, continues to make significant investments and improvements in our drug detection capabilities and interdiction technology. Our highly-trained officers use narcotic detection canines and a variety of technologies to detect the presence of illicit drugs, including illicit opioids, in all operating environments.

CBP's canine program continues to demonstrate its significant contribution to our efforts to intercept dangerous illicit drugs and disrupt TCO activity. In fiscal year 2022, CBP canine teams assigned to the Office of Field Operations and U.S. Border Patrol assisted in the seizure of more than $19 million in undeclared or illicit drug-related currency, more than 400 firearms, and nearly 290,000 pounds of drugs, including nearly 13,000 pounds of fentanyl—approximately 87 percent of CBP's fentanyl seizures—valued at more than $2.5 billion. The effectiveness of our canine teams is demonstrated daily. For example, in a single event on April 18, 2023, a canine team in Otay Mesa, California, aided in the seizure of 776 pounds of fentanyl pills valued at more than $21 million.[8]

CBP canine teams often work alongside officers conducting other inspection activities. CBP has deployed more than 350 large-scale and 4,500 small-scale NII X-ray and gamma-ray imaging systems to detect the presence of illicit substances, including synthetic drugs such as fentanyl. This technology enables detection of these illicit substances hidden within passenger belongings, cargo containers, commercial trucks, rail cars, and privately-owned vehicles, as well as express consignment carrier and international mail parcels. In fiscal year 2022, CBP officers used large-scale NII systems to scan more than 7.6 million conveyances, which resulted in the interdiction of more than 100,000 pounds of narcotics and approximately $2 million of undeclared U.S. currency.

Canine teams and NII technology are complementary detection and inspection capabilities that are critical to the continued success of CBP's interdiction operations at the POEs. At the core of these efforts are specially-

[8] https://www.cbp.gov/newsroom/local-media-release/we-re-spilling-beans-211-million-worth-fentanyl-pills-concealed-within.

trained officers and specialists using their expertise and experience to maximize technological capabilities and resources. Every seizure we make at the border is important. It stops the flow of drugs into our communities, contributes to investigations, and increases our awareness of emerging trends and illicit networks.

Advance Information and Targeting

CBP's interdiction efforts begin well before a conveyance or shipment arrives at a POE. Advance electronic shipping information,[9] actionable intelligence, and information-sharing partnerships are critical components of CBP's ability to quickly identify, target, and deter the entry of dangerous illicit drugs in all operational environments.

All advance shipment information is automatically fed into the National Targeting Center's (NTC) Automated Targeting System (ATS), an enforcement and decision support system. At CBP's NTC, advance data converges with law enforcement and intelligence records to facilitate the targeting of persons, conveyances, and items of cargo that pose the highest risk to our security in all modes of transportation. Advance information is a critical and effective component of CBP's targeting and interdiction efforts. We continue to pursue solutions to expand advance information opportunities to the land POEs, where—unlike travel processes over air and sea—CBP often receives no advance traveler information, limiting traveler vetting conducted before an individual arrives at a land POE.

In addition to targeting illicit substances directly, CBP and Homeland Security Investigations (HSI) target precursor chemicals shipped through the United States to destinations in Mexico and other countries. While many of the precursor chemicals used to synthesize methamphetamines and synthetic illicit opioids such as fentanyl have legitimate uses, CBP and HSI coordinate with the Drug Enforcement Administration (DEA) to intercept and seize precursors if they can be identified as having been brought into the United States in violation of U.S. law, such as Title 21 of the U.S. Code. CBP also targets production-related equipment such as pill presses and tableting machines. The DEA regulates pill press/tableting machines, and the HSI diversion coordinator works on behalf of DHS to coordinate the investigations

[9] See section 343 of the Trade Act of 2002 (Pub. L. 107-210), as amended; the Security and Accountability for Every Port Act or SAFE Port Act of 2006 (Pub. L. 109-347); and the Synthetics Trafficking and Overdose Prevention (STOP) Act (Pub. L 107-210) of 2018.

of pill press/tableting machine imports being diverted for illicit uses. The HSI diversion coordinator works closely with the NTC to identify and target individuals importing and diverting pill press/tableting machines to produce illicit fentanyl and other synthetic drugs.

The increasing ability of TCOs to produce sophisticated forms of synthetic drugs and develop new ways to smuggle is a challenge to CBP's counter-narcotic efforts. In addition to CBP's advance detection and targeting efforts, CBP's laboratory testing and analysis capabilities are invaluable to the timely identification of suspect substances and the disruption of drug-trafficking networks. These capabilities not only contribute to our targeting and interdiction success, but also aid our intelligence and investigative partners in their criminal prosecution efforts.

Analysis and Intelligence

Just as TCOs rapidly evolve their illicit production and smuggling operations, CBP must advance its capabilities to quickly and reliably identify the dangerous substances it encounters and provide analysis for targeting and other enforcement and investigative actions.

Sound analytical methodology centers on providing timely and actionable intelligence to our front-line officers and agents, decision makers, and partners. To strengthen our intelligence posture in responding to this complex threat environment, CBP's Intelligence Enterprise (IE) was established in 2017 as a cohesive, threat-based, data-driven, and operationally-focused effort to leverage the collective intelligence capabilities and expertise across CBP's operational components.

To enhance its intelligence capacity, CBP IE established investment priorities that support a whole-of-agency approach to countering various border threats, such as the use of a common reporting platform to timely share and disseminate threat information to disparate offices. CBP's IE was also responsible for launching the CBP Watch, a situational awareness facility that provides trend analysis and real-time feedback to better support the agency's operational front line 24 hours a day, 7 days a week.

Laboratory Testing

CBP's ability to swiftly and accurately identify suspect substances is a critical part of our ability to determine new production trends and seize illicit drugs, but also a critical tool for partner investigative agencies, such as HSI, to make law enforcement-controlled deliveries that could lead to arrests and the shutting down of criminal networks. CBP officers use various field-testing devices and leverage CBP's 24/7 Narcotic Reachback program to obtain a swift, presumptive identification of a suspect substance from a CBP Laboratories and Scientific Services (LSS) scientist. CBP has also positioned Forward Operating Labs (FOL) at strategic locations where new or emerging substances enter the United States. At the FOLs, LSS can triage quickly if a potentially new analogue of an illicit substance or designer drug is encountered and send it to the LSS INTERDICT Science Center for comprehensive testing. These newly-encountered substances, particularly synthetic opioids or other significant chemicals of interest, are added to the user libraries of the handheld field-testing devices used by CBP officers and agents to rapidly screen suspected substances. Since January 2022, 170 new spectra have been added to the equipment's factory library. Since the start of the designer drug wave in 2009, LSS has identified over 550 new substances.

CBP scientists participate in weekly operational roundtable discussions with intelligence personnel and law enforcement partners from Federal, State, and local agencies to share information on the latest analysis on encountered substances. Based on pollen analysis and suspected controlled substance analysis results, CBP develops intelligence products to share with CBP officers and agents, intelligence analysts, policy makers, and relevant external partners at Federal, State, local, and international organizations to maintain a consistent understanding of the fentanyl threat picture nationally, not just at the borders.[10]

Collaboration and Information Sharing

Shifting trends and sophisticated TCO tactics mean that now, more than ever, efforts to counter TCO activity require coordination and cooperation across the law enforcement community. CBP leverages collaboration with our Federal, State, local, Tribal, and international partners to address drug

---

[10] https://www.cbp.gov/document/fact-sheets/cbp-fentanyl-factsheet.

trafficking and other transnational threats across all our operational environments. This includes working closely with the Office of National Drug Control Policy's High-Intensity Drug Trafficking Area program and continuous work with other laboratories and the medical community, including coroners and medical examiners, to identify emerging drug threats.

CBP works closely with key partners, including HSI, DEA, the United States Postal Inspection Service, the Federal Bureau of Investigation, and other Federal, State, local, Tribal, and international partners, to share information, coordinate enforcement actions, and facilitate investigations regarding intelligence and seizures. For seizures that do not meet a Federal threshold, intelligence and information derived from these seizures are provided to local, State, and regional task forces for situational awareness and further investigative and prosecutorial actions.

CBP regularly hosts briefings with Federal, State, local, territorial, and Tribal partners regarding the current State of the border, providing a cross-component, multi-agency venue for discussing trends and threats. Engagements focus on interdictions and arrests at both the border and interior areas within the United States. These briefings also include participants from the governments of Canada and Mexico.

Strong international partnerships are a critical part of CBP's ability to respond to the global challenges that affect our border operations. CBP works closely with our foreign partners and contributes to multilateral forums by sharing information and leveraging partner capabilities to combat transnational threats and advance our national security.

CBP also participates in joint operations and multi-agency enforcement teams composed of representatives from international and Federal law enforcement agencies. Working together with State, local, and Tribal agencies, these operations target drug and transnational criminal activity, and often contribute to investigations involving national security and organized crime.

Our partnerships are also invaluable to our enforcement efforts. For example, CBP and HSI recently concluded Operation Blue Lotus, a 2-month, multi-agency effort led by CBP and HSI focused on narcotics smuggling attempts at POEs in Arizona and California. Through targeted inspections at border crossings, cross-border investigations, and the leveraging of advanced analytics and intelligence capabilities, approximately 8,000 pounds of fentanyl, more than 4,600 pounds of methamphetamine, more than 1,050 pounds of cocaine, and more than 72 pounds of heroin were seized—leading to more than 250 arrests by CBP and HSI. U.S. Border Patrol ran a complementary operation between POEs and at checkpoints near the border, leading to additional seizures of approximately 2,500 pounds of fentanyl, 6,500 pounds of methamphetamine, 330 pounds of marijuana, 620 pounds of cocaine, and 60 pounds of heroin.

Following the success of these enforcement efforts, DHS recently announced the next special operations of its surge campaign to target and prevent fentanyl from entering the United States.[11] Operation Artemis, led by CBP and supported by HSI, will leverage intelligence and investigative information derived from Operation Blue Lotus to focus on critical junctures in the illicit production and international trafficking of fentanyl and other synthetic drugs by targeting precursor chemicals, pill presses and parts, movement of finished substances, and illicit proceeds. Concurrently, Operation Rolling Wave will surge inspections at U.S. Border Patrol checkpoints along the Southwest Border, covering every sector and leveraging predictive analysis and intelligence sharing. CBP will run a parallel intelligence and analysis operation, Operation Argus, to provide trade-focused analysis in support of Artemis. In collaboration with multiple Department of Justice components, in particular the Bureau of Alcohol, Tobacco, Firearms, and Explosives, CBP and HSI also lead Operation Without a Trace, a joint platform for our personnel to target and investigate smuggling networks to disrupt and dismantle their illegal gun trafficking operations. Since the initiative's inception in fiscal year 2020, Operation Without a Trace has achieved significant success preventing Mexico-bound gun trafficking, resulting in the initiation of 803 investigations, the execution of 555 arrests, and the seizure of 1,213 firearms, more than 723,203 rounds of ammunition, and $16.5 million in illicit currency.[12]

Finally, CBP established the Southern Border Intelligence Center in April 2023. The Southern Border Intelligence Center, located in Tucson, Arizona, will integrate CBP's Southwest Border Intelligence Enterprise through collaboration within CBP and with the interagency into a single intelligence focal point. The Southern Border Intelligence Center will build and maintain a trans-regional intelligence understanding of the entire Southern Border by integrating CBP's intelligence efforts and collaborating with the interagency.

---

[11] https://www.dhs.gov/news/2023/06/22/next-phase-dhs-campaign-stop-fentanyl-will-focus-interdiction-and-supply-chain.

[12] As of March 28, 2023.

Conclusion

With continued support from Congress, CBP, in coordination with our partners, will continue to deploy critical resources to our Nation's borders to refine the effectiveness of our detection, interdiction, and identification capabilities and combat transnational threats and the entry of illegal drugs into the United States.

CBP will continue investing in our front-line and intelligence capabilities, which are vital to all our law enforcement efforts. CBP will also pursue new partnerships and innovative technology to aid in our layered enforcement strategy to support our fight against this ever-evolving threat.

Thank you for the opportunity to testify today. I look forward to your questions.

Mr. HIGGINS. Thank you, Mr. Mandryck.

I now recognize Mr. Papadopoulos for 5 minutes to summarize his opening statement.

Statement of George Papadopoulos, Acting Chief of Operations, Drug Enforcement Administration, U.S. Department of Justice

Mr. PAPADOPOULOS. Good afternoon, Chairman Higgins, Ranking Member Correa, and distinguished Members of the subcommittee. On behalf of the Department of Justice and, in particular, the more than 9,000 employees of the Drug Enforcement Administration, it's my honor to appear before you today.

Today's hearing comes at a critical moment in our country's history, and I thank the committee for bringing attention to this important topic.

Our Nation is in the midst of a devastating drug poisoning epidemic that claimed the lives of nearly 110,000 people in 2022. That's about one death every 5 minutes, or more than 300 mothers and fathers, sisters, and brothers, and most tragically, children dying every day, with countless more nonfatal drug poisonings.

I've had the privilege of being a DEA special agent for 27 years, and have served in locations as diverse as Detroit, Michigan and Athens, Greece. I worked at the DEA Special Operations Division and, most recently, was deputy chief for operations, responsible for all foreign offices. I can assure you that the drug poisoning epidemic that our country is facing today is unprecedented.

In 2022, DEA seized more than 58 million fentanyl-laced pills and 13,000 pounds of fentanyl powder. That's nearly 400 million deadly doses that didn't reach American streets and more than enough to kill everyone in the United States.

The men and women of the DEA are relentlessly focused day in and day out on saving lives by combating the deadly drug poisoning epidemic and bringing those responsible to justice.

As the primary U.S. Government agency responsible for investigating drug trafficking, the DEA leads and coordinates the whole-of-Government law enforcement response to defeat the two cartels responsible for flooding the United States with fentanyl: the Sinaloa and Jalisco cartels.

This is our top operational priority, because these cartels pose the greatest criminal drug threat that the United States has ever faced. They are ruthless and violent global criminal enterprises with members, associates, facilitators, and brokers in all 50 States and in at least 100 countries throughout the world.

The cartels use treachery and deceit to drive addiction and deaths in our country. They mix fentanyl with other drugs, like cocaine, heroin, and methamphetamine, and press it into pills that look like legitimate prescription medication. But the pills that look safe and familiar do not contain any prescription medication. Instead, they contain deadly fentanyl. Many people that died didn't even know they were taking fentanyl. Instead, they believed they were taking a different drug or a real prescription pill.

To save lives and defeat these cartels, the DEA created two counterthreat teams, one for the Sinaloa Cartel and one for the Jalisco Cartel. These teams synthesized DEA intelligence for a data-driven approach to mapping and strategically targeting the cartels' entire network and infrastructure, and to identify key nodes that can be exploited. Our counter-threat teams regularly send target packages to DEA offices across the country and around the world that are used to initiate or enhance investigations.

Along with our interagency partners, we've had some recent success against the cartels. In April, we announced the results of an 18-month undercover investigation, Operation Royal Flush, which resulted in the indictment of 28 members of Sinaloa Cartel, including Chapo Guzman's sons.

The indictment describes the cartel's entire network and supply chain from China to Mexico to Main Street. During this investigation, which included 32 DEA offices around the world and operational activities in 10 countries, we seized more than 22 million potentially deadly doses of fentanyl.

In May, we announced the results of Operation Last Mile, which focused on the cartel's U.S. distributors. During this year-long effort, we arrested more than 3,300 people in the United States, seized more than $104 million in cash and assets, and took nearly 8,500 guns off the street. Most importantly, we stopped more than 193 million potentially deadly doses of fentanyl before they reached U.S. communities.

Just last month, we announced the results of Operation Killer Chemicals, which focused on the precursor chemicals needed to manufacture fentanyl. We charged 8 Chinese nationals and, for the first time, 4 Chinese companies with conspiracy to manufacture and import fentanyl into the United States. These individuals and companies sold enough precursor chemicals to produce millions of potentially deadly doses of fentanyl.

While we've had some success, there is clearly more work to do. The men and women of the DEA are committed to saving lives and defeating the Sinaloa and Jalisco cartels and will relentlessly pursue cartel leaders, members, associates, and facilitators to ensure that they face justice for their crimes.

Thank you for the opportunity to testify before you today on this important topic. I look forward to your questions.

[The prepared statement of Mr. Papadopoulos follows:]

Prepared Statement of George Papadopoulos July 12, 2023

Chair Higgins, Ranking Member Correa, and distinguished Members of the committee: On behalf of the Department of Justice (Department), and in particular the over 9,000 employees working at the Drug Enforcement Administration (DEA), thank you for the opportunity to appear before you today to discuss DEA's work to save lives and to combat the deadly drug poisoning epidemic in our country.

Americans today are experiencing the most devastating drug crisis in our Nation's history. This is because one drug—fentanyl—has transformed the criminal landscape. Fentanyl is exceptionally cheap to make, exceptionally easy to disguise, and exceptionally deadly to those who take it. It is the leading cause of death for Americans between the ages of 18 to 45, and it kills Americans from all walks of life, in every State and community in this country. The criminal organizations responsible for bringing fentanyl into this country are modern, sophisticated, and extremely violent enterprises that rely on a global supply chain to manufacture, transport, and sell fentanyl, and rely on a global illicit financial network to pocket the billions of dollars in revenue from those sales.

DEA has been hard at work to undertake a transformation of its own to meet this moment. DEA has acted with urgency to set a new vision, target the global criminal networks most responsible for the influx of fentanyl into the United States, and raise public awareness about how just one pill can kill. We have transformed our vision by focusing on fentanyl—the drug killing the most Americans—and the criminal organizations responsible for flooding fentanyl into our communities—the Sinaloa Cartel and the Jalisco New Generation (Jalisco) Cartel. We have transformed our plan by building an entirely new strategic layer—our counter-threat teams for the Sinaloa Cartel and the Jalisco Cartel—that map the cartels, analyze their networks, and develop targeting information on the members of those networks wherever they operate around the globe. We have transformed our execution by providing that targeting information to our 334 offices world-wide, drawing from our global intelligence and law enforcement teams here and abroad, and working as One DEA to take the networks down. And we are seeing results—as demonstrated earlier this year with the indictment of 28 members and associates of the Chapitos network of the Sinaloa Cartel; the arrest of 3,337 associates of the Sinaloa and Jalisco Cartels in the United States who were responsible for the last mile of fentanyl and methamphetamine distribution on our streets and through social media; and the indictment of 4 chemical companies and 8 individuals in the People's Republic of China (PRC) for providing criminal actors in the United States and Mexico with the precursor chemicals and scientific know-how necessary to make fentanyl.

The Drug Poisoning Epidemic

In 2022, nearly 110,000 people in the United States lost their lives to drug poisonings. Countless more people are poisoned and survive. These drug poisonings are a national crisis.

A majority of the drug poisoning deaths in the United States involve synthetic opioids, such as fentanyl, that are being distributed in new forms. Fentanyl is being hidden in and being mixed with other illicit drugs such as cocaine, heroin, and methamphetamine. Drug traffickers are also flooding our communities with fentanyl disguised in the form of fake prescription pills.

These fake pills often are made to appear legitimate using pill presses and marketed by drug traffickers to deceive Americans into thinking that they are real, diverted prescription medications. In reality, these pills are not made by pharmaceutical companies, but drug trafficking organizations; they are highly addictive and are often deadly. DEA lab testing reveals that 6 out of 10 of these fentanyl-laced fake prescription pills contain a potentially lethal dose.

The availability of fentanyl throughout the United States has reached unprecedented heights. In 2022, DEA seized more than 58 million fake pills containing fentanyl, and 13,000 pounds of fentanyl powder, equating to nearly 400 million deadly doses of fentanyl. This is enough fentanyl to supply a potentially lethal dose to every member of the U.S. population. These seizures occurred in every State in the country.

The Drug Enforcement Administration

As the single mission agency tasked with enforcing our Nation's drug laws, DEA's top operational priority is to relentlessly pursue and defeat the two Mexican drug cartels—the Sinaloa Cartel and the Jalisco Cartel—that are primarily responsible for driving the current fentanyl and drug poisoning epidemic in the United States. In April of this year, the administration announced its Strengthened Approach to Crack Down on Illicit Fentanyl Supply Chains, a whole-of-Government approach to save lives by disrupting the trafficking of illicit fentanyl and its precursors into American communities. This approach synchronizes all the tools of national power to use more effectively against criminal facilitators and enablers. The administration has also increased its collaboration with key international partners to address security concerns that impact North America. For example, under the Bicentennial Framework for Security, Public Health, and Safe Communities between the United States and Mexico, the administration established a cooperative, comprehensive, and long-term approach with specific actions to promote the safety and security of our societies.

DEA is the lead agency on the law enforcement elements in the administration's whole-of-Government response to defeat the cartels and combat the drug poisoning epidemic in our communities. DEA's role in leading the law enforcement response to the fentanyl epidemic protects the safety of agents, officers, and sources. Importantly, a unified response to the fentanyl epidemic ensures that the whole-of-Government is moving in one direction that protects the safety and health of Americans. DEA operates 30 field divisions with 241 domestic offices, 93 foreign offices in 69 countries, and 9 forensic labs. DEA's robust domestic and international presence allows it to map and target the entire Sinaloa Cartel and Jalisco Cartel networks.

In addition, DEA has launched two cross-agency, counter-threat teams to execute a network-focused operational strategy to defeat the Sinaloa and Jalisco Cartels. The two teams are mapping, analyzing, and targeting the cartels' entire criminal networks. The teams are composed of special agents, intelligence analysts, targeters, program analysts, data scientists, and digital specialists. This network-focused strategy is critical to defeating the Sinaloa and Jalisco Cartels.

We already are starting to see results from our new strategy. As part of the network-focused strategy, DEA investigations recently resulted in charges against 28 members and associates of the Sinaloa Cartel, including leaders, suppliers, brokers, smugglers, and money launderers in multiple countries, for operating the global criminal enterprise that manufactures and traffics most of the fentanyl that comes into the United States.

DEA is simultaneously focused on American communities. We are targeting the drug trafficking organizations and violent gangs located in the United States that are responsible for the greatest number of drug-related deaths and violence. DEA's Operation Overdrive uses a data-driven, intelligence-led approach to identify and dismantle criminal drug networks operating in areas with the highest rates of violence and drug poisoning deaths. In each of these locations, DEA is working with local and State law enforcement officials to conduct threat assessments identifying the criminal networks and individuals that are causing the most harm. DEA works with State, local, Tribal, and Federal law enforcement and prosecutorial partners to pursue investigations and prosecutions that will reduce drug-related violence and drug poisonings. Phase one of Operation Overdrive took place in 34 locations across the United States, and phase two is currently occurring in 57 locations. So far in Operation Overdrive, DEA and its partners have made over 1,700 arrests, seized over 1,300 firearms, and seized over 13 million potentially deadly doses of fentanyl. In 2021, DEA launched the "One Pill Can Kill" enforcement effort and public awareness campaign. Through that, DEA and our law enforcement partners have seized millions of fake fentanyl-laced prescription pills and hundreds of pounds of fentanyl powder—equating to millions of potentially lethal doses of fentanyl, which could have entered our communities. Hundreds of these cases were linked to social media platforms, including Snapchat, Facebook, Instagram, and TikTok.

DEA is combating the sale of fentanyl on social media. Drug traffickers are using social media platforms to recruit associates, find customers, and sell fentanyl and other deadly drugs. In particular, drug traffickers use social media to deceptively advertise fake prescription pills—pills that look like Xanax, Percocet, or Oxycodone but actually contain fentanyl—directly to young people and teenagers. DEA has investigated more than 150 cases directly linked to the sale of fake pills containing fentanyl on social media.

DEA also works closely with families who have lost loved ones to drug poisonings. These families are often brave advocates for change, and help ensure that people in their communities are aware of the dangers of fentanyl and fake pills.

DEA is working closely with our local, State, Tribal, territorial, Federal, and international counterparts to target every part of the illegal drug supply chain and every level of the drug trafficking organizations that threaten the health and safety of our communities. To succeed, we must use every tool to combat this substantial threat that is being driven by the Sinaloa and Jalisco Cartels, as well as the Chinese-sourced precursor chemicals and global money-laundering operations that facilitate the cartels' operations.

Mexican Cartels and Drug Trafficking

The Sinaloa and Jalisco Cartels pose the greatest criminal drug threat the United States has ever faced. These ruthless, violent, criminal organizations have associates, facilitators, and brokers in all 50 States in the United States, as well as in more than 100 countries around the world.

The Sinaloa Cartel and the Jalisco Cartel and their affiliates control the vast majority of the fentanyl global supply chain, from manufacture to distribution. The cartels are buying precursor chemicals in the PRC; transporting the precursor chemicals from the PRC to Mexico; using the precursor chemicals to mass produce fentanyl; using pill presses to process the fentanyl into fake prescription pills; and using cars, trucks, and other routes to transport the drugs from Mexico into the United States for distribution. It costs the cartels as little as 10 cents to produce a fentanyl-laced fake prescription pill that is sold in the United States for as much as $10 to $30 per pill. As a result, the cartels make billions of dollars from trafficking fentanyl into the United States.

The business model used by the Sinaloa and Jalisco Cartels is to grow at all costs, no matter how many people die in the process. The cartels are engaging in deliberate, calculated treachery to deceive Americans and drive addiction to achieve higher profits.

The Sinaloa Cartel

The Sinaloa Cartel, based in the Mexican state of Sinaloa, is one of the oldest drug-trafficking organizations in Mexico. The Sinaloa Cartel controls drug-trafficking activity in various regions in Mexico, particularly along the Pacific Coast. Additionally, it maintains the most expansive international footprint of the Mexican cartels. The Sinaloa Cartel exports and distributes wholesale amounts of fentanyl, methamphetamine, heroin, and cocaine in the United States by maintaining distribution hubs in cities that include Phoenix, Los Angeles, Denver, and Chicago. Illicit drugs distributed by the Sinaloa Cartel are primarily smuggled into the United States through crossing points located along Mexico's border with California, Arizona, New Mexico, and Texas. The Sinaloa Cartel reportedly has a presence in 19 of the 32 Mexican states. It has been identified that there are currently more than 26,000 members, associates, facilitators, and brokers affiliated with the Cartel in more than 100 countries.

The Jalisco Cartel

The Jalisco Cartel is based in the city of Guadalajara in the Mexican state of Jalisco, and was originally formed as a spin off from the Milenio Cartel, a subordi nate to the Sinaloa Cartel. The Jalisco Cartel maintains illicit drug distribution hubs in Los Angeles, Seattle, Charlotte, Chicago, and Atlanta. Internationally, the Jalisco Cartel has a presence and influence through associates, facilitators, and brokers on every continent except Antarctica. The Jalisco Cartel smuggles illicit drugs such as fentanyl, methamphetamine, heroin, and cocaine into the United States by accessing various trafficking corridors along the Southwest Border that include Tijuana, Mexicali, Ciudad Jua´rez, Matamoros, and Nuevo Laredo. The Jalisco Cartel's rapid expansion of its drug-trafficking activities is characterized by the organization's willingness to engage in violent confrontations with Mexican government security forces and rival cartels. The Jalisco Cartel reportedly has a presence in 21 of the 32 Mexican states. It has been identified that there are currently more than 18,800 members, associates, facilitators, and brokers affiliated with the Cartel in more than 100 countries.

People's Republic of China and Precursor Chemicals

Chemical companies within the PRC produce and sell the majority of precursor chemicals that are used today by the Sinaloa and Jalisco Cartels to manufacture fentanyl and methamphetamine. These precursor chemicals from companies within the PRC are the foundation of the fentanyl and methamphetamine that are manufactured and transported from Mexico into the United States and that are causing tens of thousands of drug-related deaths in our country.

According to the State Department's 2023 International Narcotics Control Strategy Report, there are at least 160,000 chemical companies in the PRC. Chemical companies within the PRC distribute and sell precursor chemicals that are used in fentanyl and methamphetamine production around the world. Some companies within the PRC, for example, engage in false cargo labeling and ship chemicals to Mexico without tracking the customers purchasing the chemicals from the PRC and elsewhere.

In recent weeks, DEA has had productive engagements with Chinese counterparts in Beijing and Washington, DC focused on increasing cooperation between our countries. DEA remains ready to work with the PRC and all willing partners to reduce the flow of precursor chemicals and the deadly synthetic drugs they produce.

Chinese Money-Laundering Operations and the Cartels

The Sinaloa and Jalisco Cartels utilize Chinese Money-Laundering Organizations (CMLOs) in the United States and around the world to facilitate laundering drug proceeds. CMLOs use mirror transfers, trade-based money laundering, and bulk cash movement to facilitate the exchange of foreign currency. The use of CMLOs by the cartels simplifies the money-laundering process and streamlines the purchase of precursor chemicals utilized in manufacturing drugs.

These money-laundering schemes are designed to remedy two separate issues: (1) the desire of Mexican cartels to repatriate drug proceeds into the Mexican banking system, and (2) wealthy Chinese nationals who are restricted by the PRC's capital flight laws from transferring large sums of money held in Chinese bank accounts for use abroad. To address these issues, CMLOs acquire U.S. dollars held by Mexican cartels as a means to supply their customers in the PRC.

Recent Enforcement Actions Against the Sinaloa and Jalisco Cartels and Prc-Based Chemical Suppliers

The Chapitos Network of the Sinaloa Cartel

On April 14, 2023, DEA announced indictments against the Chapitos—the leaders of the Sinaloa Cartel—and their criminal network.

The Sinaloa Cartel supplies the majority of the fentanyl trafficked into the United States, which has resulted in the United States' unprecedented fentanyl epidemic. The Chapitos, the sons of the cartel's notorious former leader Joaquin "El Chapo" Guzman, currently lead the most violent faction of the Sinaloa Cartel. El Chapo was once the world's most dangerous and prolific drug trafficker. Now his sons have stepped in to fill their father's void by flooding the United States with deadly fentanyl and leaving a wake of destruction across families and communities throughout the United States.

Following their father's arrest and subsequent extradition and conviction, we allege that the Chapitos expanded their enterprise with sophisticated fentanyl laboratories in Culiacan, Mexico. We allege that the Chapitos now run the largest, most violent, and most prolific fentanyl trafficking operation in the world. The cartel is highly organized and sophisticated, employing military-grade weapons and vehicles and hundreds of people who protect the cartel and its leadership at all costs. In ad dition, we allege that the Chapitos use extreme violence and intimidation, including murder, torture, and kidnapping, to ensure dominance and expand their territory. The Chapitos pioneered the manufacture and trafficking of fentanyl, and are responsible for the massive influx of fentanyl into the United States over the past 8 years. The Chapitos oversee and control every step in their fentanyl trafficking process and will stop at nothing to ensure the expansion of their operations and the flow of fentanyl into the United States. From procuring fentanyl precursors from illicit sources of supply in the PRC; to distribution in the United States, and, ultimately, reaching the hands of Americans; to the surreptitious repatriation of massive proceeds through money launderers to avoid detection, the cartel has direct involvement—and culpability. Investigations found that even when test subjects died as a result of high-potency fentanyl, the cartel sent the deadly batch to the United States anyway—knowingly poisoning Americans for their own profit.

The indictments charged 28 members of the Chapitos network. These include suppliers of fentanyl precursor chemicals based in the PRC, a broker based in Guatemala assisting with the transport of those chemicals from the PRC to Mexico, managers of clandestine fentanyl laboratories based in

Mexico converting the precursor chemicals into fentanyl pills and powder, weapons traffickers and assassins perpetuating extreme violence in Mexico to protect and expand the fentanyl production operation, smugglers transporting the fentanyl from Mexico into the United States, and illicit financiers laundering the proceeds of fentanyl sales from the United States back to Mexico through bulk cash smuggling, trade-based money laundering, and cryptocurrency.

These indictments reflect the work of 32 DEA offices in the United States and abroad, as well as our law enforcement partners and other Department of Justice components, such as the U.S. Attorney's Office. As part of the investigation, the DEA conducted operations in ten countries and seized staggering amounts of illicit materials, including 2,557,000 fentanyl-laced pills, 105 kilograms of fentanyl powder, and 37 kilograms of fentanyl precursor chemicals, amounting to 22,747,441 potentially lethal doses of fentanyl.

Seven of the charged defendants were arrested pursuant to the investigation—in Colombia, Greece, Guatemala, and the United States—with the assistance of DEA's law enforcement partners in the United States and abroad. Ovidio Guzman-Lopez was arrested earlier this year by military officials in Mexico.

Simultaneously with the announcement of these indictments, the Department of State has announced up to nearly $50 million in monetary rewards for information leading to the capture of the defendants who remain at large, and the Department of the Treasury Office of Foreign Assets Control announced sanctions against 2 chemical companies that operate in the PRC, and 5 individuals associated with those companies, for supplying precursor chemicals to drug cartels in Mexico for the production of illicit fentanyl intended for U.S. markets.

Operation Last Mile

On May 5, 2023, DEA announced the results of Operation Last Mile, a year-long national operation targeting operatives, associates, and distributors affiliated with the Sinaloa and Jalisco Cartels who were located in the United States and responsible for the last mile of fentanyl and methamphetamine distribution on our streets and on social media.

In Operation Last Mile, DEA tracked down distribution networks across the United States that are connected to the Sinaloa and Jalisco Cartels. The Operation shows that the Sinaloa and Jalisco Cartels use violent local street gangs and criminal groups and individuals across the United States to flood

American communities with huge amounts of fentanyl and methamphetamine, which drives addiction and violence and kills Americans. It also shows that the Cartels, their members, and their associates use social media applications—like Facebook, Instagram, TikTok, and Snapchat—and encrypted platforms—like WhatsApp, Telegram, Signal, Wire, and Wickr—to coordinate logistics and reach out to victims.

Operation Last Mile comprised 1,436 investigations conducted from May 1, 2022 through May 1, 2023, in collaboration with Federal, State and local law enforcement partners, and resulted in 3,337 arrests and the seizure of nearly 44 million fentanyl pills, more than 6,500 pounds of fentanyl powder, more than 91,000 pounds of methamphetamine, 8,497 firearms, and more than $100 million. The fentanyl powder and pill seizures equate to nearly 193 million deadly doses of fentanyl removed from communities across the United States, which have prevented countless potential drug poisoning deaths. Among these investigations, more than 1,100 cases involved social media applications and encrypted communications platforms, including Facebook, Instagram, TikTok, Snapchat, WhatsApp, Telegram, Signal, Wire, and Wickr.

Operation Killer Chemicals

On June 23, 2023, DEA announced Operation Killer Chemicals and the indictments of 4 chemical companies and 8 individuals—all based in the PRC—for knowingly providing customers in the United States and Mexico with the precursor chemicals and scientific know-how to manufacture fentanyl. These indictments are the first-ever charges against fentanyl precursor chemical companies. Two PRC nationals were taken into custody pursuant to the investigation. DEA also seized more than 200 kilograms of precursors in these investigations alone, enough to make millions of deadly doses of fentanyl.

As alleged, these Chinese chemical companies, and the individuals working for them, not only provided customers with the ingredients for fentanyl, they also gave advice on how to mix and substitute ingredients to more efficiently make fentanyl, and employed chemists to troubleshoot and provide expert advice when customers had questions. The individuals also spoke freely about having clients in the United States and Mexico and, specifically, in Sinaloa, Mexico, where the Sinaloa Cartel is based.

The companies went to great lengths to conceal the chemicals during transport. They falsified shipping labels and customs paperwork, claiming the shipments were "dog food" or "raw cosmetic materials" rather than fentanyl precursors. They even disguised the chemicals at a molecular level—adding a molecule to "mask" the precursors so they would not be detected as banned substances during transport, and teaching their customers how to remove that molecule after receipt.

Operation Killer Chemicals made clear that fentanyl precursors are exceptionally cheap. Fentanyl precursors cost less than one cent per deadly dose of fentanyl. In just one example, a defendant sold two kilograms of fentanyl precursors for approximately $1,000, which can make 1.75 million lethal doses of fentanyl. The amount of fentanyl that can be made depends only on the amount of chemicals that can be purchased.

The Operation also showed that fentanyl precursors are easily bought online. Although based in the PRC, the chemical companies and individuals reached customers across the world because they advertised fentanyl precursors on social media (on Facebook and LinkedIn), used encrypted applications like WhatsApp to speak with customers and coordinate shipments, and took payment in Bitcoin and other cryptocurrencies.

Conclusion

DEA will continue our relentless pursuit of the Sinaloa and Jalisco Cartels—the criminal networks most responsible for fentanyl-related deaths in our country—and we will continue to work tirelessly to defeat these cartels and dismantle every part of their global supply chain, in order to protect the American people. Thank you again for the opportunity to appear before the committee today. I look forward to answering your questions.

Mr. HIGGINS. Thank you, Mr. Papadopoulos.

I now recognize Mr. Durham for 5 minutes to summarize his opening statement.

Statement of Tyrone Durham, Director, Nation-State Threats Center, Office of Intelligence and Analysis, U.S. Department of Homeland Security

Mr. DURHAM. Good afternoon. Chairman Higgins, Ranking Member Correa, and distinguished Members of the subcommittee, thank you for the opportunity to appear before you today.

I'm honored to be here representing the Department of Homeland Security's Office of Intelligence and Analysis and the dedicated intelligence professionals working diligently to keep the homeland safe, secure, and resilient.

As previously stated, the fentanyl drug overdose crisis in the United States, which is fueled by Mexican transnational criminal organizations and their Chinese suppliers of precursor chemicals, continues at epidemic proportions.

As you know, the drug overdose deaths rose from 2019 to 2021, with more than 100,000-plus deaths reported in 2021. Those deaths specifically involving synthetic opioids, primarily fentanyl, continued to rise during the same time period with more than 70,000 overdose deaths reported at that same time period.

So let's talk about who's responsible. You previously heard about the two Mexican cartels responsible for the activity, the Sinaloa Cartel and the Jalisco New Generation Cartel. These cartels supply U.S.-based affiliates with fentanyl for further distribution and retail-level sale. U.S.-based traffickers then sell fentanyl to users seeking the synthetic opioid. They mix fentanyl with other controlled substances, and they distribute it in the form of counterfeit prescription pills to drive addiction.

China's role in the global fentanyl trade is also a serious concern. China is the source of most of the precursor chemicals required for fentanyl production. A cartel associate brokers the sale and shipment of fentanyl precursor chemicals from China to clandestine labs in Mexico, where the fentanyl is manufactured.

Moreover, as law enforcement scrutiny or legal restrictions increase, suppliers adapt by modifying or changing chemical compounds of precursors, subsequently falling outside the purview of existing controls, to mimic the desired effect. Some Chinese chemists have focused on precursors to precursors, many of which have legitimate uses and are therefore hard to regulate.

There are several reasons why China is such a major source of fentanyl production. First, China has a large and sophisticated chemical and pharmaceutical industry that can produce its precursor chemicals at will and at scale. Second, China has a lax regulatory environment for chemicals, making it easy for traffickers to acquire the precursors they need for fentanyl manufacturing. Third, China's borders are porous, making it easy for fentanyl precursors to be smuggled out of the country, ultimately making their way to Mexico.

The Office of Intelligence and Analysis is producing finished intelligence on drug trafficking and other transborder threats to strengthen engagement between U.S. officials and foreign partners. Specific to drug trafficking threats, our analysis is aimed at identifying key transnational criminal organized crime leadership figures, organizational networks, logistical supply chains, smuggling routes, and the efforts of corruption that stand in the way of dismantling these organized crime groups.

Intelligence products draw upon national-level reporting from the intelligence community fused with DHS-unique data from components, as well as information from our law enforcement partners across all levels of government. This finished intelligence product related to TCOs are written at the widest possible dissemination level for distribution to our Federal, State, local, Tribal, and territorial partners and, when appropriate, shared with our foreign partners in Mexico.

I&A has deployed intelligence personnel, worked closely with DHS components, State and major urban area fusion centers, and other law enforcement agencies to gather, analyze, and report information that is uniquely available from these partners.

Thank you again for the opportunity to appear before you today to discuss this critical threat and for your continued support of the Office of Intelligence and Analysis.

We remain committed to keeping the homeland safe, secure, and resilient, and will continue our efforts at home and abroad to uphold the national security and public safety of the United States.

I look forward to your questions.

Mr. HIGGINS. Thank you, Mr. Durham.

Members will be recognized by order of seniority for their 5 minutes of questioning. An additional round of questioning may be called after all Members have been recognized.

I now recognize myself for 5 minutes of questioning.

Mr. Papadopoulos, I'd like to ask you: In your opening statement, you cited that you've identified major distribution hubs in cities, including Phoenix, Los Angeles, Denver, and Chicago. Is that in your opening statement?

Mr. PAPADOPOULOS. Yes, sir.

Mr. HIGGINS. OK. So a general question would be: Obviously without revealing on-going law enforcement investigations and operations, if you've identified the major hubs of narcotics distributions in these cities—Phoenix,

Los Angeles, Denver, and Chicago— can we look forward to major arrests in Phoenix, Los Angeles, Denver, and Chicago?

Mr. PAPADOPOULOS. Yes, sir. As you know, the DEA is constantly working these investigations. I mentioned Operation Last Mile, which was announced in May, which is a year-long effort focusing on the U.S. distributors of these cartels, where we arrested over 3,300 people, seized $104 million in cash and assets, and took about 8,500 guns across—off the street. That was across the entire United States.

Mr. HIGGINS. Understood. The American citizenry asked common-sense questions, and we're sworn by our oath to convey those questions, and it's a good question. If you've identified a narcotics hub and you—that means you're watching it. So we expect those people to be arrested.

The volume of drugs seized and the arrests made is reflective of the realities of effective law enforcement, but also the overwhelming amount of trafficking that we're dealing with and the criminal activity. It's at a level we've not seen in America, and we expect—we expect large numbers of arrests. If we identify these guys, we've got to break their back, make them hate each other. It's just fine with me.

Director Cagen, last Congress, I introduced the Homeland Security Fentanyl Enforcement Act. You're familiar, sir, this bill is written to expand Homeland Security Investigations' authority to investigate narcotics cases under Title 21. Can you explain why HSI is currently unable to conduct independent narcotics investigations?

This gets into some jurisdictional authority that Congress should be involved in, so I—I ask you to clarify.

Mr. CAGEN. Mr. Higgins, thank you for the support on this topic. HSI enjoys a great, long history and long relationship with the DEA, 25 years-plus, and we look forward to the next 25 years. Right now, our authority is derived from DEA's designation, which allows us to work together, us to focus on our foreign counterparts, our foreign customs authorities, working with our TCIUs overseas, and to continue to work—actually, Mr. Papadopoulos and I worked in the same fusion center building together here in the District of Columbia a long time ago and had a great relationship. So we'd just look forward to having that continued relationship moving forward.

Mr. HIGGINS. We—we understand and we appreciate the fact that long-standing relationships have been developed between the law enforcement agencies and working on the ground. But we must ensure that you have the legal pathway—statutory pathway to conduct your investigations, sometimes in cooperation with other agencies but with an independent capability that we must ensure.

So I look forward to speaking with my colleagues more about the Homeland Security Fentanyl Enforcement Act.

Mr. Chester, China is the main country of origin for precursor chemicals for synthetic opioids. These chemicals are then taken by the cartels, who make drugs like fentanyl. We all understand that. You've made that clear.

Can you characterize the coordinated effort between the cartels and China to create and distribute illicit drugs like fentanyl, and how is that changing as we speak?

Mr. CHESTER. Thank you for the question, Congressman. So the first major change happened in 2019, when China scheduled—at the United States' request, scheduled fentanyl as a class. What that did was it had the effect of reducing finished fentanyl from China to the United States to almost zero, and the traffickers got into the precursor business selling those to Mexican cartels for production.

The coordination happens on a couple of different levels. The first one is there's—there is a broker, usually located in Mexico, that works with a broker in the PRC in order to order the chemicals, often from a legitimate chemical company, who fills the bill. Those chemicals are transported and shipped, usually on an unwitting carrier, to one of the ports in Mexico or via air where at the port of entry it is delivered—diverted and then delivered to the drug manufacturers. That's the raw materials.

Then the payment for that is usually done through—through illicit finance enablers and brokers located in the PRC and in Mexico. It is this network of brokers between the drug producers and the raw material suppliers that gives this entire global illicit supply chain its life.

Mr. HIGGINS. Thank you, Mr. Chester. It's a massive network. We intend to break it.

My time has expired.

I recognize the Ranking Member, my friend and colleague, Mr. Correa, the gentleman from California.

Mr. CORREA. Thank you, Mr. Chairman.

I wanted to follow up on the Chairman's last comment on China, their role.

Their cooperation, has it been better in the past? Two-thousand-nineteen, they helped us, classified fentanyl, stopped it. Now you've got the issue of precursors, precursors to precursors, harder to regulate.

Has China helped us over the last year or two? Have you seen that level of cooperation maybe not as good as it's been in the past?

Mr. CHESTER. Thank you for your question. Your question is very prescient, and the answer is cooperation in the past actually has brought results. In fact, in the—in the words of Chinese diplomats, counternarcotics cooperation between the United States and the PRC has been a bright spot.

We were able to do—there was routine law enforcement cooperation. We were able to get fentanyl scheduled as a class. As of late, over more than a year, for a variety of reasons, the PRC has decided not to engage with the United States on—on counternarcotics and a number of other issues.

The United States would like that level of cooperation again, and we have made it clear to the PRC a few things. The first one is we're not blaming the PRC government for this. There are criminal elements within China and Mexico and the United States who keep this global illicit supply chain alive. That's the first thing.

The second thing is our cooperation is absolutely essential in order to help us with that, and we have made some very specific asks of the Chinese government that they could implement very easily in order to be able to help us to do that.

Mr. CORREA. Gentlemen, I just want to say thank you for your good work. You've done a stellar job of doing what you're paid to do.

We talk about commercial disruption, precursors, pills, shipping. It's as though every time you stop one place, something else explodes. I've heard lately that—there is intel now a lot of the precursors are coming in through our ports of entry, pill presses coming into the United States. So every time you bottle something up, another source, another supply seems to emerge.

The one issue that I think probably holds everything together is the finances, the laundering of this money. What can we do to better enable you to stop the flow of these profits?

HSI, you talked about—you know, the Chairman asked you about maybe some other tools you may need. But I would ask all of you: What else can we do as Members of Congress to strengthen your hand to stop the flow of the profits? Because, you know, you dry up the money and the whole machine comes to a stop.

You know, right now, what we are witnessing in this country is a massive transfer of wealth from American pocketbooks to somewhere around the country—excuse me—around the world.

Please, open it up for comments.

Mr. CAGEN. Since you mentioned HSI, I'll—I'll take that.

You know, money is moved in multiple ways, and they're everevolving. You just mentioned the fact that—you know, that we stop one thing that the Chinese are doing, and they move in a different way. The same thing happens with money laundering. It's bulk cash, it's trade-based money laundering, it's cryptocurrency movement of money right now.

One thing—and I come back to, you know, begin and end in China. China has taken over. Chinese money-laundering organizations have taken over the network, the money movement network, which we're all focused on as—you know, everybody sitting up here is focused on that. They're able to charge much lower percentages than other people have in the past because of their vast network around the world.

But we are—HSI is—that's what we do. We like to go after their money. We like to go after their toys. Because when you take their money away, then they can't flourish. So we're continuing to——

Mr. CORREA. I asked you directly—I called you out because I've seen you work, and I've seen some of your results. When I've been down to San Isidro, I've taken a tour of your operations.

Mr. CAGEN. Yes, sir.

Mr. CORREA. All of you are doing a stellar job. In the half minute that I have left, I would just ask you all as a challenge to let us know what we can do as Congress to strengthen your hand when it comes to money laundering. It's not an easy solution.

You've got 20 seconds. You're not going to give me the answer. But I'd love all of you to go back and give us some, you know, wish lists, legislatively what tools and what resources you need to stop the flow of drug money.

In my opinion, that's the best punch you can give these folks when it comes to fentanyl.

Thank you, Mr. Chairman. Time is up. I turn it over back to you.

Mr. HIGGINS. The gentleman yields.

The gentleman from Oklahoma, Mr. Brecheen, is recognized for 5 minutes for questioning.

Mr. BRECHEEN. Thank you, Mr. Chairman.

I appreciate you all being here today. There is no doubt this is a crisis. Just in Oklahoma alone, the State that I'm a Representative for, we've seen a 735 percent increase in fentanyl deaths, and that has occurred from 2018 to 2022: 326 deaths in 2022 in Oklahoma. In 2018, it was 39.

I think probably every Member of this committee has some personal point of contact with somebody that they know of who has lost their life or has a direct connection. It's really sad.

I guess what I want to zero in on—and I'll open this up to anyone—if you—if 6 out of the 10 pills that you all are looking at— one of your testimonies a minute ago—are containing lethal overdose elements to the point that you take it unsuspectingly, it can kill you, why are they doing that?

There's an addictive element, right. You're trying to use the addictive element, 10 cents to make, and $30—10 to $30 sold, massive increase in profit.

So can you—I'd be interested in some comments if you—if you can help bring about why they are enabling such a lethal concoction in their pills?

Mr. CHESTER. Congressman, I can start, and then I can turn it over to my colleagues.

I think—I think the first thing is that—that our image of these drug producers and traffickers, I think, traditionally has been that they're evildoers who are out to hurt people when in reality they are disinterested businesspeople who really only want a few things. They want to lower their production costs. They want to lower their risk of detection and interdiction. They want to increase their customer base and increase their profits.

By—and—and a mechanism to do that is to provide the drug user an experience that they did not expect. This is what we saw back in 2015 when we started to see synthetic opioids like fentanyl introduced into the heroin supply chain. This is—this was the door that opened this up for the United States. What it did, it provided the individual a qualitative effect that they did not expect, and it was used as kind-of a branding.

Because these things are so potent and because they are so potentially lethal, a milligram in the wrong direction will take you from having a qualitative experience that you didn't expect to an overdose death. In a lot of cases, these things are not uniformly mixed, and they're not done well, and it's a lot of cross-contamination that actually leads to the overdose deaths.

The last thing I'll tell you is, in a lot of cases, the unwitting user who may not have an active substance use disorder or does not intend to take fentanyl gets it in another counterfeit pill that they did not expect, like Xanax or Adderall or something like that. This is done in the interest of making money with a casual disinterest as to whether people are harmed or not.

Mr. BRECHEEN. So I want to pivot, because I think somebody else maybe on the panel can answer this. Are you seeing it utilized as a revenge element to—so you're saying, you know, that there's nothing that's in this more than profit margin, but there's a—an evil intent that can lead to murder purposefully.

In your investigations, are you seeing that?

Mr. PAPADOPOULOS. Sir, I can jump in.

So the answer is yes. We have evidence in some of the char-— previous cases I mentioned where the cartels knew that there was deadly fentanyl. The amount of fentanyl that they were sending to United States was deadly, because they tested it on human beings in Mexico, and they still sent it anyway.

As Mr. Chester was saying, these are not mixed in labs. They're not sterile situations. We've seen pills with less than a milligram of fentanyl all the way up to 8 milligrams of fentanyl. The average dose is 2.4 milligrams, and 1 milligrams is considered a potentially deadly dose.

Mr. BRECHEEN. In regards to human trafficking, "Sound of Freedom" is a movie that's, you know, getting a lot of attention right now nationally, and you can sell a drug one time, common—commonly being discussed is—as the human trafficking element, that you can sell an individual multiple times.

What are you seeing with the human traffic—in all of your investigations, where are you seeing the overlap with those that are engaged in human trafficking, prostitution, also alongside the fentanyl trade?

Mr. MANDRYCK. Thank you for the question, sir. So, historically, we had seen the transnational criminal groups focus on narcotics, were solely focused on narcotics. They would charge a piso, or a tax, for migrants to cross.

At the beginning of COVID, where we started to see some of the closures at the ports of entry for nonessential travel, we started to see those criminal groups become more involved in the process holistically. So it wasn't just a couple-hundred-dollar tax; it was a multi-thousand-dollar program to move them throughout the whole chain.

That's what we've continued to see, is that control of the plazas along the border and that full-scale facilitation from start to finish.

Mr. BRECHEEN. Mr. Chairman, would you allow—would you allow if anybody else has any—I know my time has expired. Does anybody else have any—any comments on that?

Mr. CAGEN. I can draw a distinction a little bit between the human smuggling and human trafficking aspect, which I think is where your question was going.

We don't see a direct link between your large-scale criminal organizations that are operating and moving people trafficking-wise, human traffickingise, across the border like the transnational criminal organizations. A lot of those folks are already here. People are smuggled into the United States. Then, once in the United States, transnational—or organizations prey on vulnerable populations, and that's when they're turned into trafficking victims.

Mr. BRECHEEN. Thank you.

Mr. HIGGINS. The gentleman yields.

Mr. Thanedar is recognized for 5 minutes for questioning.

Mr. THANEDAR. Thank you, Chairman Higgins. Thank you, gentlemen, for your testimony.

I have heard from both sides of the aisle that transnational criminal organizations and the smuggling of illicit drugs like fentanyl is not just a U.S. problem; it is a global issue. There are bad actors all over the world looking to profit from these deadly drugs. That's why it is important to foster relationships with law enforcement partners and international governments to disrupt and dismantle transnational criminal organizations.

Mr. Cagen, you mentioned this point in your testimony. So my question is for you, Mr. Cagen, and also for Mr. Papadopoulos. Can you—and, in fact, I have three questions. Let me just state those and allow you, either of you, to comment on.

Can you discuss how HSI and the DEA are working and sharing information across the Federal Government, as well as State and local law enforcement partners, to investigate and prosecute these criminal organizations?

No. 2, can you discuss how HSI and DEA are fostering relationships internationally to prevent these deadly drugs from reaching our borders?

No. 3, in April 2023, the Justice Department announced charges against Federal leaders of the Sinaloa Cartel. What role did this partnership play in these critical investigations?

Mr. CAGEN. Thank you very much for the question. I think it's a fantastic question.

I've mentioned it in my opening statement and in a statement already before, HSI and DEA have a long history of working together. I mentioned that we both worked together in the same building, which is actually a fusion center, where we bring in information, intelligence, and 30-plus Federal agencies sit in this building where we share information and ensure that we're taking a whole-of-Government approach toward attacking the cartels and the transnational criminal organizations.

We both have very similar tactics as well when we're working with our international partners. Both have investigative units. Ours is called a Transnational Criminal Investigative Unit. Very different but the same structure. Ours, we've got the ability to work with the Mexican Customs, where we can stop things that are coming over the ports, like precursor chemicals that are shipped from China over the sea, things like that.

I think that we have a very good international relationship with Mexico and other countries on the working level, which is how we all get our job done to go after transnational criminal organizations.

Mr. THANEDAR. Thank you.

Mr. PAPADOPOULOS. Thank you for the question, sir. So as far as information sharing, we are in, as I mentioned, unprecedented times right now, which I think calls for unprecedented collaboration across the Federal, State, and local governments. We are committed to that. We are using every tool that we have available, including sanctions and rewards for justice, to get the word out.

As far as our international relationships, we have a big international presence also, and that's because we want to be proactive. Most drugs are manufactured outside of the United States, and then they need to be transported here through other countries. So when we're outside of the United States working with our international counterparts, we are being proactive, instead of reactive, waiting for the drugs to get here.

As far as the case that you mentioned, we did work closely on that investigation with other districts and other agencies to put that case together.

Mr. THANEDAR. Thank you so much.

Mr. Chairman, my time is up, so I yield back.

Mr. HIGGINS. The gentleman yields.

My colleague from Texas, Mr. Gonzales, is recognized for 5 minutes for questioning.

Mr. GONZALES. Thank you, Chairman, and thank you for holding this hearing.

I want to talk—I want to use my time to talk about fentanyl as it relates to drones. I think this is an area that the landscape is changing.

If you're watching the war in Ukraine, you're seeing that drones are the future of conflict, and that's no different from fentanyl. What I'm seeing is I'm seeing on a regular basis cartels are using drones to penetrate the United States air space, and they're dropping off packages of fentanyl. Remember, you don't need large quantities in order to make a lot of money off of this. Then they're taking that and they're moving it around.

Well, let me just set the tone. Imagine if you're in a soccer field and all of a sudden there's a drone that flies over with fentanyl and it doesn't drop it to get picked up and get sold somewhere, it just drops it in the stadium. Could we live in that world? Well, guess what? We already live in that world.

So I'm very concerned with the drones that are happening, in particular in the cartels and how it's all related to fentanyl.

My first question is for Mr. Mandryck. Can you speak to any trends or observations you have seen with the recent rise in the use of drones to smuggle drugs across the border?

Mr. MANDRYCK. Thank you, sir. Historically, we have seen drones almost entirely used for surveillance along the border, whether that's at a port of entry or between ports of entry, where scouts located on the Mexican side would monitor the movements and then facilitate cross-border movement from there.

We have started to see an increased number of sUAS incursions crossing the border, some of which are for surveillance purposes, but we have seen increased use of smuggling of some narcotics, primarily hard narcotics, those that, as you mentioned, don't require larger quantities for movement. We have in place a very strong counter-UAS program with our U.S. Border Patrol and our Air and Marine Operations Center that we would love to give you a more in-depth briefing on the specific capabilities of that.

Mr. GONZALES. Great. Thank you.

I was just in El Paso a few weeks ago, and I visited two areas. One, I visited the Clint Station, Border Patrol station. This is an area in the El Paso Sector, but it's not the main one. It's not what you see on TV. It's one of the sectors that is in the Lower Valley, and it is historically known that this is the area that is most trafficked.

So I was asking the agents there, I was like, How many agents do you have on duty at one time? The answer was two agents. OK. My next question was, How much contraband have you apprehended this year? Guess what the answer was? Zero. OK.

So the most trafficked area in El Paso County, you only have two agents on duty, and they've apprehended nothing. OK.

Go a little further. You know, outside the city limits of El Paso is a brand-new soft-sided facility. It's like going to the Dallas Cowboys Stadium. OK. It's like Disneyland: 360,000 square feet, larger than six football fields. It's costing taxpayers $400 million a year. Guess how many agents were in that facility? Two hundred eight. What I'm getting at is we're putting all our resources into the humanitarian piece of it, and there's nobody on the field to actually stop some of the traffic that's happening.

One of the agents told me, Hey, look, I see drones—Tony, I see drones coming back and forth all the time, and I feel powerless. There is nothing I can do as a field agent down on the ground.

What I'm also seeing too is all these procedures—you have to go through all these procedurals to be able to go all the way up the chain in order to get a response back.

Once again, we are living in a different environment where things are tactical. You've got to be able to give the agent the tools that they need to succeed in a real-time environment if we're going to save lives.

I've got 1 minute left. Let me ask one more question. Once again for you, Mr. Mandryck. What can the committee do to ensure that CBP and other appropriate agencies have what they need to combat drones that are illegally crossing our border?

Mr. MANDRYCK. Sir, what a lot of it comes down to is just the adaptability of where we are with the technology, the speed at which that grows. They're very cheap to collect, to produce, so it's kind of a twofold effort. So it's actually attacking logistical supply chains behind those to prevent those being moved into the hands of TCOs to use for facilitation, but also support in the technology to, not just detect, but also safely bring down those pieces of aircraft, and then the exploitation after that significant investment from a technology and an expertise standpoint.

Mr. GONZALES. Well, I'd love to take you up on your offer and sit down and walk through this, in particular to these UAS vehicles that we can defeat, and talk about it, not only in regards to the Homeland Security Committee, but I also sit on the Appropriations Committee. How can we give real money to real programs that work? I'm very interested in that. Would love to follow up with you.

Mr. Chairman, I'm out of time. I yield back.

Mr. HIGGINS. The gentleman yields.

The gentlewoman, Mrs. Ramirez, is recognized for 5 minutes for questioning.

Mrs. RAMIREZ. Thank you, Chairman Higgins and Ranking Member Correa, of the Border Subcommittee for convening today's hearing.

However, I do wish that we could be focused on addressing the root causes of migration rather than having to debunk myths and respond to Republican fearmongering. I sincerely hope we can look beyond the politics and work together to achieve comprehensive immigration reform and address the causes and the concerns we have around this opioid crisis.

We know that nearly 90 percent of hard drugs, such as fentanyl, heroin, and methamphetamines, are seized by CBP at our ports of entry rather than between them. Even when hard drugs are seized between ports of entry, the vast majority are seized at vehicle checkpoints.

Mr. Mandryck, can you confirm that nearly 90 percent of hard drugs seized are at ports of entry? Is that a yes or no?

Mr. MANDRYCK. Yes, ma'am.

Mrs. RAMIREZ. Thank you. Mr. Mandryck, is it true that the vast majority of opioids seized between ports of entry are seized at vehicular checkpoints?

Mr. MANDRYCK. That's correct, ma'am.

Mrs. RAMIREZ. Thank you.

Mr. Mandryck and Mr.—I'm going to do my best because pronunciation is important to me—Mr. Papadopoulos—Papadopoulos. Papadopoulos. Did I get it right? My understanding is that more than 85 percent of the people convicted for smuggling fentanyl are U.S. citizens. Is that accurate?

Mr. MANDRYCK. So, ma'am, I can talk about the seizures and the turnover for the actual prosecutions. When we look at those encounters at the ports of entry, so Office of Field Operations, there's two ways to look at that. That's by weight and by number of events. If we look at it from events, so individual encounters, this fiscal year we're at 73.1 percent are U.S. citizens, the balance being Mexican nationals. If we look at that by weight, we're looking at about 56 percent U.S. citizens. The delta between those two is a lot of the U.S. citizens we see are very small quantity personal use.

Mrs. RAMIREZ. What about convicted for smuggling fentanyl? Is it U.S. citizens, the majority?

Mr. PAPADOPOULOS. Ma'am, I'm going to have to get back to you on that. I don't know the answer to that, but I'll be happy to get back with you.

Mrs. RAMIREZ. Yes, I appreciate it. Thank you.

So, Mr. Mandryck, would it be fair to say that the majority of seizures in between ports of entry, because even with the percent ages you gave me, are also from U.S. citizens and U.S. persons more so than from Mexican nationals?

Mr. MANDRYCK. It's a fairly close breakdown. We will have to get back with you on specifics.

Mrs. RAMIREZ. Thank you. Mr. Mandryck, can you also share the percentage of opioids CPB seized on migrants not in vehicles during the fiscal year? Do you have that information?

Mr. MANDRYCK. It's a very small percentage of those who were actually on migrants for opioids. We don't have the firm percentage. We can get back to you.

Mrs. RAMIREZ. So a very small percentage, correct?

Mr. MANDRYCK. Yes, ma'am.

Mrs. RAMIREZ. That's what I thought.

So just to clarify, Mr. Mandryck, would you agree that undocumented persons traveling on foot between ports of entry represent a very small fraction of the people trafficking opioids across our borders?

Mr. MANDRYCK. Yes, ma'am. There's a variety of reasons behind that: the ability to exploit illegal travel with, you know, millions of people each day back and forth, easy concealment techniques, operational security with a countersurveillance of individuals.

Mrs. RAMIREZ. Thank you. Thank you.

We know the alarming number of fentanyl overdoses is emblematic of a larger drug abuse public health crisis that our country is experiencing and has been for decades. I deeply sympathize with the losses that many families, including in the Third Illinois District, are facing. But this issue is broader than one of border security. In the words of Mr. Chester, and I quote, you said that the— hold on 1 second. I want to get it right. Ending the opioid crisis doesn't start at the border and it won't end in the border.

We need—and so I think we need to treat the demand driving this epidemic, and we need comprehensive health care and access to education, treatment for everyone.

Mr. Chester, knowing that, what initiatives is this administration pursuing to prevent substance abuse in our communities and support these in recovery?

Mr. CHESTER. Thank you very much. You stated it correctly, right, the efforts that we take to keep these drugs out of our country have got to be complemented by strong public health efforts in order to be able to reduce their demand. It really starts with prevention, particularly youth prevention. We out of ONDCP manage the drug-free communities program, which is enormously successful, more than 700 coalitions funded around the country, focused at the local level in order to prevent drug use.

The second thing is reducing barriers to treatment, whether those barriers are monetary or regulatory, ensuring that everyone who needs treatment is able to get it. Sadly, about 8 out of 10 Americans who need treatment don't have access to it.

Then the final thing is to create communities and workplaces that are recovery ready, so that individuals in recovery can continue their sustained recovery, stay with their families, get a good job, and not tragically enter back into the population of those using drugs.

Mrs. RAMIREZ. Thank you for your time.

I yield back.

Mr. HIGGINS. The gentlewoman's time has expired.

Mr. D'Esposito, my colleague from New York, is recognized for 5 minutes.

Mr. D'ESPOSITO. Well, thank you, Mr. Chairman, and thank you for allowing me to waive on to the subcommittee this afternoon.

To all of you, thank you for being here.

Prior to serving as a Member of Congress, I was even prouder, I think, to be a Member of the New York City Police Department, retiring there as a detective. I know that just working in the five boroughs of New York City you get to see different district attorneys and what their priorities are, their prosecutorial priorities.

So I guess this is really a question for Mr. Papadopoulos, but it's really open to all of you. Do you see that the people that you're arresting and hopefully eventually prosecuted, are you dealing with different prosecutors with different priorities, and is that hindering your ability to take illegal narcotics?

Mr. PAPADOPOULOS. Sir, thank you for the question. As you know as former law enforcement, you know, we collect the evidence, we gather the evidence, and present it to a grand jury or to a prosecutor's office, and they decide the most appropriate charges. So we don't factor into that, other than collecting the evidence.

Mr. D'ESPOSITO. Right. But what I'm asking is, have you seen it become more difficult with different prosecutors, the effective— really the prosecution of drug arrests? Has it become more difficult as we see different prosecutors having different priorities?

I mean, we see it throughout the United States of America, whether it's in cities like New York or places like California where, you know, crime is rampant, because we see over and over again repeat offenders, people that are—they're being arrested, they're being sometimes prosecuted, and then they are let out to commit more crimes. One of the biggest things that we've seen is repeat offenders.

So have we seen—and the issues on our Southwest Border when we're dealing with, specifically in this hearing, the trafficking of narcotics and fentanyl, have we seen repeat offenders, and has the ability of prosecutors and perhaps their priorities had an effect on the way that you guys are able to really take criminals off the street, and I think most important, keep them off the street?

Mr. PAPADOPOULOS. Yes, sir. So for the border, I'll defer to DHS on what they're seeing there. I will say that, you know, DEA strives to prosecute Federally, not at the local level.

Mr. D'ESPOSITO. Of course.

Mr. PAPADOPOULOS. What we see when we do that is that—more of an impact in terms of crime reduction and sentencing.

Mr. D'ESPOSITO. Right. But even Federal prosecutors, different offices have different priorities, and sometimes we see things headed in a different direction.

So I guess for the border, I'll hand it over to you guys.

Mr. CAGEN. I don't oversee our domestic operations branch, but I will tell you that I don't believe that we have seen much of a change. There's a consistent cadre who works day in and day out on the law enforcement, either CBP or HSI side, that works continuously with U.S. attorneys to take cases to the Federal level.

I can take that as a get-back. If there's something different, I can let you know.

Mr. D'ESPOSITO. OK. Perfect.

Mr. MANDRYCK. Sir, I'd have to go with our DEA and HSI colleagues. When we get seizures, they're turned over to them for the prosecution.

Mr. D'ESPOSITO. Great.

I yield back. Thank you, Chairman.

Mr. HIGGINS. The gentleman yields.

My colleague, Mr. Ivey, is recognized for 5 minutes for questions.

Mr. IVEY. Thank you, Mr. Chairman.

Before I start asking questions, I'd like to commend the Chair for putting this hearing together. I waived in to the committee today and had just come over from another hearing, so I just picked up the witness testimony. I came in and asked—I looked at the list, and I asked staff, Well, who are their witnesses and who are our witnesses? They said, Well, this looks like it's pretty much straight down the middle.

I must agree. I appreciate the fact that you put together a balanced hearing that's been very informative. It's the first one I've had like this since I got to Congress.

Mr. HIGGINS. You're always welcome.

Mr. IVEY. Thank you, sir.

I did want to follow up on Mr. Gonzales' questions about the drones issue. Because when we went down to—I guess it was in Brownsville, and we were talking with some of the Border Patrol agents, they were echoing what he said. They said there's a lot of drones, that it's increased a lot, that more of them are being used to now ship the drugs, and that they were outnumbered. The ratio of 17:1 sticks out in my mind for some reason.

I think, Mr. Correa, we were trying to get some—and I don't know if it happened or not—but some language in the bill that we passed to try and see if we could get additional funding to increase your capability to get drones to try and respond to the amount that they're using. I know they're very well-funded, they're keeping up with technology, and we have to hustle to keep up with them.

But I did want to make sure that that's something that would be helpful to you. We—you know, resources are short, but if you need additional help with the drone counter push on our part, you know, I would like to hear what your position is on that.

Mr. MANDRYCK. Absolutely, sir. Drones are something that's not going away. We're going to continue to see those, whether it's surveillance or narcotics movement.

We also support the vast majority of seer activities that take place, so Super Bowl, large-scale events with the counter-UAS approach. So it's a holistically beneficial program.

Mr. IVEY. Yes. I think there's legislation that's coming through the House, but it's got multiple committees because there's multiple types of jurisdiction. So that means it's got a hard path to travel, but hopefully we can get there. With your push, it might help to move it forward. So thank you for that.

I wanted to ask you too about China and some of their activities. I think one of you said that they have porous borders, and so it's easy for, you know, bad actors to ship precursors and the drugs out. Then I believe it was Mr. Chester who mentioned that, to the extent China is being cooperative, it can really enhance our efforts to reduce the drug flow.

What kinds of additional steps can we take, in your view? I know this is ticklish. You're not State Department necessarily. But what can we do to help to address that? Because if we can help to cut it off at the source, that would really help our issues here.

Mr. CHESTER. You know, thanks very much. I work with my State Department colleagues on this literally every day, and they do a remarkable job, help managing this relationship.

I think the first thing is we need dialog with the PRC government, routine collaboration like we've had in the past. That's the first thing.

The second thing that we've specifically asked them to do is we've presented them with what we call the three asks. The first one is implement quality know-your-customer standards, so that the shippers of precursors, pill presses, dye molds, encapsulating machines know that they're going to go to a legitimate business and they're just not filling every single order. The second one is to properly label those items in accordance with World Trade Organization standards, so that pill press parts are labeled as pill press parts, so that they can be inspected, and motorcycle parts are labeled as motorcycle parts. The third thing is to agree with the United States and other countries on the—and it's a finite list, of legitimate uncontrollable chemicals because they have so many legitimate uses that can be combined and turned into precursor chemicals for making synthetic opioids or other synthetic drugs.

Three things that are really just due diligence on the part of any responsible country that not only the PRC but all countries—and we've talked to all countries about doing this—in order to be able to help dry up this permissive environment in which these items can move around in plain sight.

The last thing is the PRC needs to join with us in partnership at the global level, and this is particularly true in light of the establishment of this global coalition. They hold a major role in this problem, and they should, as any great nation, hold a major role in its solution as well. We look forward to them engaging with us and doing that.

Mr. IVEY. I thank you for that.

I yield back the balance of my time. Thank you again, Mr. Chairman.

Mr. HIGGINS. The gentleman yields.

My colleague from Texas, Ms. Jackson Lee, is recognized for 5 minutes for questioning.

Ms. JACKSON LEE. Let me thank the Chairman and Ranking Member. I was just in Judiciary, so I'm somewhat delayed and may be asking questions that have already been asked.

But let me start with the principal deputy administrator of the DEA, Mr. Papadopoulos, and really hone in on the DEA's work with respect to opioids and the fact that fentanyl, which is synthetic, is found in drugs for medical use, and it is sometimes used to lace other drugs, and as well sold on-line, come in pink pills, multicolored pills.

How difficult is the fight for fentanyl, and what are the elements the DEA uses? I know there's some on the criminal side. You deal with scheduling of drugs, not yet scheduled fentanyl. But how difficult is this fight?

Mr. PAPADOPOULOS. Yes. Thank you, ma'am. So we are using all the tools that we have available and the authorities that we have been given to battle this unprecedented epidemic that we're facing right now. As you mentioned, we are having millions of pills come into the United States. Six out of 10 have a potentially lethal dose. That's up from 4 out of 10 last year.

So we are committed to doing everything we can to prevent the overdose deaths that are hap- pening throughout the country.

Ms. JACKSON LEE. Well, what is your—let me get you to be more extensive. Everything you can. But what are the—are you targeting certain areas? How do you incorporate the fact that there's medical uses? You know, are you seeing a criminal element that is separate and apart from the cartels? Because fentanyl is everywhere. Can you comment on that, please?

Mr. PAPADOPOULOS. Yes. So we are—domestically, I mentioned Operation Last Mile, which resulted in the distributors—cartel distributors arrests in the United States. Also, we have Operation Overdrive, which is data-driven, and it focuses on areas of the country that have high number of overdose deaths and drug-related violence. We're working with our State and local partners to identify those areas.

Most recently, we are in 57 cities in 36 States. Phase 1, which ended last year, resulted in significant decreases in fatal shootings and homicides in Philadelphia in the Kensington area. Phase 2 is on-going, and phase 3 is coming soon. So we're doing that.

We also have Operation Overdose Justice, which focuses on deaths resulting from fentanyl, where we partner with local counter—State and local counterparts to bring the most appropriate charges when somebody does die either through a fake prescription pill or if it's fentanyl that's mixed with another drug.

Ms. JACKSON LEE. Let me thank you very much. I am in the business of stopping fentanyl and particularly the impact that it's had on our children. I want to ask Mr. Chester what is being done as relates to research or treatments on opioid addiction, but particularly the impact on school children.

At this time, Mr. Chairman, I'd like to introduce into the legislation—my legislation, which is Stop Fentanyl Now Act of 2023. I hope that there will be an opportunity for this legislation to be reviewed in this committee, Judiciary, and I know that there's an Energy and Commerce component. But included in here is the ability for more institutions to use the strips. Some States outlawed them as being a criminal element.

So, Mr. Chester, you want to comment particularly focused on school children and the crisis we have?

Mr. CHESTER. Yes, Congresswoman. Thank you very much. The first thing is our strong emphasis, and particularly in the National Drug Control Strategy, on youth prevention. This is not only preventing at the individual level but looking at the environmental factors that may lead to eventual substance use. That's the first thing.

The second thing, as you mentioned, fentanyl test strips. I would also like to mention naloxone and increasing the availability of naloxone to get it in the hands of everyone who needs it so that anyone who suffers an opioid overdose, who doesn't need to die, that overdose can be reversed with the use of naloxone. Those are two important components of harm reduction. In the National Drug Control Strategy, this is the first time that harm reduction has been mentioned in a National Drug Control Strategy.

The last thing, when you talk about treatment, we have wonderful professionals at the National Institutes of Drug Addiction, at NIDA, who do research on this. I think the most important thing that we can do now is reduce barriers to treatment, particularly medication treatment for opioid use disorder, to ensure that everyone who needs treatment has access to it. That's probably the most critical important thing that we can do in order to take the oxygen out of this illicit supply that's being pulled across our borders.

Ms. JACKSON LEE. Mr. Chester, thank you. But I wanted to end on your testimony, because if we can cut the desire, then the supply has nowhere to go. It is in our schools. My legislation, Stop Fentanyl Now Act, does naloxone, does the strips, and you have indicated it is a holistic approach.

I just want to end, Mr. Chairman, by—I'm not sure if I did get a answer, but I'm asking unanimous consent to introduce in the record the Stop Fentanyl Now Act.

Mr. HIGGINS. Without objection. [The information follows:]

H. R. 4272

To provide public awareness and outreach regarding the dangers of fentanyl,to expand the grants authorized under the Comprehensive Opioid Abuse Grant Program, to expand treatment and recovery services for people with opioid addictions, and to increase and to provide enhanced penalties for certain offenses involving counterfeit pills.

In the House of Representatives

June 22, 2023

Ms. JACKSON LEE (for herself, Mr. NADLER, Mr. EVANS, Mr. ESPAILLAT, Mr. IVEY, Mr. SCHIFF, Ms. ROSS, Ms. CROCKETT, Mr.

DAVIS of Illinois, Mr. COHEN, Mrs. CHERFILUS-MCCORMICK, Ms. WILSON of Florida, Mr. DOGGETT, Mrs. BEATTY, Mr. MFUME, Mr. JACKSON of Illinois, Mr. NEGUSE, Mr. JOHNSON of Georgia, Mr. THOMPSON of Mississippi, Mr. CLEAVER, Ms. KAMLAGER-DOVE, Mrs. SYKES, Mr. HORSFORD, Ms. SEWELL, Mr. CARTER of Louisiana, Ms. CLARKE of New York, Mrs. MCBATH, Mr. VARGAS, Mr. ROBERT GARCIA of California, Mr. THANEDAR, Ms. WILLIAMS of Georgia, Mr. GARC′IA of Illinois, Mr. GRIJALVA, Mr. PAYNE, Mr. CARSON, Mr. RASKIN, Ms. LEE of California, Mr. MEEKS, Mr. LIEU, Mr. BOWMAN, Ms. MOORE of Wisconsin, Mr. SHERMAN, and Ms. BROWN) introduced the following bill; which was referred to the Committee on Energy and Commerce, and in addition to the Committee on the Judiciary, for a period to be subsequently determined by the Speaker, in each case for consideration of such provisions as fall within the jurisdiction of the committee concerned.

A BILL

To provide public awareness and outreach regarding the dangers of fentanyl, to expand the grants authorized under the Comprehensive Opioid Abuse Grant Program, to expand treatment and recovery services for people with opioid addictions, and to increase and to provide enhanced penalties for certain offenses involving counterfeit pills.

Be it enacted by the Senate and House of Representatives of the United States of America in Congress assembled,

SECTION 1. SHORT TITLE.

This Act may be cited as the “Stop Fentanyl Now 5 Act of 2023.”

SEC. 2. FINDINGS.

Congress finds the following:

(1) The United States is in the midst of the worst opioid epidemic in history.

(2) Illicit fentanyl is typically mixed into heroin or pressed into counterfeit pills made to look like controlled prescription drugs such as oxycodone, hydrocodone, and Xanax.

(3) From September 29 through December 15, 2021, the DEA seized more than 1,500 pounds of substances containing fentanyl and 8.4 million fentanyl-laced, fake prescription pills. The seizures were directly linked to at least 39 overdose deaths and included at least 76 cases that involved buying and selling drugs on social media apps. Over the course of that year, the DEA seized over

15,000 pounds of substances containing fentanyl and 20.4 million fake pills, with roughly four out of every 10 pills containing lethal doses of fentanyl.

(4) The widespread availability of illicit fentanyl, the proliferation of counterfeit pills resembling prescription drugs but containing illicit fentanyl or other illicit drugs, and the ease of purchasing pills through social media have increased fatal overdose risk among adolescents.

(5) According to the Centers for Disease Control, overdose deaths reached a historic high of more than 90,000 drug overdose deaths in 2020, a 31 percent increase compared with the previous year and in 2021, there were more than 106,000 reported drug overdose deaths in the U.S., with deaths involving synthetic opioids (primarily fentanyl) numbering 1470,601.

(6) Between 2019 and 2021, more than 2,200 adolescents overdosed, 96 percent of whom were between the ages of 15 and 19. Fentanyl was involved in 84 percent of the deaths. While counterfeit pill evidence was present in 25 percent of adolescent overdose deaths, this is likely an undcrestimate because pills present at the scenes of the overdose deaths were not always tested.

(7) Many overdose deaths are preventable with public health interventions such as education, harm reduction, and treatment access.

(8) Public education campaigns can teach teenagers, parents, and others on the dangers of fentanyl and counterfeit pills and educating individuals on mitigating practices can be beneficial, including emphasis on not initiating drug use, not using drugs while alone, using fentanyl test strips, and having overdose reversal drugs readily available.

(9) Opioid antagonists, such as naloxone, can be used during emergencies to reverse opioid overdoses and are effective at preventing fatal drug overdoses.

(10) The Centers for Disease Control and Prevention reported that despite an increase in prescriptions for emergency opioid antagonists, not enough of the medication is getting into the hands of those who need it most.

(11) Expanding access to emergency opioid antagonists and encouraging people to obtain emergency opioid antagonists are in the best interest of the health and safety of the public.

(12) Increasing access to medications like methadone and buprenorphine that effectively treat opioid use disorder can save lives.

(13) Greater access to drug detection tools such as fentanyl strips are a low-cost method of helping prevent drug overdoses and reducing harm.

Sec. 3. Comprehensive Opioid Abuse Grant Program

Section 3021 of title I of the Omnibus Crime Control and Safe Streets Act of 1968 (34 U.S.C. 10701(a)) is amended—

(1) in subsection (a), by adding at the end the following:

''(11) Developing, implementing, or expanding a program that provides training and resources for teachers and other school officials in public or private middle schools, high schools, institutions of higher education (as such term is defined in section 101 of the Higher Education Act of 1965), or area career and technical education schools (as such term is defined in section 3 of the Carl D. Perkins Career and Technical Education Act of 2006) on—

''(A) carrying and administering an opioid overdose reversal drug or device approved or cleared by the Food and Drug Administration;

or

''(B) acquiring such a drug or device for teachers and other school officials who have re ceived such training to so carry and administer such a drug or device.''; and

(2) by adding at the end the following:

''(g) PREFERENTIAL CONSIDERATION.—In awarding grants under this part, the Attorney General may give preferential consideration to an application from an applicant in a State that—

"(1) has in effect a law that exempts from criminal and civil liability teachers and other school officials who carry or administer in good faith an opioid overdose reversal drug or device approved or cleared by the Food and Drug Administration if trained to carry or administer such drug or device;

or

"(2) has in effect a law that exempts from criminal or civil liability the possession, sale, or purchase of fentanyl drug testing equipment, including fentanyl test strips."

Sec. 4. Prevention and Treatment of Fentanyl-Laced Substance Use

(a) PREVENTION.—The Secretary of Health and Human Services, in consultation with the Attorney General, shall develop and implement a national strategy to prevent the use of fentanyl, fentanyl-related substances, and fentanyl-laced substances. The strategy shall include the following elements:

(1) Education and outreach to the public about the dangers of fentanyl, fentanyl-related substances, and fentanyl-laced substances.

(2) Development of treatment programs for individuals who are addicted to fentanyl and fentanyl-related substances.

(b) TREATMENT.—The Secretary of Health and Human Services shall provide grants to States and localities to support the development and implementation of treatment programs for individuals who are addicted to fentanyl and fentanyl-related substances.

SEC. 5. Enhanced Law Enforcement Efforts

(a) INCREASED RESOURCES.—The Attorney General shall increase the resources available to law enforcement agencies to combat the trafficking of fentanyl, fentanyl-related substances, and fentanyl-laced substances. The Attorney General shall prioritize the following activities:

(1) Investigation and prosecution of individuals who traffic fentanyl, fentanyl-related substances, and fentanyl-laced substances.

(2) Disruption of the supply chain for fentanyl, fentanyl-related substances, and fentanyl-laced substances.

(3) Prevention of the importation of fentanyl,
fentanyl-related substances, and fentanyl-laced substances into the United States.

(b) INTERAGENCY COORDINATION.—The Attorney General shall establish an interagency task force to coordinate the efforts of Federal, State, and local law enforcement agencies to combat the trafficking of fentanyl, fentanyl-related substances, and fentanyl-laced substances.

SEC. 6. Research

The Secretary of Health and Human Services shall conduct research on the following topics:

(1) The effects of fentanyl, fentanyl-related substances, and fentanyl-laced substances on human health.

(2) The development of new treatments for individuals who are addicted to fentanyl and fentanyl-related substances.

(3) The best practices for preventing the use of fentanyl, fentanyl-related substances, and fentanyl-laced substances.

Sec. 7. Increase in Punishment

Section 303(b) of the Federal Food, Drug, and Cosmetic Act (21 U.S.C. 333(a)) is amended by adding at the end the following:

"(9)(A) Notwithstanding subsection (a)(1), any person who violates subsection (a), (b), (c), or (g) of section 301 with respect to any drug, if such violation results in—

"(i) serious bodily injury, shall be imprisoned not more than 10 years, fined not more than $1,000,000, or both; or

"(ii) death, shall be imprisoned for any term of years or for life, fined not more than 10 $5,000,000, or both.

"(B) Notwithstanding subsection (a)(2), any person who violates subsection (a), (b), (c), or (g) of section 301 with respect to any drug with the intent to defraud or mislead, if such violation results in—

"(i) serious bodily injury, shall be imprisoned not more than 20 years, fined not more than $5,000,000, or both; or "(ii) death, shall be imprisoned for any term of years or for life, fined not more than 20 $10,000,000, or both.

"(C) Any person who violates subsection (a), (b), (c), or (g) of section 301 with respect to any drug promoted or sold online shall, in addition to the punishment provided for such violation, be sentenced to a term of imprisonment of not more than 5 years."

Sec. 8. Exclusion of Fentanyl Drug Testing Equipment from Treatment as "Drug Paraphernalia"

Section 422(f) of the Controlled Substances Act (21 U.S.C. 863(f)) is amended—

(1) in paragraph (1), by striking "or" at the end;

(2) in paragraph (2), by striking the period at the end and inserting "; or"; and

(3) by adding at the end the following:

"(3) the possession, sale, or purchase of fentanyl drug testing equipment, including fentanyl test strips."

Sec. 9. Sense of Congress

It is the sense of Congress that fentanyl deaths should be addressed by—

(1) increasing funding for prevention and treatment programs, including—

(A) programs that provide education and treatment for people who are at risk of opioid addiction or overdose; and

(B) school-based programs, community outreach programs, and treatment centers;

(2) expanding access to naloxone (a medication that can reverse the effects of an opioid overdose) such as by making naloxone available over-the-counter or by providing subsidies for its purchase;

(3) cracking down on the trafficking of fentanyl, including—

(A) increased efforts both domestically and internationally;

(B) increased funding for law enforcement agencies;

(C) increased penalties for fentanyl trafficking; and

(D) working with other countries to stop the flow of fentanyl across borders;

(4) improving data collection and analysis, including the improvement of Federal data collection and analysis on fentanyl deaths, to better understand the scope of the problem and identify effective prevention and treatment strategies; and

(5) supporting research on new treatment options, including—

(A) support for research on new treatment options for opioid addiction and overdose; and

(B) funding for research on new medications, new delivery methods, and new approaches to treatment.

Ms. JACKSON LEE. Additionally, I want to introduce into the record, "Fentanyl is dominating headlines, but there's a more comprehensive drug problem happening in Texas." It goes on to talk about the broader crisis, synthetic opioids are not taken alone, and so health care and law enforcement officials are dealing with multiple deadly drugs at once. That means we must cut into the desire. I use that term because it's desire because you're addicted.

[The information follows:]

Submitted for the Record by Honorable Jackson Lee
Fentanyl Is Dominating Headlines, But There's a More Comprehensive Drug Problem Happening in Texas

Lawmakers are passing laws in an attempt to slow the rise in fentanyl overdoses, but drug advocates warn the opioid is mostly a booster for other illegal drugs.

by Stephen Simpson
June 19, 2023, 5 AM Central

Fentanyl has been in the headlines across Texas, grabbing the attention of State leaders worried about the drug crossing over the State's border with Mexico and overdose deaths among young people.

But often left out of the discussion is that the drug is one part of a broader addiction crisis in the State. The synthetic opioid is rarely taken alone, and health care and law enforcement officials are dealing with multiple deadly drugs at once.

The illicit use of fentanyl began increasing in Texas around 2015, quickly spark- ing a crisis. Obtained with a doctor's prescription, the synthetic opioid can be an effective pain reliever. But there's been a rise both in the illegal use of the drug and now the manufacture of counterfeit prescription drugs that contain fentanyl but are packaged to look like something else, in an effort to cause addiction and generate repeat buyers.

"It's certainly, at this moment, the drug and the drug supply that is the most dangerous," said Katharine Neill Harris, a drug policy fellow at Rice University's Baker Institute for Public Policy.

Opioids, including heroin, prescription pills, and fentanyl, have caused the most overdose deaths in Texas, according to a Texas Health and Human Services report that studied death certificate data from 2010 to 2019.

And because opioids are often mixed with other drugs, there's been a rise in deaths known as polysubstance overdoses. The most recent state data shows those deaths reaching a rate of four per 100,000 people in 2019.

The most prevalent drug combinations were commonly prescribed pills, like hydrocodone and oxycodone, mixed with depressants like benzodiazepines and psychostimulants that include amphetamine and methamphetamine.

"That is the reason I caution very much against focusing on one drug," Neill Harris said. "Fentanyl is certainly a big problem. But I don't think it's necessarily the last drug crime crisis that we are going to face."

The role of methamphetamine in the illegal drug market has been pushed aside in headlines as images of drug use in the South turned from exploding meth labs to potentially deadly fentanyl pills. But drug experts say meth has made an unwanted comeback as meth manufacturers have begun making a stronger product. "Meth is eating everybody's lunch and nobody's talking about it. Meth is crawling up on everybody," said Peter Stout, president and chief executive officer of the Houston Forensic Science Center. "Meth fatalities are way up even if you look at the Texas numbers."

Experts say if Texas wants to solve the overdose problem, officials here must fully realize the state has an overall drug issue that goes beyond fentanyl. Here's a look at the broader drug situation across Texas.

What Are the Drug Trends?

When the University of Texas at Austin's Addiction Research Institute studied calls made to poison control centers, admissions to drug treatment programs and drug seizures in 2021, researchers found the most common drugs flowing across the State's southern border from Mexico were methamphetamine, heroin, cocaine, marijuana, fentanyl, benzodiazepines like Xanax, and synthetic cannabinoids more commonly known as "spice" or K2.

While marijuana is still popular in Texas, its role in the illegal drug market has diminished greatly as 25 states across the country so far have passed laws to legalize it. When Texas legalized hemp in 2019, the prosecution of low-level pot cases declined due to the costly testing needed to determine if a vape pen liquid or a gummy contains marijuana or hemp because both come from the same plant species. But hemp contains less than 0.3 percent of tetrahydrocannabinol, or THC, the ingredient in marijuana that gets you high. Anything with less THC is hemp.

Synthetic narcotics like fentanyl, meanwhile, have shot up the ranks of causes of overdose deaths. In the past 5 years, deaths from synthetics have surpassed deaths from other opioids, heroin and depressants.

Illegally manufactured fentanyl is a perilous chemical experiment, a stew of synthetic opioids.

Opium derived from poppies has long been used as a painkiller and recreational drug. Opioids like fentanyl or oxycodone are chemical concoctions that duplicate those effects.

Fentanyl was created in 1960 and approved for use in America in 1968. It's most commonly used as a sedative and pain reliever for patients. Legally obtained fentanyl is usually administered to patients through pills, intravenous therapy, skin patches or nasal spray.

But it can also be distilled and blended to produce a fine powder that can be easily added to other drugs.

Its potent molecules scurry straight to the brain, where thousands of receptors, similar to tiny satellite dishes, pull in signals from cells in the body. They have different jobs, some gathering information to control organ functions, others emotions or moods.

Fentanyl latches on to the receptors that signal pain and shuts them down. And when those receptors are turned off, the human body reacts in ways that can be fatal, including shutting down lungs and other vital organs.

The drug is considered 100 times more potent than morphine and 50 times more potent than heroin.

Fentanyl isn't the only drug mixture that has the Federal Drug Enforcement Administration concerned as the growing threat of xylazine is starting to make its way into Texas.

Xylazine: A New Threat

Xylazine is a tranquilizer, as opposed to a painkiller, doing its work by numbing nerves rather than switching off receptors in the brain. It targets the central nervous system, the nerve highways running in and out of the spinal column that carries messages to the rest of the body.

Developed in 1962, it's used by veterinarians to keep elephants and horses calm enough to be examined or have their teeth cleaned. It mostly comes in liquid form and is sold in vials or preloaded syringes.

When tranquilizers are used, the spinal column sends messages to the brain to slow down a bit. This produces a sense of calm and elation, which is why tranquilizers are also used to treat anxiety, panic attacks and sleep disorders.

The Drug Enforcement Administration reported the first instances of this tranquilizer being used in illegal drug activity in the early 2000's by drug dealers in Puerto Rico when they began mixing it with other substances. The practice has now spread across the United States and has been found recently in Texas mixed with fentanyl.

Xylazine has been found in a growing number of overdose deaths across the country and is commonly encountered in combination with fentanyl, cocaine, heroin and a variety of other drugs.

Meth

Methamphetamine is a white, odorless, crystalline powder that was developed early in the 20th century from its parent, amphetamine, and was originally used in nasal decongestants and inhalers. It can come in liquid form, which is easily made into a crystal form by drug traffickers. The highly addictive stimulant outpaced all others in the 2021 UT study of Texas drug trends.

The drug targets the brain and the spinal cord to create a sense of well-being or euphoria. Symptoms can include talkativeness, decreased appetite and a pleasurable sense of well-being. Meth also speeds up the body's systems to sometimes lethal levels by increasing blood pressure and heart and respiratory rates.

Texas drug labs have recently started seeing meth being placed in counterfeit Adderall pills, meaning a segment of meth users might be unaware they are even addicted to the drug.

Heroin

Heroin is made from morphine, a natural substance taken from the seed pod of an opium poppy plant typically grown in Asia, Mexico and Colombia. It's often portrayed in film and television as a needle drug, but the substance can also be snorted or smoked. In the past, heroin was often mixed with crack cocaine, but fentanyl has become the primary substance being added to poppy plant extract. Dealers will often "cut" heroin with other substances to allow them to sell more of it at a higher price.

The 2021 UT study of drug trends showed that Texas has avoided the heroin overdose crisis seen in other states because Mexican black tar heroin is the most common version of the drug found in the state. Black tar heroin tends to have an average purity of 28 percent and cannot be easily mixed with fentanyl.

"Tar" heroin is usually sold in small balloons from which the user extracts the sticky substance from the balloon by mixing it with water over heat.

Cocaine/Crack

Cocaine, the highly addictive stimulant made from coca leaves, was used more than a century ago to treat a wide variety of illnesses and was often used by early surgeons to block pain before local anesthetics were developed. Frequent use can alter brain structure and function. Users can inject or snort the powdered version of cocaine. "Crack" is the term often given to cocaine after it has been refined into a smokable substance.

What Can Be Done?

Lawmakers in Texas have recently tried to tackle the state's overdose problem by aggressively attacking fentanyl distribution and use by means of enforcement and awareness.

Last week, Gov. Greg Abbott signed four bills to combat the growing fentanyl crisis, including House Bill 6, which classifies overdoses from the synthetic opioid as "poisonings," triggering murder charges for those convicted of giving someone a fatal dose of the synthetic opioid.

"These four laws will forever change Texas through new protections that will help save lives," he said in a press release. "In 2022, more than 2,000 people died from fentanyl in Texas—more than five a day. It is the No. 1 killer of Americans ages 18–45."

Other measures signed by Abbott will establish a Fentanyl Poisoning Awareness Month in October and require public schools to provide students with staff to assist with fentanyl abuse prevention and drug poisoning awareness. A fourth law will allow the distribution of Narcan or other opioid antagonists to Texas colleges and universities.

However, bold substance abuse measures like legalizing test strips were once again rejected by lawmakers.

Neill Harris, the drug policy fellow at Rice University's Baker Institute for Public Policy, said to combat fentanyl and the next impending drug crisis, the state must increase access to medical substance abuse treatments over enforcement measures. "Until we have policies that address the demand, we're going to continue to have a problem with drug use," she said. "Law enforcement has always had problems with reducing the drug supply. We look back over decades and it has never been effective at slowing down the supply. Because there's always a demand. It's just simple economics."

Michele Steeb, a senior fellow at the Texas Public Policy Foundation, a conservative think tank, said their organization views addiction as a complex brain disorder disease.

"Well-supported scientific evidence shows that brain disruptions reduce brain function which inhibits the ability to make decisions and regulate one's actions, emotions, and impulses," she said. " . . . Diseases require treatment."

If the State can't control the supply, Neill Harris said, it's time to focus on reducing the harm of drug use by legalizing testing strips, making substitute drug treatment like methadone more available and giving more substance use options to the uninsured.

Ms. JACKSON LEE. So I thank you, Mr. Chairman. I hope you will consider—and the Ranking Member, your courtesies—but I hope you will consider the legislation because we have to find a multiple level of dealing this.

To the other witnesses, my time is gone, so I just want to express my recognition of your presence here, Mr. Cagen, Mr. Mandryck, Mr. Durham. I did not get a chance, but I'm well aware of the work that you're doing and the challenges that we all have.

I yield back.

Mr. HIGGINS. Yes, ma'am. The gentlewoman yields.

The Ranking Member and I and perhaps our colleague, Ms. Lee, have other questions. So I'm going to open for a second round of questioning and recognize myself.

Mr. Papadopoulos, some things are law and some percentages and statistics are law enforcement-sensitive, so I recognize that. But I'm going to ask you to share with America, to the extent that you can, so that the citizenry can comprehend just what an overwhelming challenge we face regarding the fentanyl that's already in our country.

As we consider the volume seized, which is an unprecedented amount. You guys are pretty much seizing everything you have operational capability to seize, and it's an incredible job that you're doing. But regarding the volumes seized, regardless of at ports of entry or between ports of entry, can you share with America what you would consider to be a number that the public could consume and would not interfere with the operations—what's the percentage of seizures versus the totality of volume that has come into our country?

Mr. PAPADOPOULOS. Sir, thanks for the question. I don't—I think DEA strives to seize as much—as many drugs as possible. We don't find any acceptable amount of drugs entering the United States.

Mr. HIGGINS. Of course.

Mr. PAPADOPOULOS. So we continue to do whatever we can.

Mr. HIGGINS. Of course. You're seizing all you—I would imagine if you had twice the staff, you'd be seizing twice the volume that you have right now. There's so much out there.

A drug dealer told me last year, he said, Cap, we have so much fentanyl, we're giving it away. It's why people are dying. They want their product to be more popular on the streets, so they're making it heavier. This is a guy who's been in the game for quite some time, is incarcerated. He said that they essentially are giving volumes away, and when people start dying, they reel it back. He said that they abandoned volumes of fentanyl if they're going to cross State lines, if they're moving an operation to another State, because it's so much cheaper to replace the fentanyl than it is to risk the inter-State trafficking.

So you're seizing unbelievable volumes of fentanyl. But how does that volume compare with what, in your estimation, would be the total? Are you seizing 25 percent, 50 percent, 15?

Mr. PAPADOPOULOS. Sir, I'd like to consult our intelligence division on that. I don't know that—I would want to give you a more precise answer.

Mr. HIGGINS. Right next to you.

Mr. PAPADOPOULOS. This is DHS, but yes.

Mr. MANDRYCK. Sir, so a little explanation first. The challenge with something like fentanyl is being synthetic, there's no agriculture-based place to get an initial estimate. So unlike cocaine or marijuana where we can kind of do an oversight to see general cultivation estimates, we can't do that with synthetics like fentanyl or methamphetamine.

When we look at it holistically from an intelligence perspective, it's probably within that 25 percent mark based off demand.

Mr. HIGGINS. Thank you. I think that's an honest answer. That's an honest answer, and this will paint the picture for America of the challenge that we face.

I yield the balance of my time and recognize the Ranking Member for additional questions.

Mr. CORREA. Thank you, Mr. Chairman.

I'm going to follow up on your question from a different perspective. Ports of entry, Mr. Mandryck—and correct me if I'm wrong here—but only 2 or 3 percent of our passenger cars are actually inspected right now with nonintrusive technology. Fifteen to 17 percent of our commercial vehicles are inspected, and you have these record volumes of seizures. It's—the Biden administration now is talking about going to 40 percent inspection of vehicles coming through and maybe 70 percent of commercial vehicles by 2026.

I'm going to ask you to straight line and speculate. What's it going to do to the seizures at the border?

Mr. MANDRYCK. Sir, as part of the layered approach, the non-intrusive inspection has become a key part of it. With that, you know, 2 percent in the passenger vehicles, that's yielded a significant volume of overall seizures. So that extrapolation from that 2 percent to 40 percent, we'll have significant increase in seizures. Once you layer in things like the officer intuition, the canine capabilities, those seizure volumes are going to continue to increase.

Mr. CORREA. Again, if I heard you earlier, all of you, your testimony, you're looking at drones now being a way, by the way, of actually bringing in fentanyl into the United States. Is that correct?

Mr. MANDRYCK. There certainly is that potential, yes, sir.

Mr. CORREA. I mean, I don't know what a drone costs, and I don't know what the value of a payload would be. But if we do a cost-benefit analysis, I'd imagine you can just flood any part of our border or borders to come up with a very profitable situation.

Mr. MANDRYCK. Yes, sir. The majority of the drones we've seen commercially available, things like the DJI, a couple hundred dollars to a thousand dollars of payload capacity is, you know, 5-ish kilograms, plus or minus, depending on what you're willing to pay.

Mr. CORREA. How much would that be in terms of value of fentanyl?

Mr. MANDRYCK. Depending on if it's——

Mr. CORREA. You've got a $200 drone. What's the value of the payload?

Mr. MANDRYCK. You could easily have, you know, a million dollars' worth per flight and continuous flights throughout the day.

Mr. CORREA. How much?

Mr. MANDRYCK. Easily have a million dollars per——

Mr. CORREA. A million dollars. So that's a pretty good return on your investment.

I know, this last week I was in my district, and I took a tour of a contractor that's about to put out a manu-—manufacturing really a system, not only of radar, but radar to interfere with the controls of drones as they move forward. I would imagine that's also in your horizon in terms of investing for our national defense and border defense? Yes? No?

Mr. MANDRYCK. Yes, sir.

Mr. CORREA. Again, gentlemen, I would just come back to my earlier statement and challenge that I made, which is, let us know what we, the Members of Congress, need to look at to help you do a better job of defending our country against fentanyl and other negative things that come in. You're the experts. You know, we look at little patterns, little tidbits of what's going on, but you're the experts, and you need to let us know what it is that you need. So thank you, Mr. Chairman. I yield the rest of my time to you.

Mr. HIGGINS. The gentleman yields.

The gentlewoman, Ms. Lee, is recognized for additional questions.

Ms. JACKSON LEE. I thank the Chairman.

I want to just follow the line of questioning that I did not get a chance, and it might be redundant, redundant, redundant, but maybe asked in a different way.

Whether it's the DEA or whether it's CBP and others, can I get— was it said—total amount in dollar value that's coming into the United States? Second, is most of it coming through the ports of entry, legal ports of entry?

Mr. MANDRYCK. Ma'am, I can begin to answer that question for you. So, so far in fiscal year 2023, we're at just about 20,000 pounds of fentanyl seized by CBP along the border, 18,000 pounds of that with our Office of Field Operations at our ports of entry, and a little over 2,000 pounds with the U.S. Border Patrol.

Ms. JACKSON LEE. Would you be able to capture what that might be in street value or any value?

Mr. MANDRYCK. It's a little bit tougher, depending on the purity levels, powder versus pill format. With Operation Blue Lotus, as I had mentioned, alongside Four Horsemen, we've seized about 10,000 pounds that had a street value of about $90 million.

Ms. JACKSON LEE. DEA, do you have a different number of what you've been able to deal with?

Thank you. Thank you very much.

Mr. PAPADOPOULOS. Ma'am, we've seized, this fiscal year, approximately 57 million pills, which is about the same amount that we seized last year, and about 13,000 pounds of fentanyl powder. Again, the amounts vary. Pills can run anywhere from a few dollars if you're buying wholesale, all the way up, you know, if you're just buying a single pill, $10 to $20 a pill. So it's hard to estimate.

Ms. JACKSON LEE. What have you found—how difficult is the— first of all, to say what you've seen, if you're working with collaborative agencies of on-line sales and how difficult it is to catch the on-line sales. I give the example that is so tragic and so difficult, loving parents, great athlete, middle schooler, high schooler, A student, or average student, loved by all. One moment they're going upstairs to go to bed, and the next moment, in the morning hours, they are not with us. Pink pills, the on-line sales, the sale to children.

Mr. PAPADOPOULOS. Yes, ma'am. Social media and on-line sales are an increasing problem that we are keeping a very close eye on. The cartels are advertising and selling on social media. In Operation Last Mile, which I mentioned earlier, which was the U.S. distributors, it was over 1,400 cases. About 40 percent of them in volved social media. So it is a certain issue that we are keeping an eye on.

As you mentioned, all these deaths are tragedies, of course. I would point out that we had family members last summer come into DEA headquarters and tell us their stories, and they shared stories similar to what you just mentioned. We started the Faces of Fentanyl, which is in our lobby. It started with a couple of hundred pictures. It is now up to 5,000 pictures. It covers 8 walls in the DEA headquarters lobby that every DEA employee has to walk past to get to work that works at headquarters. The youngest person on that wall is 17 months old and the oldest person is 70 years old. A lot of them did buy the pills that ended up killing them over social media.

Ms. JACKSON LEE. This—our approach to getting that—again, my legislation deals with enhanced penalties that's on the back side of it for those utilization on social media to sell pills. So it's on the criminal end, it has the treatment end, as Mr. Chester emphasized. But, anyhow, you know how do we do an eagle eye on that, those sales on that phone or that iPad or when you're alone and you order them and they come in whatever package or you send it to somebody else and you have pink pills and you take them?

Mr. PAPADOPOULOS. Yes, ma'am. That goes back to getting the word out. Public awareness is a big part of this, in addition to enforcement. The social media companies, frankly, have to do more. When I was growing up, if you wanted to buy drugs, you needed to know somebody that had them or where to go to get them. Right now, everybody with a smartphone knows a drug dealer, unfortunately, and that includes our kids. So getting the word out is going to help with that.

I mentioned earlier, we're in an unprecedented crisis which requires unprecedented collaboration, including with social media companies, because with that collaboration we will save lives.

Ms. JACKSON LEE. Thank you very much. I think you're absolutely right. I am a rabid supporter of the First Amendment, but we have a crisis of—you've got 5,000 and growing. We have a crisis around children, and there is a level of responsibility that we must demand. I thank you for these numbers.

Thank you. I yield back.

Mr. HIGGINS. The gentlewoman yields.

I thank the witnesses for their valuable testimony and Members for their questioning.

Members of the subcommittee may have some additional questions for the witnesses and we would ask that the witnesses respond to these in writing. Pursuant to committee rule VII(D), the hearing record will be held open for 10 days.

Without objection, the subcommittee stands adjourned. [Whereupon, at 4:04 p.m., the subcommittee was adjourned.]

Fentanyl Is Dominating Headlines, but There's a More Comprehensive Drug Problem Happening in Texas

Lawmakers are passing laws in an attempt to slow the rise in fentanyl overdoses, but drug advocates warn the opioid is mostly a booster for other illegal drugs.

Fentanyl is dominating headlines, but there's a more comprehensive drug problem happening in Texas (Noe Ortega - CBS7)

By STEPHEN SIMPSON

Published: Jun. 19, 2023 at 9:33 AM EDT

Fentanyl has been in the headlines across Texas, grabbing the attention of state leaders worried about the drug crossing over the state's border with Mexico and overdose deaths among young people.

But often left out of the discussion is that the drug is one part of a broader addiction crisis in the state. The synthetic opioid is rarely taken alone, and health care and law enforcement officials are dealing with multiple deadly drugs at once.

The illicit use of fentanyl began increasing in Texas around 2015, quickly sparking a crisis. Obtained with a doctor's prescription, the synthetic opioid can be an effective pain reliever. But there's been a rise both in the illegal use of the drug and now the manufacture of counterfeit prescription drugs that contain fentanyl but are packaged to look like something else, in an effort to cause addiction and generate repeat buyers.

"It's certainly, at this moment, the drug and the drug supply that is the most dangerous," said Katharine Neill Harris, a drug policy fellow at Rice University's Baker Institute for Public Policy.

Opioids, including heroin, prescription pills and fentanyl, have caused the most overdose deaths in Texas, according to a Texas Health and Human Services report that studied death certificate data from 2010 to 2019.

And because opioids are often mixed with other drugs, there's been a rise in deaths known as polysubstance overdoses. The most recent state data shows those deaths reaching a rate of four per 100,000 people in 2019.

The most prevalent drug combinations were commonly prescribed pills, like hydrocodone and oxycodone, mixed with depressants like benzodiazepines and psychostimulants that include amphetamine and methamphetamine.

"That is the reason I caution very much against focusing on one drug," Neill Harris said. "Fentanyl is certainly a big problem. But I don't think it's necessarily the last drug crime crisis that we are going to face."

The role of methamphetamine in the illegal drug market has been pushed aside in headlines as images of drug use in the South turned from exploding meth labs to potentially deadly fentanyl pills. But drug experts say meth has made an unwanted comeback as meth manufacturers have begun making a stronger product.

"Meth is eating everybody's lunch and nobody's talking about it. Meth is crawling up on everybody," said Peter Stout, president and chief executive officer of the Houston Forensic Science Center. "Meth fatalities are way up even if you look at the Texas numbers."

Experts say if Texas wants to solve the overdose problem, officials here must fully realize the state has an overall drug issue that goes beyond fentanyl. Here's a look at the broader drug situation across Texas.

What Are the Drug Trends?

When the University of Texas at Austin's Addiction Research Institute studied calls made to poison control centers, admissions to drug treatment programs and drug seizures in 2021, researchers found the most common drugs flowing across the state's southern border from Mexico were methamphetamine, heroin, cocaine, marijuana, fentanyl, benzodiazepines like Xanax, and synthetic cannabinoids more commonly known as "spice" or K2.

While marijuana is still popular in Texas, its role in the illegal drug market has diminished greatly as 25 states across the country so far have passed laws to legalize it. When Texas legalized hemp in 2019, the prosecution of low-level pot cases declined due to the costly testing needed to determine if a vape pen liquid or a gummy contains marijuana or hemp because both come from the same plant species.

But hemp contains less than 0.3% of tetrahydrocannabinol, or THC, the ingredient in marijuana that gets you high. Anything with less THC is hemp.

Synthetic narcotics like fentanyl, meanwhile, have shot up the ranks of causes of overdose deaths. In the past five years, deaths from synthetics have surpassed deaths from other opioids, heroin and depressants.

What Is Fentanyl?

Illegally manufactured fentanyl is a perilous chemical experiment, a stew of synthetic opioids.

Opium derived from poppies has long been used as a painkiller and recreational drug. Opioids like fentanyl or oxycodone are chemical concoctions that duplicate those effects.

Fentanyl was created in 1960 and approved for use in America in 1968. It's most commonly used as a sedative and pain reliever for patients. Legally obtained fentanyl is usually administered to patients through pills, intravenous therapy, skin patches or nasal spray.

But it can also be distilled and blended to produce a fine powder that can be easily added to other drugs.

Its potent molecules scurry straight to the brain, where thousands of receptors, similar to tiny satellite dishes, pull in signals from cells in the body. They have different jobs, some gathering information to control organ functions, others emotions or moods.

Fentanyl latches on to the receptors that signal pain and shuts them down. And when those receptors are turned off, the human body reacts in ways that can be fatal, including shutting down lungs and other vital organs.

The drug is considered 100 times more potent than morphine and 50 times more potent than heroin.

Fentanyl isn't the only drug mixture that has the federal Drug Enforcement Administration concerned as the growing threat of xylazine is starting to make its way into Texas.

Xylazine: A New Threat

Xylazine is a tranquilizer, as opposed to a painkiller, doing its work by numbing nerves rather than switching off receptors in the brain. It targets the central nervous system, the nerve highways running in and out of the spinal column that carries messages to the rest of the body.

Developed in 1962, it's used by veterinarians to keep elephants and horses calm enough to be examined or have their teeth cleaned. It mostly comes in liquid form and is sold in vials or preloaded syringes.

When tranquilizers are used, the spinal column sends messages to the brain to slow down a bit. This produces a sense of calm and elation, which is why tranquilizers are also used to treat anxiety, panic attacks and sleep disorders.

The Drug Enforcement Administration reported the first instances of this tranquilizer being used in illegal drug activity in the early 2000s by drug dealers in Puerto Rico when they began mixing it with other substances. The practice has now spread across the United States and has been found recently in Texas mixed with fentanyl.

Xylazine has been found in a growing number of overdose deaths across the country and is commonly encountered in combination with fentanyl, cocaine, heroin and a variety of other drugs.

Meth

Methamphetamine is a white, odorless, crystalline powder that was developed early in the 20th century from its parent, amphetamine, and was originally used in nasal decongestants and inhalers. It can come in liquid form, which is easily made into a crystal form by drug traffickers. The highly addictive stimulant outpaced all others in the 2021 UT study of Texas drug trends.

The drug targets the brain and the spinal cord to create a sense of well-being or euphoria. Symptoms can include talkativeness, decreased appetite and a pleasurable sense of well-being. Meth also speeds up the body's systems to sometimes lethal levels by increasing blood pressure and heart and respiratory rates.

Texas drug labs have recently started seeing meth being placed in counterfeit Adderall pills, meaning a segment of meth users might be unaware they are even addicted to the drug.

Heroin

Heroin is made from morphine, a natural substance taken from the seed pod of an opium poppy plant typically grown in Asia, Mexico and Colombia. It's often portrayed in film and television as a needle drug, but the substance can also be snorted or smoked. In the past, heroin was often mixed with crack cocaine, but fentanyl has become the primary substance being added to poppy plant extract. Dealers will often "cut" heroin with other substances to allow them to sell more of it at a higher price.

The 2021 UT study of drug trends showed that Texas has avoided the heroin overdose crisis seen in other states because Mexican black tar heroin is the most common version of the drug found in the state. Black tar heroin tends to have an average purity of 28% and cannot be easily mixed with fentanyl.

"Tar" heroin is usually sold in small balloons from which the user extracts the sticky substance from the balloon by mixing it with water over heat.

Cocaine/Crack

Cocaine, the highly addictive stimulant made from coca leaves, was used more than a century ago to treat a wide variety of illnesses and was often used by early surgeons to block pain before local anesthetics were developed. Frequent use can alter brain structure and function. Users can inject or snort the powdered version of cocaine. "Crack" is the term often given to cocaine after it has been refined into a smokable substance.

What Can Be Done?

Lawmakers in Texas have recently tried to tackle the state's overdose problem by aggressively attacking fentanyl distribution and use by means of enforcement and awareness.

Last week, Gov. Greg Abbott signed four bills to combat the growing fentanyl crisis, including House Bill 6, which classifies overdoses from the synthetic opioid as "poisonings," triggering murder charges for those convicted of giving someone a fatal dose of the synthetic opioid.

"These four laws will forever change Texas through new protections that will help save lives," he said in a press release. "In 2022, more than 2,000 people died from fentanyl in Texas — more than five a day. It is the No. 1 killer of Americans ages 18-45."

Other measures signed by Abbott will establish a Fentanyl Poisoning Awareness Month in October and require public schools to provide students with staff to assist with fentanyl abuse prevention and drug poisoning awareness. A fourth law will allow the distribution of Narcan or other opioid antagonists to Texas colleges and universities.

However, bold substance abuse measures like legalizing test strips were once again rejected by lawmakers.

Neill Harris, the drug policy fellow at Rice University's Baker Institute for Public Policy, said to combat fentanyl and the next impending drug crisis, the state must increase access to medical substance abuse treatments over enforcement measures.

"Until we have policies that address the demand, we're going to continue to have a problem with drug use," she said. "Law enforcement has always had problems with reducing the drug supply. We look back over decades and it has never been effective at slowing down the supply. Because there's always a demand. It's just simple economics."

Michele Steeb, a senior fellow at the Texas Public Policy Foundation, a conservative think tank, said their organization views addiction as a complex brain disorder disease.

"Well-supported scientific evidence shows that brain disruptions reduce brain function which inhibits the ability to make decisions and regulate one's actions, emotions, and impulses," she said. "... Diseases require treatment."

If the state can't control the supply, Neill Harris said, it's time to focus on reducing the harm of drug use by legalizing testing strips, making substitute drug treatment like methadone more available and giving more substance use options to the uninsured.

Truth in Testimony Disclosure Form

In accordance with Rule XI, clause 2(g)(5)* of the *Rules of the House of Representatives*, witnesses are asked to disclose the following information. Please complete this form electronically by filling in the provided blanks.

Committee: Homeland Security

Subcommittee: Border Security and Enforcement

Hearing Date: 07/12/2023

Hearing Title :

"Protecting the U.S. Homeland: Fighting the Flow of Fentanyl from the Southwest Border"

Witness Name: George Papadopoulos

Position/Title: Acting Chief of Operations

Witness Type: ● Governmental ○ Non-governmental

Are you representing yourself or an organization? ○ Self ● Organization

If you are representing an organization, please list what entity or entities you are representing:

Drug Enforcement Administration

FOR WITNESSES APPEARING IN A NON-GOVERNMENTAL CAPACITY

Please complete the following fields. If necessary, attach additional sheet(s) to provide more information.

Are you a fiduciary—including, but not limited to, a director, officer, advisor, or resident agent—of any organization or entity that has an interest in the subject matter of the hearing? If so, please list the name of the organization(s) or entities.

N/A

Please list any federal grants or contracts (including subgrants or subcontracts) related to the hearing's subject matter that you or the organization(s) you represent have received in the past thirty-six months from the date of the hearing. Include the source and amount of each grant or contract.

N/A

Please list any contracts, grants, or payments originating with a foreign government and related to the hearing's subject that you or the organization(s) you represent have received in the past thirty-six months from the date of the hearing. Include the amount and country of origin of each contract or payment.

N/A

Please complete the following fields. If necessary, attach additional sheet(s) to provide more information.

☑ I have attached a written statement of proposed testimony.

☑ I have attached my curriculum vitae or biography.

*Rule XI, clause 2(g)(5), of the U.S. House of Representatives provides:

(5)(A) Each committee shall, to the greatest extent practicable, require witnesses who appear before it to submit in advance written statements of proposed testimony and to limit their initial presentations to the committee to brief summaries thereof.

(B) In the case of a witness appearing in a non-governmental capacity, a written statement of proposed testimony shall include— (i) a curriculum vitae; (ii) a disclosure of any Federal grants or contracts, or contracts, grants, or payments originating with a foreign government, received during the past 36 months by the witness or by an entity represented by the witness and related to the subject matter of the hearing; and (iii) a disclosure of whether the witness is a fiduciary (including, but not limited to, a director, officer, advisor, or resident agent) of any organization or entity that has an interest in the subject matter of the hearing.

(C) The disclosure referred to in subdivision (B)(ii) shall include— (i) the amount and source of each Federal grant (or subgrant thereof) or contract (or subcontract thereof) related to the subject matter of the hearing; and (ii) the amount and country of origin of any payment or contract related to the subject matter of the hearing originating with a foreign government.

(D) Such statements, with appropriate redactions to protect the privacy or security of the witness, shall be made publicly available in electronic form 24 hours before the witness appears to the extent practicable, but not later than one day after the witness appears.

False Statements Certification

Knowingly providing material false information to this committee/subcommittee, or knowingly concealing material information from this committee/subcommittee, is a crime (18 U.S.C. § 1001). This form will be made part of the hearing record.

Witness signature

7-6-2023

Date

Chapter 3

The Silent Epidemic: Fentanyl and Older Americans*

U.S. Senate Committee on Aging

Findings

- Fentanyl and other synthetic opioids have devastated communities all over the United States, fueling the worst drug crisis in American history.
- While fentanyl is the leading cause of death for Americans under 50, older Americans are increasingly confronting surging overdose rates as well.
- Among Americans 65 and older, overdose deaths quadrupled across the last two decades, and there's increasing evidence that synthetic drugs like fentanyl are adding to these fatalities.
- Despite this dramatic increase in overdoses due to synthetics, prevention messaging for older adults still reflects traditional concerns about prescription opioid misuse but does not focus on synthetics like fentanyl increasingly infecting drugs taken by older Americans.
- Older Americans susceptible to overdoses on synthetics are often long- term, stable users whose drugs become infected by synthetics or people who turn to black-market prescription drugs due to cost or

* This is an edited, reformatted and augmented version of U.S. Senate Committee on Aging Publication, dated December 2023.

In: Understanding the Fentanyl Crisis
Editor: Michael K. Reyes
ISBN: 979-8-89113-830-8

to supplement their demand for medication after being cut off from legal channels.

- Synthetics are surging in counterfeit pills, which seniors are particularly vulnerable to unknowingly purchase. The Drug Enforcement Administration reported in October 2023 that seven out of every ten pills it seizes now contain a lethal dose of fentanyl.
- America's drug crisis is so severe compared to other countries because of its position in drug supply chains.
- Mexican cartels import synthetic chemicals from China and make synthetic drugs like fentanyl at very low cost, which are then smuggled through the southern border.
- In 2020, U.S. Border Patrol seized 4,600 pounds of fentanyl along the southern border. In 2023, the amount of fentanyl seized skyrocketed to 26,700 pounds, a 480 percent increase.
- While Congress has taken steps to increase treatment, and treatment and recovery services are vital for many older adults, the drug crisis can't be solved without supply reduction.
- Overdoses are increasing the number of grandfamilies, in which grandparents raise grandchildren, spiking healthcare costs, and decreasing life expectancy.
- There is a pressing need to rethink how and why older adults are impacted by substance use, reduce stigma, and raise awareness about growing substance use among older populations.

Recommendations

- Reduce the supply of synthetic drugs
    - Congress and the administration should take immediate action to enhance border security and confront China in order to tackle the drug crisis at its core—the Chinese Communist Party (CCP) and cartels' drug supply. Curbing production of synthetics like fentanyl in China and in territory run by drug cartels is ultimately necessary for long-term gains in the drug crisis.
- Raise awareness among seniors
    - Prevention messaging should be tailored to older adults. Policymakers and stakeholders should sound the alarm to raise awareness about synthetics' threat to older adults, especially

counterfeit pills. Just one can kill. The public should understand and recognize that synthetics are extremely lethal, mixed in other drugs —both licit and illicit—and increasingly found in common pills like Oxycodone, Xanax, and Adderall. Public health systems should also update their consideration of older Americans and substance use to reflect changing patterns of behavior and new drug developments.

- Collect more data on synthetic drug use by seniors.
    - Policymakers and stakeholders should ensure that adequate research and data are available to fully understand the scale of synthetics' impact on older Americans. There is a clear need for additional research on older Americans and substance use, and for federal agencies to coordinate with states on improved data. More information, and higher quality surveys and reporting, especially on synthetics, would help guide policy responses.

The Silent Epidemic: Fentanyl and Older Americans

Over 100,000 Americans a year now die from overdoses, the vast majority of which are caused by or linked to synthetics [1]. It's easy to assume that older Americans are scarcely affected by this overdose crisis and that it primarily impacts younger Americans. While it is true that fentanyl is the leading cause of death for Americans under 50, older Americans are increasingly confronting surging overdose rates as well. Among Americans 65 and older, overdose deaths quadrupled across the last two decade, and there's increasing evidence that synthetic drugs like fentanyl are adding to these fatalities [2]. Older Americans' now have the fastest-growing overdose death rate.

Research and data on overdose deaths makes clear that synthetics are increasingly killing older Americans. The CDC found that overdose deaths from synthetics among older Americans increased by 53 percent in just one year [3]. Synthetics are being added to pills they take, or laced into other drugs they use. However, information, research, and data on substance use among older Americans is limited, which in turn limits effective policy responses. This has led to prevention messaging for older adults that still reflects traditional concerns about prescription opioid misuse but does not focus on synthetics like fentanyl increasingly infecting drugs taken by older Americans. There is a pressing need to rethink how and why older Americans are impacted by substance use, reduce stigma, and raise awareness about growing substance use among older populations. There is also a pressing need to address the fentanyl crisis at its source.

Chinese suppliers continue to provide Mexican cartels with chemicals that the cartels cheaply and efficiently turn into synthetics like fentanyl and smuggle across the southern border, which is overwhelmed by a migration crisis. In 2022, the Drug Enforcement Agency (DEA) seized over 379 million deadly fentanyl doses, enough to kill every American [4]. The current administration is unwilling to meet the challenge. Older Americans, like every demographic, aren't going to find relief until Congress and the Biden administration combat the drug crisis at its source and take border security, law enforcement, and public safety seriously.

The country's current response to the drug crisis is woefully inadequate and until more action is taken, overdose death rates will continue to grow. In states like Indiana, frontline service providers are encountering larger numbers of older Americans at risk of synthetics overdoses. It is time for everyone to rethink older Americans and substance use. Policymakers and stakeholders must do more to improve data on synthetic drug use among old Americans, raise awareness among seniors of the dangers of synthetics, and reduce the supply of synthetic drugs coming into the country.

Older Americans, Substance Use, and Overdoses

There's increasing public awareness of the health risks that substance use poses to older Americans, especially around the potential risks of overprescription, prescription combinations, and alcohol use. Policymakers, healthcare professionals, educators, and community leaders have launched campaigns to stress these risks and support treatment and recovery options. They have highlighted a range of factors that put older Americans at higher risk of developing substance use problems [5], such as: aging decreasing the body's metabolic tolerance to drugs [6], chronic health conditions leading to more prescription drugs and risky drug interactions [7], and pain, social isolation, and loneliness being linked to addiction [8, 9]. They have established and taken steps to address the reality that, in some cases, older Americans have fewer treatment options or are screened less for substance misuse [10].

For example, the U.S. Senate Special Committee on Aging held a hearing in 2018, "Preventing and Treating Opioid Misuse Among Older Americans," that highlighted steps to identify and curb older Americans' opioid dependence and the importance of expanded treatment options [11]. However, since that time, research and reports indicate that there's a neglected substance use problem for older Americans: synthetic drugs. Synthetics are drugs made from separate chemicals in labs rather than from plants. They include fentanyl, a hyper-potent synthetic opioid 50 times stronger than heroin, and its analogues (drugs chemically related to fentanyl); methamphetamines; and tranquilizers like xylazine [12]. The key difference for public health consideration of synthetics is that even one small dose, one use, can be enough to kill.

In the first phase of the opioid crisis, prescription opioid painkillers dominated. In the second phase, heroin displaced prescriptions, and in the third and current phase, synthetics supplanted both in the drug market [13]. Overdose deaths from cocaine, heroin, and other substances are now frequently caused by synthetics mixed into those drugs [14]. Alone or mixed in other drugs, synthetics accounted for 66 percent of drug overdose deaths in 2021—70,000 out of 106,699 fatalities. The opioid epidemic has become a synthetics crisis. Older Americans, though less likely to die from synthetics than younger cohorts, have not been spared. In November 2022, the Centers for Disease Control and Prevention's (CDC) National Center for Health Statistics reported that "Fentanyl and other synthetic opioids have had a big impact on the older population as well" [15]. From 2019 to 2020, the study reported, the rate of fatal drug overdoses from synthetics among adults 65 and over increased by 53 percent [16].

Over the last two decades, overdose deaths among Americans 65 and older quadrupled.

[17] 83 percent of these overdoses were unintentional, and 74 percent of those were caused by drugs like fentanyl, cocaine, methamphetamines, and heroin. Over 79,000 Americans 55 and older died from an opioid overdose between 1999 and 2019, and 79 percent were between the ages of 55 and 64 [18].

These numbers represent an increase of 1,886 percent. In 2021, 6,702 Americans 65 and older died from overdoses. This dramatic rise is reflected in the growing overdose rate for this age group, which rose from three overdose deaths per 100,000 in 2002 to 12 per 100,000 in 2021. From 2020 to 2021, Americans 65 or older had a 28 percent spike in overdose deaths, the largest increase of any group [19].

There are also racial and ethnic disparities in addiction and overdose fatalities among older Americans, where the timing of recent surges in overdose deaths underscores how synthetics like fentanyl are likely leading to more death [20]. Nationwide, black men 55 and older have an opioid overdose rate four times larger than the overall same-age rate.

[21] From 2017 to 2022, 72 percent of opioid overdose deaths in Washington., D.C., were among older Americans, skewing higher among those 50-59 [22].

That synthetics account for a share of overdose deaths among older Americans may seem surprising. The standard demographic assumption of the typical drug epidemic victim is that he or she is either younger or middle-aged, and individuals struggling with severe addiction often die before having the chance to grow old. It's also rare for older Americans to develop an addiction in old age. But there are distinct factors that can still put older Americans at risk. Over the course of their lives, aging Baby Boomer have likely approached drug use with more permissive and experimental attitudes than prior generations [23]. Some continue this behavior as they age and die from overdoses when substances they use are adulterated with synthetics. There are also older populations of long-term, stable substance users whose supply of drugs like heroin or cocaine, previously devoid of synthetics, is increasingly infected by them.

In one Florida county, people 40 or older accounted for over half of overdose deaths [24]. One man told local news that drugs overwhelm the area and said, "They put fentanyl in everything [like] depressant pills with fentanyl." Another county's medical official added that "You don't think of the seventy-year-old grandmother, late 60-year-old grandmother going in buying drugs on the street, yet that is exactly what is happening here." A headline in a Seattle Times' story this year said, "In Seattle, fentanyl's tentacles reach all the way up to seniors" [25].

"There are more older adults than you might think going to open-air drug markets," said Charles Fain Lehman, Manhattan Institute Fellow, in comments to the Committee. "We might pass them on the way to work and not even think about it." Some of the most vulnerable older Americans are increasingly facing some of the highest risks.

Linda Grove-Paul, Vice President at Centerstone, a nonprofit providing mental health and substance use treatments and services for all ages, told the Committee that in Indiana, "Synthetic use has become prolific. It's proportionately impacting older adults just as much as the rest of the population."

Centerstone finds that increased social isolation is a contributing cause, along with housing shortages and unstable housing. Increasingly, the organization's crisis response teams are serving older adults. Grove-Paul said that these older recipients of treatment are highly vulnerable, "just as vulnerable if not more to synthetic opioids."

The Committee has also heard from several experts reporting that counterfeit pills laced with synthetics are a rising threat to older Americans who don't generally use substances. There are three ways in which this older group is at risk. First, some older adults taking prescription medication develop higher tolerance and look for stronger medication in illicit markets, often through online vendors purporting to offer inexpensive, readily available pills. Second, some lose access to or run up against limits in acquiring medicine they need for pain management and also turn to illicit markets. Finally, some look to illicit markets because of lower costs.

In September 2023, the CDC found that overdose fatalities from counterfeit pills have more than doubled in recent years and, in some states, tripled [26]. While younger Americans made up the majority of deaths in the CDC's study, around 9 percent occurred among adults 55 and over, the data is limited by underestimated drug fatalities in coroner reports. In comments to the Committee, an expert said that the counterfeit problem is getting worse for older Americans as the supply of fake pills only increases and enforcement authorities seize record levels of counterfeits.

The Drug Enforcement Administration (DEA) in October 2023 reported that seven out of every ten pills it seizes now contain a lethal dose of fentanyl, a rise from four out of ten in 2021 and six out of ten in 2022 [27]. In 2023, DEA has seized 86 million fentanyl pills, up from 58 million in 2022. Its "One Pill Can Kill" campaign presents images of authentic and counterfeit versions of Oxycodone, Xanax, and Adderall to alert the public of barely distinguishable differences between reality and deadly fakes.

Substance Use and Aging: Grandfamilies and Falling Life Expectancy

As the population ages, the number of resources required to address older adults' substance use problems will only increase. The overall number of older Americans with substance use and addiction-related challenges has been rising in recent decades, so the scale of suffering is not limited to older Americans who die from overdoses and their loved ones [28]. The crisis reaches many older Americans who struggle with their addictions daily and may never be counted in official statistics. It extends to declining living standards, with decreases in older Americans' labor force participation and a higher likelihood of being unemployed [29]. It covers grandfamilies, with grandparents often raising their grandchildren because parents have died from or been rendered incapacitated by overdoses from synthetics [30]. The Administration for Community Living (ACL) notes that the number of grandfamilies has increased substantially because of synthetics-caused overdose deaths [31].

Paul Larkin, Senior Legal Research Fellow in the Meese Center for Legal and Judicial Studies at the Heritage Foundation, told the Committee that he has three friends who've lost a child to drug overdoses. "That's a critical group to keep in mind—don't forget the children and grandchildren, don't forget grandparents. They know what it means to lose people." Grandfamilies can face several challenges, including increased stress, stigma, relationship problems, and social stigma [32]. "There are too many grandparents raising their grandkids," Jim Carroll, former Director of the Office of National Drug Control Policy (ONDCP), told the Committee. "We need to think about that, the burden they face, how great the work they undertake is."

Carroll also pointed to a related aging problem with synthetics—life expectancy. Synthetics are increasingly killing older Americans while limiting younger Americans' chances to grow old. In 2022, U.S. life expectancy limped to 77.5 years after dramatically falling to 76.4 in 2021, its lowest point since 1996 [33]. The Covid pandemic accounted for some of this decline, but U.S. life expectancy hasn't recovered from the pandemic the way life expectancy has in other peer countries [34]. Synthetics are one significant reason for this lack of recovery [35]. From 2020 to 2021, the death rate from unintentional injuries increased by over 12 percent, with overdoses making up a third of the total [36]. Falling American life expectancy looks worse in a larger context. The United States has much higher living standards than other peer countries, but worse life expectancy. The life expectancy gap between the United States and peer countries is growing even though this key metric for assessing population health generally increases with countries' wealth [37].

Responding to the Crisis: Improving Data, Research, and Prevention

Support for services and treatment are critical to addressing the synthetics crisis and its impact on American aging—rising rates of addiction and overdoses, more grandfamilies and family suffering, higher costs, lower life expectancy—and expanded access to services is helping older adults.

However, there's still less recognition of just how deadly the synthetics crisis is, and what drives it. Lehman told the Committee that policymakers, experts, and the public don't recognize that the drug landscape has shifted from a health problem to a mortality problem. Prior American drug epidemics just didn't kill as many people because the drugs weren't as deadly as synthetics.

Policymakers and stakeholders should ensure that adequate research and data are available to fully understand the scale of synthetics' impact on older Americans. There is a clear need for additional research on older Americans and substance use, and for federal agencies to coordinate with states on improved data. The Committee heard from several experts that data on older adults and substance use is limited. In some instances, limits may reflect traditional difficulties with collecting information on substance use, including the difficulties in determining cause of death, dependence on voluntary reporting, and challenges in reaching vulnerable populations. Mental Health America of Indiana's Stephen McCaffrey and Stephanie Anderson told the Committee that stakeholders mostly don't focus on older populations and substance use, which leads to data gaps and a perverse feedback loop—without adequate information, there's less incentive for anyone to take older adults drug challenges seriously.

With synthetics increasingly affecting older Americans, the need is becoming more urgent. Public health systems should also update their consideration of older Americans and substance use to reflect changing patterns of behavior and new drug developments, especially the threat of synthetics like fentanyl. Health systems and community partners should increase efforts to combat stigma. Policymakers and stakeholders should sound the alarm to raise awareness about synthetics' threat to older adults, especially counterfeit pills.

Prevention is sometimes criticized because messaging can be goofily aggressive or make target audiences curious about drugs, but this is not true of the synthetics crisis, when one use of a drug can actually kill people [38]. Policymakers and the public still think of the drug crisis in terms of the opioid epidemic and fail to see the rapid changes, creating a gap of understanding between prevention efforts and what will accurately warn people of the fast lethality of synthetics. Derek Maltz, a retired Special Agent in Charge with the DEA's Special Operations Division, observed that, "They're targeting kids, but the elderly can be at risk, too. I haven't seen a good PSA for the elderly on synthetics. It would be a great and very proactive move to warn and alert older people."

"We have to address prevention," Carroll told the Committee. "The only education right now is for youth. But we need to educate older adults. They don't necessarily understand the dangers that are out there."

Older adults should not simply receive instructions about the risks of overprescription and prescription combinations. They should be told that illicit synthetics are abundant, kill quickly in small doses, and can harm both long-term users and older adults who rarely or never use illicit substances. Older Americans should also be made aware that having naloxone, a medication that rapidly reverses overdoses, at home is an indispensable tool for saving lives from fentanyl poisonings. Government agencies, healthcare professionals, and community partners should develop prevention messages tailored to older adults, especially on the dangers of counterfeit pills and fentanyl adulteration. We must also address the importance of combatting stigma. Stigma makes it harder for older adults to talk to family, friends, and healthcare professionals, and it makes older adults' social networks and healthcare teams less likely to engage with those problems or notice them in the first place.

In Indiana, Centerstone's crisis response teams try break down stigma by directly engaging with some of the most vulnerable populations, including many older adults. Centerstone identifies clients at risk of an overdose through its Overdose Risk Pathway. Clients receive a risk assessment and, if they meet admission criteria, a continuously updated safety plan. Centerstone's teams work with clients to develop a treatment course and also assess recovery capital like social connections, jobs, and employment, which are considered in the Pathway's discharge process. Centerstone's innovative work combines prevention, effective responses, and decreased stigma.

Finally, the reason other countries don't face drug epidemics of similar scale and severity is that they are integrated into different drug markets—they avoid China and Mexico's expansive and unchecked synthetics supply chain [39]. The drug crisis won't get better for older Americans, or anyone else, until Congress and the administration confront China and Mexico. Curbing production of synthetics like fentanyl in China and in territory run by drug cartels is ultimately necessary for long-term gains in the drug crisis.

Responding to the Crisis: Supply Reduction and Border Security

China has the largest pharmaceutical production in the world [40]. Black and "gray" market firms found that they could make tidy profits by exploiting

China's abundant chemical resources and production to manufacture fentanyl and ship it to the United States [41]. Increasingly, the country's illicit drug market operations have shifted from the production of synthetics like fentanyl to manufacturing fentanyl "precursors," key chemical ingredients [42]. Mexican criminals on the ground act as brokers to collect the imported precursors and distribute them to producers [43]. The producers, or "cooks," are hired by Mexico's powerful cartels, transnational criminal and drug trafficking organizations running substantial sections of the country [44].

Synthetics are lighter than heroin and other drugs, easier to hide, and more potent. This efficiency exponentially improves the cartels' smuggling operations, which thrive at the United States' southern border [45]. The Mexican government is at war with the cartels, to little effect or gain, with tens of thousands of murders a year linked to cartel-related violence and the country increasingly becoming what Lehman refers to as "a de facto narco state" [46]. Unimpeded migration across the border enables drug trafficking. It allows the cartels' traffickers, who control travel routes to the border, to exploit a massive crisis and more effectively smuggle drugs into the United States. They can more easily sneak across the border, avoiding detection and enforcement authorities.

Unprecedented flows of migration overwhelm Customs and Border Patrol (CBP) agents and resources, directing their efforts away from fighting the flow of drugs, and similarly tax Immigration and Customs Enforcement (ICE) capacity, with a 12 percent decline in arrests of serious offenders during one border surge [47].

The border crisis has escalated significantly under President Biden's lax enforcement policies, and the drug crisis has escalated alongside it. President Biden campaigned on and pledged once in office to pursue amnesty for illegal immigrants. Joined to Democrats' broader opposition to CBP and ICE and steadfast devotion to sanctuary cities, President's Biden rhetoric and positioning created powerful messages and incentives for aspiring migrants to seek entry into the United States, and for traffickers to tell them that they are welcome [48]. The border crisis is driven by outdated and confused laws and court orders that allow economic migrants to arrive at the southern border, incorrectly claim asylum, and take advantage of limited detention periods and delayed asylum hearings to settle in the United States.

Authorities' encounters with migrants at the border have reached record highs under the Biden administration, rising to over 200,000 a month [49]. Senator Braun has noted that there are now 2.4 million encounters at the southern border, a 40 percent increase from just two years ago [50]. With such a magnitude of border encounters and crossings, it's hard to imagine how border personnel and resources meant to combat drugs would not be diverted and drained. In November 2023, Senator Braun joined the Indiana Sheriff's Association and other law enforcement officers to see the expanding crisis at the southern border firsthand. "No community is immune from the border crisis," he said, referring to it as a "dire threat to our national security."

Senator Braun also said, "Fentanyl is killing Hoosiers every day, and we've had 600,000 'gotaways' enter our country from nearly every nation on Earth. With 169 people on the terrorist watchlist stopped at our border in the last year."

The Drug Enforcement Agency (DEA) announced that in 2022, it seized over 379 million deadly fentanyl doses, enough to kill every American [51]. It's of course a positive sign that enforcement agents are able to stop large amounts of drugs, but it reflects discouraging trends in the growth of dangerous synthetics entering the country—over 100,000 Americans are dying from overdoses while border seizures increase. As one expert commented, "If they're seizing a lot, it's because a lot is coming in" [52].

"This is a mass poisoning issue," David W. Murray, Senior Fellow in Drug Policy at Hudson Institute, said in comments to the Committee. "Mexico is our first leverage point, vulnerable to our pressure, sanctions and rewards, carrots and sticks." Murray and Hudson Institute President John P. Walters have called fentanyl a public health and national security threat, and released a strategy on confronting China, cracking down on the cartels, and expanding treatment [53].

Murray added that "The movement and trafficking of people is as significant as drugs. Migrants are being used by the cartels, by gangs. The border is consequential for human trafficking, for drugs, and money-laundering—it's a linked problem at multiple levels."

Larkin echoed Murray in comments to the Committee. "The cartels decide who crosses the border. What do you think is in these backpacks?" he said. Larkin has also analyzed synthetics' deadliness and endorsed a supply-reduction approach focusing on China and the cartels [54].

"We're not making any real effort on border security, or with the Mexican government," Larkin said. "We have leverage but we aren't using it even though it's a country controlled to a substantial degree by the cartels."

The Biden administration's indifference to the border crisis has allowed more fentanyl to flood onto America's streets and put more older Americans at risk. Stopping deadly synthetic drugs and securing the border requires immediate relief and prompt solutions to the crisis, but it also calls for more extensive strategic efforts from policymakers. Senator Braun backs legislation to tackle the border crisis and fix the broken, convoluted asylum rules that fuel dangerous surges. He is a coauthor of the Secure the Border Act, also known has H.R.2, which passed the House on May 11, 2023. This bill would force the administration to restart construction of the border wall, deploy technology to the southern border, increase the number of Border Patrol agents and provide bonus pay. It would also require transparency regarding illegal crossings from the Department of Homeland Security, strengthen current law to protect unaccompanied children from human trafficking, end catch-and-release, end abuse of executive immigration authority, and strengthen and streamline the asylum process.

Senator Braun also believes more can be done to crack down swiftly and aggressively on fentanyl. Senator Braun co-authored the Felony Murder for Deadly Fentanyl Distribution Act, which would impose severe penalties on drug trafficking by making fentanyl distribution that results in death punishable by felony murder charges, carrying a minimum life sentence and eligibility for the death penalty. The Controlled Substances Act currently requires a 20-year minimum sentence and no more than a life sentence for distributing drugs that end up killing people, but the law is too weak for fentanyl's deadliness—dealing fentanyl should at least be treated like arson, kidnapping, and other felony murder crimes.

Under current law, fentanyl traffickers face mandatory minimum sentences, or five years in prison, for possession of 40 or more grams of the drug, or ten or more grams of its analogues. But fentanyl is so powerful that much smaller amounts can kill. The Fairness in Fentanyl Sentencing Act, supported by Senator Braun, would apply mandatory minimums to possession of 2 grams of fentanyl or 0.5 grams of its analogues. National Fentanyl Awareness Day was May 9, 2023, when Senate Republicans tried to pass the Fairness in Fentanyl Sentencing Act. Senate Democrats blocked the bill, arguing that it would increase incarceration when too many people are already in jail.

A current regulation makes fentanyl analogues a Schedule I controlled substance under the Controlled Substances Act, which carries stricter penalties and gives law enforcement more tools to crack down on trafficking. This classification lets law enforcement stay ahead of traffickers because it applies to new fentanyl analogues— they can't evade stiffer punishment by tweaking analogue ingredients to meet a lower classification. Senator Braun co-authored the Stopping Overdoses of Fentanyl Analogues (SOFA) Act, which would permanently classify fentanyl analogues as Schedule I substances, empowering law enforcement to quickly act against new fentanyl variants and giving them certainty that the policy won't change. Here again, congressional Democrats largely object to the policy over concerns about excessive incarceration.

Senator Braun understands the importance of helping law enforcement engage emerging fentanyl-related threats. In April 2023, he sent a letter to DHS Secretary Alejandro Mayorkas and DEA Administrator Anne Milgram asking for clarity on the status of xylazine-related border countermeasures. Xylazine is a horse tranquilizer, known as "tranq", that is increasingly being mixed with fentanyl as an illicit and dangerous street drug. It causes fatal poisoning, severe skin wounds, and rots human tissue. Assessing the administration's approach to this rising threat will help policymakers develop tools to blunt it.

The Fentanyl Eradication and Narcotics Deterrence (FEND) Off Fentanyl Act would help the United States fight back against the cartels and their Chinese suppliers. It would impose sanctions on the cartels and key figures involved in international fentanyl trafficking and allow the Treasury to use special measures to go after money-laundering from the fentanyl trade. Taking the fight against fentanyl to China and its partners in the Mexican cartels, the underlying sources of the drug crisis, is one of the best options available for protecting the country.

Conclusion

Reducing stigma, raising awareness, filling gaps in research and data, and tailoring prevention messages in a synthetics crisis won't just help older Americans access needed services. These steps can help save lives. As the Committee has heard repeatedly in conversations and engagement with experts and stakeholders, American society needs to rethink substance use and its implications for older Americans—to reconsider how and why older Americans are at risk, how we approach them about addiction and substance use challenges, and how social systems can respond with speed and sensitivity.

This report also urges policymakers and the public to realize that synthetics alter prior drug policy playbooks, including for older adults. The supply side of the current drug crisis can't be ignored. President Biden has gestured at the severity of the drug crisis, referencing vague commitments to curb fentanyl production. The administration's National Drug Control Strategy does not offer a response suitable to the size of the crisis, nor does it offer new approaches [55]. Though their convictions may waver at times when shocking statistics or tragic events too painful to ignore capture headlines, administration officials' attachment to minimalist border security policy, and their open defiance of evidence, are a confession of weakness and apathy.

Older Americans are one window into the effects of overlapping crises: soft treatment of foreign adversaries, vicious cartels, and a porous border. Congressional Republicans are pressing for commonsense steps to address these crises, and hope that the Biden administration might start to listen.

The Following Tips Can Help You or a Loved One Avoid Overdose

Know that synthetics like fentanyl are extremely potent, dangerous, and abundant substances. Two milligrams of fentanyl is considered deadly. One pill can kill.

Understand that synthetics like fentanyl are impacting older populations too: synthetics are increasingly infecting drugs like heroin and cocaine.

Avoid illicit markets for prescription access or discounts—there are surging rates of counterfeit pills laced with synthetics like fentanyl.

Trust licensed medical professionals and legitimate pharmacies on prescriptions. Make sure your doctor is aware of all medication you are taking.

Take only prescribed medication as prescribed, and never take anyone else's medication. Never mix pain medicines with alcohol, sleeping pills, or illicit substances.

Understand that prior substance misuse and continued substance misuse make individuals more susceptible with age.

Talk to friends and loved ones about the risks of substance misuse and dangers of fentanyl.

Tell friends and loved ones to talk to their doctors if concerned about them. Be aware of the signs of an overdose in loved ones and friends, including:

- Difficulty breathing and slow heartbeat
- Lips and fingernails changing color (often becoming blue or purple)
- Vomiting
- Loss of consciousness

Seek immediate medical attention for a suspected overdose and call 911 immediately. Timely responses by emergency medical professionals are critical to saving lives.

Know that help is available—naloxone, a medication, can quickly reverse the effects of an opioid overdose and save a life.

Treatment and recovery options are available to older adults and allow them to fight addiction and go on to flourish.

References

[1] Merianne Rose Spencer, Arialdi M. Miniño, and Margaret Warner, Drug Overdose Deaths in the United States, 2001-2021, NCHS Data Brief No. 457, Dember 2022, https://www.cdc.gov/nchs/products/databriefs/db457.htm#:~:text=In%20both%20 2020%20and%202021%2C%20rates%20were%20highest%20for%20adults,%2C %20with%20a% 2028%25%20increase.

[2] Keith Humphreys and Chelsea L. Shover, Twenty-Year Trends in Drug Overdose Fatalities Among Older Adults in the US, JAMA Psychiatry, March 29, 2023, https://jamanetwork.com/journals/jamapsychiatry/article-abstract/2802945? resultClick=3.

[3] Ellen A. Kramarow and Betzaida Tejada-Vera, Drug Overdose Deaths in Adults Aged 65 and Over: United States, 2000-2020, National Center for Health Statistics, Center for Disease Control and Prevention, November 2022, https://www.cdc.gov/ nchs/data/databriefs/db455.pdf.

[4] Drug Enforcement Administration, DEA Washington Division Announces the Seizure of Over 8 Million of Deadly Doses of Fentanyl in 2022, January 26, 2023, https://www.dea.gov/press-releases/2023/01/26/dea-washington-division-announces-seizure-over-8-million-deadly-doses#:~:text=The%20DEA%20 Laboratory%20estimates%20that,fentanyl%20to%20kill%20every%20American.

[5] Maryann Mason, Rebekah Soliman, and Howard Kim, Disparities by Sex and Race and Ethnicity in Death Rates Due to Opioid Overdose Among Adults 55 Years or Older, 1999 to 2019, JAMA Network Open, January 11, 2022, https:// jamanetwork.com/journals/jamanetworkopen/fullarticle/2787930.

[6] Sarah Larney, Amy S.B. Bohnert, Dara Ganoczy, Mark A. Ilgen, Matthew Hickman, Fred C. Blow, Louisa Degenhardt, Mortality among older adults with opioid use disorders in the Veteran's Health Administration, 2000–2011, Drug and Alcohol Dependence, Volume 147, February 1, 2015, https://www.sciencedirect.com/ science/article/abs/pii/S0376871614019991?via%3Dihub.

[7] National Institute on Drug Abuse, Substance Use in Older Adults DrugFacts, July 2020, https://nida.nih.gov/publications/drugfacts/substance-use-in-older-adults-drugfacts.

[8] Gaby Galvin, Addiction Among Older Adults Poses Complex Challenge, U.S. News and World Report, April 16, 2019, https://www.usnews.com/news/health-news/articles/2019-04-16/addiction-among-older-adults-a-complex-challenge.

[9] Anne Case, Angus Deaton, and Arthur Stone, Decoding the mystery of American pain reveals a warning for the future, PNAS, Volume 117 (40), September 21, 2020, https://www.pnas.org/doi/full/10.1073/pnas.2012350117.

[10] Maryann Mason, Rebekah Soliman, and Howard Kim, Disparities by Sex and Race and Ethnicity in Death Rates Due to Opioid Overdose Among Adults 55 Years or Older, 1999 to 2019, JAMA Network Open, January 11, 2022, https://jamanetwork.com/journals/jamanetworkopen/fullarticle/2787930.

[11] Senate Special Committee on Aging, Preventing and Treating Opioid Misuse Among Older Americans, Full Committee Hearing, May 23, 2018, https://www.aging.senate.gov/hearings/preventing-and-treating-opioid-misuse-among-older-americans.

[12] National Institute on Drug Abuse, Fentanyl DrugFacts, June 2021, https://nida.nih.gov/publications/drugfacts/fentanyl.

[13] Centers for Disease Control and Prevention, Understanding the Opioid Overdose Epidemic, Opioids, August 8, 2023, https://www.cdc.gov/opioids/basics/epidemic.html.

[14] Centers for Disease Control and Prevention, Fentanyl Facts, Stop Overdose, September 6, 2023, https://www.cdc.gov/stopoverdose/fentanyl/index.html.

[15] National Center for Health Statistics, Drug & Alcohol Deaths on the Rise Among Older Americans, Centers for Disease Control and Prevention, November 30, 2022, https://www.cdc.gov/nchs/pressroom/nchs_press_releases/2022/20221130.htm.

[16] Ellen A. Kramarow and Betzaida Tejada-Vera, Drug Overdose Deaths in Adults Aged 65 and Over: United States, 2000-2020, National Center for Health Statistics, Center for Disease Control and Prevention, November 2022, https://www.cdc.gov/nchs/data/databriefs/db455.pdf.

[17] Keith Humphreys and Chelsea L. Shover, Twenty-Year Trends in Drug Overdose Fatalities Among Older Adults in the US, JAMA Psychiatry, March 29, 2023, https://jamanetwork.com/journals/jamapsychiatry/article-abstract/2802945?resultClick=3.

[18] Maryann Mason, Rebekah Soliman, and Howard Kim, Disparities by Sex and Race and Ethnicity in Death Rates Due to Opioid Overdose Among Adults 55 Years or Older, 1999 to 2019, JAMA Network Open, January 11, 2022, https://jamanetwork.com/journals/jamanetworkopen/fullarticle/2787930.

[19] Merianne Rose Spencer, Arialdi M. Miniño, and Margaret Warner, Drug Overdose Deaths in the United States, 2001-2021, NCHS Data Brief No. 457, Dember 2022, .https://www.cdc.gov/nchs/products/databriefs/db457.htm#:~:text=In%20both%20 2020%20and%202021%2C%20rates%20were%20highest%20for%20adults,%2C %20with%20a% 2028%25%20increase.

[20] Kristin Samuelson, Older adult opioid overdose death rates on the rise, Northwestern Now, January 11, 2022, https://news.northwestern.edu/stories/2022/01/older-adult-opioid-overdose-death- rates-on-the-rise/.

[21] Maryann Mason, Rebekah Soliman, and Howard Kim, Disparities by Sex and Race and Ethnicity in Death Rates Due to Opioid Overdose Among Adults 55 Years or Older, 1999 to 2019, JAMA Network Open, January 11, 2022, https://jamanetwork.com/journals/jamanetworkopen/fullarticle/2787930.

[22] Lindiwe Vilakazi, The Deadly Wave of Fentanyl Hits Blacks and Seniors, The Washington Informer, February 15, 2023, https://www.washingtoninformer.com/the-deadly-wave-of-fentanyl-hits-blacks-and-seniors/.

[23] Gianna Melillo, Drug overdose deaths have quadrupled among seniors in the last 20 years. Why?, The Hill, April 5, 2023, https://thehill.com/changing-america/well-being/longevity/3934069-drug-overdose-deaths-have-quadrupled-among-seniors-in- the-last-20-years-why/.

[24] Phylicia Ashley and Brittany Caldwell, Central Florida fentanyl overdose numbers on the rise among elderly, WFTV, August 27, 2022, https://www.wftv.com/news/local/volusia-county/central-florida-fentanyl-overdose-numbers-rise-among-elderly/DXPQ4YN47ZDNBHJZ2OKGU32ZNU/.

[25] Danny Westneat, In Seattle, fentanyl's tentacles reach all the way up to seniors, The Seattle Times, August 19, 2023, https://www.seattletimes.com/seattle-news/in-seattle-fentanyls-tentacles-reach-all-the-way-up-to-seniors/.

[26] Julie O'Donnell, PhD; Lauren J. Tanz, ScD; Kimberly D. Miller, MPH; Amanda T. Dinwiddie, MPH; Jessica Wolff, MPH; Sasha Mital, PhD; Rochelle Obiekwe, MPH; and Christine L. Mattson, PhD, Drug Overdose Deaths with Evidence of Counterfeit Pill UseUnited States, July 2019–December 2021, Canters for Disease Control and Prevention, September 1, 2023, https://www.cdc.gov/mmwr/volumes/72/wr/mm7235a3.htm? s_cid=mm7235a3_w.

[27] Anne Milgram, A Message From DEA Administrator Anne Milgram, United States Drug Enforcement Administration, October 6, 2023, https://www.dea.gov/stories/2023/2023-10/2023-10-06/message-dea-administrator- anne-milgram.

[28] Alexis Kuerbis Paul Sacco, Dan G Blazer, and Alison A Moore, Substance abuse among older adults, National Library of Medicine, August 30, 2014, https://pubmed.ncbi.nlm.nih.gov/25037298/.

[29] Lawrance L Evans Jr., Thomas Costa, and Chuck Young, Older Workers: Opioid Misuse and Employment Outcomes, U.S. Government Accountability Office, February 23, 2022, https://www.gao.gov/products/gao-22-104491.

[30] Diane Roznowski, Jaia Lent, Danica Derriennic, and Ana Beltran, Grand Resource: Help for Grandfamilies Impacted by Opioids and Other Substance Use, Generations United, 2019, https://www.gu.org/resources/grand-resource-help-for-grandfamilies - impacted-by-opioids-and-other-substance-use/.

[31] 2022 National Strategy to Support Family Caregivers, Administration for Community Living, October 20, 2023, https://acl.gov/CaregiverStrategy.

[32] Megan L Dolbin-MacNab and Lyn M O'Connell, Grandfamilies and the Opioid Epidemic: A Systemic Perspective and Future Priorities, National Library of Medicine, January 25, 2021, https://pubmed.ncbi.nlm.nih.gov/33491118/#:~:text=As%20a%20result%20of%20the,what%20are%20known%20as%20grandfamilies.

[33] Joel Achenbach and Dan Keating, New CDC life expectancy data shows painfully slow rebound from covid, The Washington Post, November 29, 2023, https://www.washingtonpost.com/health/2023/11/29/life-expectancy-2022-united-states/.

[34] Charles Fain Lehman, Why American Life Spans Are Getting Shorter, National Review, April 27, 2023, https://www.nationalreview.com/magazine/2023/05/15/why- american-lifespans-are-getting-shorter/.

[35] Matthew Ygkesuas, Tackling America's weirdly short life expectancy should be a priority, Slow Boring, July 26, 2022, https://www.slowboring.com/p/tackling-americas- weirdly-short-life.

[36] Amber Castillo, U.S. life expectancy falls for second straight year as drug overdose and Covid deaths take toll, Stat News, December 22, 2022, https://www.statnews.com/2022/12/22/us-life-expectancy-falls-covid-drug-overdose- deaths/

[37] Matthew Ygkesuas, Tackling America's weirdly short life expectancy should be a priority, Slow Boring, July 26, 2022, https://www.slowboring.com/p/tackling-americas- weirdly-short-life.

[38] Charles Fain Lehman, How to Think about the Drug Crisis, National Affairs, Summer 2023, https://nationalaffairs.com/publications/detail/how-to-think-about-the-drug-crisis.

[39] Charles Fain Lehman, With the Taliban, and End to the Opium Trade?, The Washington Free Beacon, September 25, 2021, https://freebeacon.com/national-security/with-the-taliban-an-end-to-the-opium-trade/.

[40] Sheng Hong, Yifan Jie, Xiaosong Li, and Nathan Liu, China's chemical industry: New strategies for a new era, McKinsey & Company, March 2019, https://www.mckinsey.com/~/media/McKinsey/Industries/Chemicals/Our%20Insights/Chinas%20chemical%20industry%20New%20strategies%20for%20a%20new%20era/Chin as-chemical-industry.pdf.

[41] Liana W. Rosen, Ricardo barrios, and Susan V. Lawrence, China primer: Illicit Fentanyl and China's Role, Congressional Research Service, September 28, 2023, https://www.crs.gov/Reports/IF10890?source=search.

[42] Susan V Lawrence and Karen M Sutter, China Primer: U.S.-China Relations, Congressional Research Service, October 24, 2023, https://www.crs.gov/Reports/IF10119? source=search.

[43] Steven Dudley, Victoria Dittmar, Sara García, Jaime López-Aranda, Annie Pforzheimer, Ben Westhoff, *Luisa Acosta, Isaac Norris, Molly Schofield, Aylin Duarte, J. Yang, Parker Asmann, Marcos Vizcarra, and Carlos Arrieta, The Flow of Precursor Chemicals for Synthetic Drug Production in Mexico, InSight Crime, May 2023, https://insightcrime.org/wp-content/uploads/2023/05/The-Flow-of-Precursor-Chemicals-for-Synthetic-Drug-Production-in-Mexico-InSight-Crime-March-2023-3.pdf.

[44] Courtney Kan, Nick Miroff, Scott Higham, Steven Rich and Tyler Remmel, Overview: From Mexican labs to U.S. streets, a lethal pipeline, The Washington Post, December 12, 2022, https://www.washingtonpost.com/investigations/interactive/2022/fentanyl-crisis- mexico-cartel/.

[45] Liana W Rosen and Clare Ribando Seelke, Trends in Mexican Opioid Trafficking and Implications for U.S.-Mexico Security Cooperation, Congressional Research Service, December 9, 2022, https://www.crs.gov/Reports/IF10400?source=search.

[46] Charles Fain Lehman, Can the Fentanyl Supply be Controlled?, The Causal Fallacy, May 24, 2023, https://thecausalfallacy.com/p/can-the-fentanyl-supply-be-controlled.

[47] Charles Fain Lehman, The Next Border Crisis Will Be Biden's, City Journal, January 4, 2021, https://www.city-journal.org/article/the-next-border-crisis-will-be-bidens.

[48] Priscilla Alvarez, Smugglers spread misinformation at the border. The White House says now is not the time to come, CNN, February 10, 2021, https://www.cnn.com/2021/02/10/politics/immigration-biden-misinformation/ index.html.

[49] John Gramlich, Monthly encounters with migrants at U.S.-Mexico border remain near record highs, Pew Research Center, January 13, 2023, https://www.pewresearch.org/short-reads/2023/01/13/monthly-encounters-with- migrants-at-u-s-mexico-border-remain-near-record-highs/.

[50] Mike Braun, Border wall still best option to stem southern border crisis, The Journal Gazette, December 8, 2023, https://www.journalgazette.net/opinion/ columnists/border-wall-still-best-option-to-stem-southern-border-crisis/article_1e74e58a-92b6-11ee-8a5a- 5b01b183ba6b.html.

[51] Jarod A Forget, DEA Washington Division Announces the Seizure of Over 8 Million of Deadly Doses of Fentanyl in 2022, United States Drug Enforcement Administration, January 26, 2023, https://www.dea.gov/press-releases/2023/01/26/dea-washington-division-announces-seizure-over-8-million-deadly-doses#:~:text=The%20DEA%20Laboratory%20estimates%20that,fentanyl%20to%20kill% 20every%20American.

[52] Tommy Hicks Jr., Biden's border crisis worsens in February, The Washington Times, March 21, 2022, https://www.washingtontimes.com/news/2022/ mar/21/bidens-border- crisis-worsens-in-february/.

[53] John P Walters and David W Murray, Fentanyl is a Public Health and National Security Threat, Hudson, December 19, 2022, https://www.hudson.org/drug-policy/fentanyl-public-health-national-security-threat.

[54] Paul Larkin, Twenty-First Century Illicit Drugs and Their Discontents: The Scourge of Illicit Fentanyl, The Heritage Foundation, November 1, 2022, https://www.heritage.org/crime-and-justice/report/twenty-first-century-illicit-drugs-and-their-discontents-the-scourge.

[55] Patrick Hauf, GOP jeers Biden as he calls for fentanyl solution: 'It's your fault' the border isn't closed, Fox News, February 7, 2023, https://www.foxnews.com/politics/gop-jeers-biden-calls-fentanyl-solution-your-fault-border-isnt-closed.

Index

M

N

O

P

R

S